War of 1812

War of 1812

Kelly King Howes

Julie L. Carnagie, Editor

GALE GROUP

THOMSON LEARNING

Detroit • New York • San Diego • San Francisco
Boston • New Haven, Conn. • Waterville, Maine
London • Munich

War of 1812

Kelly King Howes

Staff

Julie L. Carnagie, *U•X•L Senior Editor*
Carol DeKane Nagel, *U•X•L Managing Editor*
Tom Romig, *U•X•L Publisher*

Pamela A. E. Galbreath, *Senior Art Director (Page design)*
Cynthia Baldwin, *Senior Art Director (Cover design)*

Shalice Shah-Caldwell, *Permissions Associate (Images)*
Kelly A. Quin, *Imaging and Multimedia Content Editor*
Robert Duncan, *Imaging Specialist*

Rita Wimberly, *Senior Buyer*
Evi Seoud, *Assistant Manager, Composition Purchasing and Electronic Prepress*

Marco DiVita, Graphix Group, *Typesetting*

Cover Photos: Washington, D.C. burning (front) and Dolley Madison (back) reproduced by permission of Corbis Corportation.

Library of Congress Cataloging-in-Publication Data

Howes, Kelly King
    War of 1812 / Kelly King Howes; Julie L. Carnagie, editor.
        p. cm.
    Includes bibliographical references (p.) and index.
    Summary: A chronological overview of the events of the War of 1812, accompanied by fifteen biographies of individuals associated with the war.
    ISBN 0-7876-5574-0 (alk. paper)
        1. United States–History–War of 1812–Juvenile literature. 2. United States–History–War of 1812–Biography–Juvenile literature. [1. United States–History–War of 1812. 2. United States–History–War of 1812–Biography.] I. Carnagie, Julie L. II. Title.
    E354 .H79 2002
    973.5'2–dc21   2001044240

Dedication

"In memory of
Gerda-Ann Raffaelle (1946–2001)."

Contents

Reader's Guide

The War of 1812 remains a mystery to many people. In fact it is sometimes called "The Forgotten War" because only a few history students can recall why or where it was fought, or by whom. It followed so closely on the heels of the more exciting American Revolution that it seems to have gotten lost in America's history.

The War of 1812 provides students with a clear understanding of the issues that caused the United States to declare war against Great Britain as well as the motivations of the people involved in the conflict. The volume explores the important battles of the war and how the victories and defeats gained by the United States evolved into a sense of patriotism by the war's end. Through primary documents contained throughout the book, *The War of 1812* also provides readers with a sense of U.S. attitudes toward Native Americans, Great Britain, and the war itself.

Format

The War of 1812 is divided into two sections: Almanac and Biographies. The Almanac contains six chapters, which chronicle the war from its origins after the American Revolution in 1783 to its end with the signing of the Treaty of Ghent in 1814. Placed throughout the chapters are primary source documents, such as diary entries, letters, and newspaper articles, that allow readers the opportunity to see how the war effected ordinary people as well as political and military leaders.

The Biographies section details the lives of fifteen people who had a strong impact during the War of 1812. Coverage includes political figures James Madison and James Monroe, first lady Dolley Madison, military leaders Isaac Brock and Thomas Macdonough, and Native American warriors Tecumseh and William Weatherford. Primary source documents are also found throughout many of the biographical entries.

The *War of 1812* includes more than fifty photos, illustrations, and maps, a timeline of key events of the war, a glossary, research and activity ideas, a general bibliography, and a subject index.

Acknowledgments

A note of appreciation is extended to the War of 1812 advisors, who provided invaluable suggestions when this work was in its formative stages:

Robert Bolt
Professor of History, Emeritus
Calvin College
Grand Rapids, Michigan

Sara Brooke
Librarian
Ellis School
Pittsburgh, Pennsylvania

Jacquelyn Divers
Librarian
Roanoke County Schools
Roanoke, Virginia

Thomas C. Mackey
Associate Professor of History
University of Louisville
Louisville, Kentucky

Bonnie L. Raasch
Media Specialist
C. B. Vernon Middle School
Marion, Iowa

Comments and Suggestions

We welcome your comments on *War of 1812*. Please write: Editors, *War of 1812,* U•X•L, 27500 Drake Rd., Farmington Hills, Michigan, 48331-3535; call toll free: 1-800-877-4253; fax: 248-414-5043; or send e-mail via http://www.gale group.com.

Words to Know

B

Battery: A set of guns.

Bayonets: Rifles that contain a steel blade at the end of the muzzle and used in hand-to-hand combat.

Bounties: One-time sums of money paid as rewards for enlisting.

Broadside: Firing all guns on one side of a warship at more or less the same time.

C

Cavalry: Soldiers mounted on horseback.

Chausseurs: Deserters from the French army who had chosen to fight on the side of the British rather than go to jail.

Commerce: Business conducted between states or with other foreign governments.

Convoys: Ships that travel in groups as protection against an attack.

Court-martialed: Tried in military court.

D

Diplomatic: Related to international relations.

E

Embargo Act: A law that barred U.S. ships from sailing to any foreign ports and thus halted U.S. trade with other countries.

Ensign: The lowest-ranking officer in the army.

F

Federalists: Members of the Federalist Party who favored a strong central government and disliked the idea of fighting a war with Britain.

Frigate: A fast, medium-sized warship that carries between twenty-four and sixty guns.

G

Gunboats: Small, armed ships used mostly for patrolling rivers and harbors.

I

Impressment: The act of British officials boarding U.S. ships to capture deserters from the British navy.

L

Land speculators: People who buy land with the hope that they will be able to sell it for a quick profit.

Louisiana Purchase: An area of land purchased by the United States from France that included the present-day states of Arkansas, Missouri, Iowa, the part of Minnesota that is west of the Mississippi River, North Dakota, South Dakota, Nebraska, Oklahoma, most of Kansas, the parts of Montana, Wyoming, and Colorado that are east of the Rocky Mountains, and Louisiana west of the Mississippi but including the city of New Orleans.

M

Magazine: Ammunitions storehouse.

Manifest destiny: The idea that it was actually the duty of white people (who viewed themselves superior to those of native peoples) to conquer the North American continent.

Martial law: Rule by a military force or government in which civil rights are suspended.

Muskets: Long-barreled guns that had been used more before rifles were invented.

Mustering: The gathering together of troops in preparation for war.

N

Neutrality rights: The right of a nation that is not at war not to be pulled into or hurt by other countries' conflicts.

Non-Importation Act: A law that stated that no British goods could be imported into the United States.

Northwest Territory: An area of land that would become the states of Ohio, Michigan, Indiana, Illinois, and parts of Minnesota.

O

Orders in Council: British laws that required anyone intending to trade with France to stop first in England and purchase a license.

P

Privateers: Private citizens employed by the government to use their ships to disrupt enemy trade by attacking enemy ships and confiscating cargo.

Prize: A captured, enemy ship.

Purchase: A traditional practice in which officers paid a fee to receive a rank.

R

Red Sticks: A hostile faction of the Creek Native Americans.

S

Schooner: A type of ship with two or more masts at its front and back ends.

Sloop: A small warship with guns on only one deck.

Sortie: A quick raid.

Smuggling: The buying and selling of illegally obtained goods.

Squadron: A group of ships assigned to a special task.

State militias: Small armies made up of troops residing in a particular state; under certain circumstances they could be called into action by the federal government.

T

Tariffs: Duties or fees paid by those importing goods into the United States.

V

Virginia dynasty: How some referred to the dominance of Virginia leaders (especially Thomas Jefferson, James Madison, and James Monroe) in national politics.

W

War Hawks: A nickname given to a group of aggressive and impatient young congressmen who favored starting a war with Great Britain.

Timeline

1775–83: Seeking independence from British rule, the thirteen American colonies wage a war against Great Britain that comes to be known as the American Revolution.

1783: With the signing of the Treaty of Paris, the United States officially gains independence from Great Britain.

1787: At the Constitutional Convention, held in Philadelphia, Pennsylvania, fifty-five delegates from twelve states meet to formulate a government structure for the nation. They decide on a democratic republic, with power balanced between three branches: the executive (the president), the legislative (the U.S. Congress), and the judiciary (the court system).

1789: The constitution is ratified (officially approved) by all of the states.

1803–15: Great Britain and its allies wage war against France in a series of conflicts called the Napoleonic Wars.

1803: Secretary of State James Monroe negotiates the Louisiana Purchase for fifteen million dollars from France. The eight hundred square miles of new territory opens up the vast lands west of the Appalachian mountains for settlement.

1803: In desperate need of seamen to fight in the Napoleonic Wars, Great Britain begins the practice of impressment, by which sailors it considers British citizens are taken from U.S. ships and forced into the British navy. Between 1803 and 1812, as many as six thousand Americans are impressed.

1807: Congress passes the Embargo Act, which is intended to punish both Great Britain and France by forbidding trade between the United States and all foreign countries.

June 22, 1807: The commanding officer of the USS *Chesapeake* refuses to allow officers from the British ship *Leopard* aboard to arrest four sailors accused of being deserters from the British navy. The *Leopard* fires on the *Chesapeake,* killing three Americans and wounding eighteen. Unprepared to defend itself, the *Chesapeake* surrenders and the British remove the four sailors.

1809: The Embargo Act is repealed. It is followed by the Non-Intercourse Act, which restores trade with all countries except Great Britain and France.

1810: A group of young, prowar representatives is elected to Congress. Known as the War Hawks and led by Kentucky representative **Henry Clay,** these congressmen feel that Great Britain's actions on the high seas and suspected involvement in stirring up Native American hostility against white settlers justifies a war.

November 1811: The Twelfth Congress convenes and passes measures (such as increasing the size of the military) to help prepare the United States for war with Great Britain. However, Massachusetts Federalist representative **Josiah Quincy** takes the lead in opposing the war.

November 7, 1811: Troops under General **William Henry Harrison,** sent to put a halt to Native American aggression, are attacked by followers of the great Shawnee war chief **Tecumseh** during the Battle of Tippecanoe. The U.S. force wins, but attacks against white settlers increase, and many Native Americans decide to join the British side in the war.

June 1812: A Federalist-owned Baltimore, Maryland, newspaper publishes an editorial expressing opposition to the war. The newspaper's supporters are violently attacked and its offices are destroyed by an enraged Republican mob. The result of what becomes known as the Baltimore Riots is the death of two people and others severely injured.

June 1, 1812: President **James Madison** sends a "War Message" to Congress, stating that Great Britain's practice of impressment, interference in U.S. trade, and involvement in Native American hostilities compel the U.S. to declare war.

June 18, 1812: The United States officially declares war against Great Britain.

August 15, 1812: A band of forty Americans (including women and children) who have been ordered to evacuate Fort Dearborn (located near present-day Chicago, Illinois) are immediately attacked by hostile Native Americans waiting outside the fort's gates. Most of the fort's inhabitants are killed.

August 16, 1812: General **William Hull** loses the town of Detroit to a British force (smaller than his own) commanded by the dynamic British general **Isaac Brock.**

August 19, 1812: The American ship USS *Constitution* wins a sea battle against the British vessel HMS *Guerriere,* an unlikely victory that bolsters U.S. morale.

October 13, 1812: The United States suffers defeat at the Battle of Queenston Heights after members of New York's militia refuse to cross into Canadian territory to join the fight. But the British also face a big loss when one of their best officers, General Isaac Brock, is killed during the clash.

January 1813: The Russian government offers to help mediate a peace treaty between the United States and Great Britain. Madison accepts the offer, but the British turn it down.

March 1813: A talented young naval officer named **Oliver Hazard Perry** takes command of the U.S. fleet on Lake Erie.

April 27, 1813: U.S. general **Zebulon Montgomery Pike** leads his troops to victory at the Battle of York (now Toronto) but is killed when an ammunition storehouse explodes. Upset by their general's death and by the discovery of a scalp in a government office, U.S. troops go on a rampage, looting and burning public buildings.

May 27, 1813: U.S. troops capture Fort George from the British.

June 1, 1813: In command of the USS *Chesapeake* when it is defeated by the HMS *Shannon,* a mortally wounded Captain James Lawrence tells his crew "Don't give up the ship!" just before he dies. The phrase becomes the motto of the U.S. Navy.

July 1813: A civil war among the Creeks—Native Americans who live in present-day Alabama and Mississippi—erupts when an aggressive faction called the Red Sticks violently resists white settlement. This conflict overlaps with the War of 1812. In the opening battle of the Creek War, U.S. soldiers attack a force of Red Sticks at Burnt Corn Creek (located about eighty miles north of Pensacola in what is now Florida) on July 27. The Americans flee, and the Red Sticks claim a victory.

August 30, 1813: About 300 Americans (including both soldiers and civilians) who had taken refuge at Fort Mims (about forty miles north of Mobile, Alabama) are surprised by a Red Stick attack. About 250 are killed, spreading terror among white settlers across the entire U.S. frontier.

September 10, 1813: On Lake Erie, Commander Oliver Hazard Perry becomes a national hero after defeating the British fleet under Captain Robert Barclay.

October 1813: Native American hopes for an alliance to resist white settlement is crushed after the great Native American war chief Tecumseh is killed while fighting for the British during the Battle of the Thames.

November 1813: Called on to aid in fighting the hostile Creeks, U.S. troops under the command of Tennessee militia general **Andrew Jackson** launch successful attacks on the Red Stick villages of Tallushatchee and Talledega.

December 1813: The United States evacuates Fort George, but on their way out they burn the nearby Canadian town of Newark after giving its residents only twelve hours notice. The British subsequently capture Fort Niagara, and in retaliation for the burning of Newark destroy the New York towns of Lewiston, Black Rock, and Buffalo.

December 1813: The British offer to begin peace negotiations. Madison quickly accepts the offer.

March 1814: The Napoleonic Wars end as the British send Napoleon into exile. With more troops now available, Great Britain can take a more offensive approach to the war in North America.

March 27, 1814: About eight hundred Native Americans are killed at the Battle of Horseshoe Bend, and the Creek War soon comes to an end. Creek leaders are later forced to sign the Treaty of Fort Jackson, by which the United States acquires twenty million acres of Creek land.

July 5, 1814: At the Battle of Chippewa, U.S. troops under General **Winfield Scott** perform brilliantly, demonstrating the results of a strict training program.

August 1814: Representatives from the United States and Great Britain arrive in Ghent, Belgium, to begin peace negotiations.

August 24, 1814: Heading for Washington, D.C., the British win an easy victory over a hastily assembled, poorly trained, and inexperienced U.S. force during the Battle of Bladensburg.

August 24, 1814: As the British approach, First Lady **Dolley Madison** flees the city and carries important government documents and other items to safety. That evening the British enter the capital and spend twenty-four hours in the city, destroying many public buildings, including the president's home.

September 11, 1814: A newly reinforced U.S. naval fleet under Commander **Thomas Macdonough** defeats a British fleet on Lake Champlain (located between the borders of New York and Vermont on the west and east and Canada on the north). The victory shatters British hopes of gaining new territory in the northeast, and makes Macdonough a national hero.

September 14, 1814: Watching the bombardment of Baltimore's Fort McHenry from a ship, Georgetown lawyer **Francis Scott Key** is moved to write *The Star-Spangled Banner,* which gains so much popularity that it eventually becomes the national anthem of the United States.

November 6, 1814: Operating on his own initiative, Andrew Jackson leads U.S. troops in a siege on Pensacola, a town in Spanish-held Florida that had earlier been taken by the British. Jackson believes that control of Pensacola is key to dominating the southeastern region.

December 15, 1814: The Hartford Convention begins with twenty-six delegates from six New England states meeting to discuss their discontent with the way the Federal government has treated their region during the war.

December 24, 1814: U.S. and British representatives sign the Treaty of Ghent, which returns conditions to their *status quo antebellum* (the way they were before the war began). However, the war will not officially end until the two countries ratify (officially approve) the treaty in February.

January 8, 1815: During the Battle of New Orleans, a much larger British force surrendered to Andrew Jackson's varied troops, which included militiamen as well as free blacks, friendly Native Americans, Creoles (people of mixed heritage), and pirates. Americans are thrilled and inspired by the victory.

February 17, 1815: The war officially ends at 11:00 P.M. Most Americans feel that the United States has emerged victorious.

April 1815: Still detained in England's Dartmoor Prison, about sixty-five hundred American prisoners of war become unruly and the British guards fire on them, killing seven and injuring thirty-one. The incident fuels anti-British feeling in the United States.

1816: James Monroe succeeds Madison as president. Because the Federalists have by now fallen completely out of favor, politics is dominated by a one-party system, and Monroe runs unopposed. His election ushers in a brief period of harmony called the "Era of Good Feeling."

Research and Activity Ideas

Debate the Pros and Cons: With several classmates, write and record a "radio" interview with residents of Baltimore, one of whom supports the war effort and one who opposes it. Stage the interview around the time of the Baltimore Riots. Or pretend you are listening in on the congressional debates about the war.

A Woman's Words: Write several journal entries of either a woman who is staying in an army camp with her soldier husband, or a woman settler in Alabama who is concerned about the increase in attacks against whites by Native Americans in her area. Try to include as many details about daily life, as well as events of the war, as you can.

Recreate a Famous Scene: Build a diorama or make a painting showing the meeting between William Weatherford or Red Eagle and Andrew Jackson after the Battle of Horseshoe Bend.

Produce a Play: With several classmates, write and act out a play dramatizing Canadian homemaker Laura Secord's daring, twenty-mile journey across difficult terrain to warn British troops about a planned American attack. Other characters in the play could include Laura's husband, James Secord, Lieutenant Colonel Charles Boerstler and other U.S. officers, an Iroquois warrior, and British Lieutenant James Fitzgibbon.

The Life of an American Soldier or Sailor: Pretend you are a young American soldier and write letters home telling your family about your experiences. You could, for example, be a member of the Tennessee militia serving under Andrew Jackson, or a crew member on the USS *Niagara* in the Battle of Lake Erie. Include details about your daily routine as well as information about events and people important in the war.

Create a Music Program: Find examples of music from the War of 1812 period (such as the *1812 Overture* and *The Star-Spangled Banner*) and put together a recording or live presentation that includes narrative commentary about the pieces (when and how they were composed, performed, preserved, etc.).

Where It Happened: Make a map that shows the sea battles of the War of 1812, the routes of some famous privateers, or focus on the events that occurred in one specific theater or area of action (such as along the Niagara River or in what are now the states of Louisiana, Mississippi, Alabama, and Florida).

Show How They Dressed: Make a series of drawings illustrating the uniforms worn by American and British soldiers as well as the clothing worn by Native American warriors who took part in the war.

Hearing Other Voices: Write and perform a monologue in the character of 1) a former slave who is now serving as a U.S. Navy sailor under Commander Oliver Hazard Perry on Lake Erie; 2) a free black man who has answered General Andrew Jackson's call to defend New Orleans against a British invasion; or 3) a Native American wife and mother who is anxiously awaiting the return of her husband, who is fighting with General Isaac Brock.

Almanac

The Forgotten War

1

His name was Zebulon Montgomery Pike (1779–1813; see biographical entry). He was a courageous, fair-minded American general well-liked by his troops. On the morning of April 27, 1813, they followed him into battle as they had so often before, this time in an attempt to overtake the British forces at Fort York (located at present-day Toronto, Canada). The general and his men crossed Lake Ontario and began their march through smoke and bullets, aided by covering fire from U.S. Navy ships on the lake behind them. It looked like the British would soon surrender, so Pike halted his troops about six hundred feet from the fort.

The general was questioning a captured British soldier when, without warning, there was a tremendous explosion. Several hundred barrels of gunpowder and a huge amount of ammunition in the fort's weapons storehouse had been ignited, sending up towers of fire and smoke and spewing rocks and other debris in all directions. More than a hundred men were immediately killed or badly wounded. Pike was slammed by a large boulder that crushed his chest and tore into his back. Passing his command to a colonel, he told his troops, "Push on my brave fellows and avenge your general."

As Pike grew weaker and weaker, he finally heard the joyful shouts of his men as they raised the American flag over Fort York. Although now unable to speak, he motioned for the captured flag of Great Britain to be brought to him. It was placed beneath his head just before he died.

By the time they reach middle school, most American students understand that the Revolutionary War (1775–83) was fought to liberate the United States from British rule. They know that the Civil War (1861–65) was a conflict between the Northern and Southern states and that it involved such issues as slavery and states' rights. The wars of the twentieth century are familiar: World War I (1914–18) and World War II (1939–45), the wars in Korea (1950–53) and Vietnam (1954–75), and the recent Persian Gulf War (1991).

The War of 1812 (1812–14), however, remains a mystery to many people. In fact it is sometimes called "The Forgotten War," because only a few history students can recall why or where it was fought, or by whom. It followed so closely on the heels of the more exciting American Revolution that it seems to have gotten lost in a mist...or perhaps in a cloud of cannon smoke!

Nevertheless, Americans do remember the War of 1812, often without realizing it. Every time we sing our national anthem, "The Star Spangled Banner" at a baseball game, we are really remembering a scene of glory and pride from the War of 1812. Every time we use the expression, "Don't give up the ship!" we are really quoting the famous words of James Lawrence (1781–1813), a naval commander of the War of 1812. If we have heard of Pike's Peak, Colorado, or the folk song, "Sweet Betsy from Pike," we are familiar with the name of the well-known and popular general (and an explorer of the American West) Zebulon Montgomery Pike from the story at the beginning of this chapter.

Contradictions and missed communications

The War of 1812 was a conflict full of contradictions and missed communications. For example, the war might have been avoided altogether if there had been some faster way to

communicate than waiting for a letter to travel across the Atlantic Ocean on a ship. At the beginning of the nineteenth century there was no telephone or even telegraph to relay the news that Great Britain was willing to change the law containing trade restrictions that Americans were getting ready to fight against. Several years later, when the war's biggest battle was fought at New Orleans, no one in the United States yet knew that a peace treaty had been signed two weeks earlier!

Pike's Peak is named after Zebulon Montgomery Pike, an explorer of the American west and a popular general during the War of 1812. *Photograph reproduced by permission of Corbis Corporation (Bellevue).*

Supposedly, the War of 1812 was all about the United States's right to carry on sea trade without being harassed, yet most of the fighting took place far inland. The Treaty of Ghent, the agreement that ended the war, resolved none of the issues that had started it. And when the dust kicked up by marching soldiers had cleared, and the smoke of cannons fired from the decks of warships had drifted off, neither side could claim victory.

Why was the war fought?

So what was the meaning of this strange, short war, and what were its results? When U.S. president James Madison (1751–1836; see biographical entry) delivered his "war message" to the Congress, in 1812 recommending that the country enter into a war with Great Britain, he stated that the British had committed some unforgivable crimes against the United States. These included the frequent violation of neutrality rights (the right of a nation that is not at war not to be pulled into or hurt by other countries' conflicts), interference with trade, and the practice of impressment, by which British officials often boarded U.S. ships to capture deserters from their own navy, often wrongfully taking American citizens in the process.

But these weren't the only reasons that many Americans sought a war with Great Britain. Some thought that Canada (then a British colony) and Florida (most of which was held by Spain) should be part of the United States, and they reasoned that war would provide a way to acquire both. It also was widely believed that Great Britain was encouraging and even helping the Native Americans in the Northwest Territory (now the states of Ohio, Michigan, Indiana, and Illinois) to attack white Americans trying to settle on Native American lands.

It also is important to remember that this conflict took place only about twenty years after the United States had won its freedom from England. The euphoria of that victory had given way to the hard realities of running a new nation and keeping it free. The War of 1812 showed Americans and others that, despite differences of opinion and a serious lack of military preparation, the United States would and could defend its independence. That is why the War of 1812 is sometimes called the Second War of Independence.

The war drew to a close in early 1815 at the Battle of New Orleans, where a ragged but plucky assortment of troops defeated a much larger British force. In the wake of this surprising and thrilling victory, many Americans felt a renewed sense of pride in and loyalty to their country. In addition, those who hoped to settle in the vast areas west of the Appalachians (the mountain range that extended from Canada into central America and had previously marked the frontier) could now do so at less risk, because the most important alliance of Native Americans had been crushed. The great Shawnee leader Tecumseh (c. 1768–1813; see biographical entry), who had tried to rally Indians of many tribal nations to join together to resist white people's encroachment on Native American land, had died in the war while fighting alongside the British.

The end of the War of 1812 marked the start of a new phase in America's development. It helped Americans feel more confident as they took up the task of building their economy, settling their land, and creating their own culture.

Native American life in the Northwest Territory before white settlers began encroaching on Native American land. *Photograph reproduced by permission of North Wind Picture Archives.*

Sources

Books

Elting, John R. *Amateurs to Arms!: A Military History of the War of 1812.* 1991. Reprint. Cambridge, Mass.: Da Capo Press, 1995.

Heidler, David S., and Jeanne T. Heidler, eds. *Encyclopedia of the War of 1812.* Santa Barbara, Calif.: ABC-CLIO, 1997.

Hickey, Donald R. *The War of 1812: A Forgotten Conflict.* Urbana: University of Illinois Press, 1989.

Mahon, John K. *The War of 1812.* 1972. Reprint. Cambridge, Mass.: Da Capo Press, 1991.

Rutland, Robert, ed. *James Madison and the American Nation, 1751–1836.* New York: Simon and Schuster, 1994.

Web sites

Discriminating Generals. [Online] http://www.militaryheritage.com/home.htm (accessed on November 26, 2001).

Documents on the War of 1812. [Online] http://www.hillsdale.edu/dept/History/Documents/War/FR1812.htm (accessed on November 26, 2001).

"War of 1812." *KidInfo.* [Online] http://www.kidinfo.com/American_History/warof1812.html (accessed on November 26, 2001).

"War of 1812." *Studyweb.* [Online] http://www.studyweb.com/links/388.html (accessed on November 26, 2001).

Thomas Warner Letters. [Online] http://www.haemo-sol.com/thomas/thomas.html (accessed on November 26, 2001).

War of 1812. [Online] http://www.galafilm.com/1812/e/index.html (accessed on November 26, 2001).

War of 1812–1814. [Online] http://www.members.tripod.com/~war1812/ (accessed on November 26, 2001).

War of 1812—Forgotten War. [Online] http://www.multied.com/1812/ (accessed on November 26, 2001).

Establishing a Democratic Republic

2

The Revolutionary War (1775–83), the conflict that sealed America's independence from Great Britain, officially ended in 1783, when both sides signed the Treaty of Paris. The first U.S. government system was based on the Articles of Confederation, which reflected the founders' fear that a strong central government—like the one from which they had just freed themselves—threatened individual liberty. Through the Articles of Confederation, the thirteen individual states (New Hampshire, Massachusetts, Rhode Island, Connecticut, New Jersey, New York, Delaware, Pennsylvania, Maryland, Virginia, North Carolina, South Carolina, and Georgia) were joined together in a "firm league of friendship" that gave the national government only limited power. Under the Articles, Congress did not have power to tax, could not regulate commerce (business conducted between states or with other foreign governments), and did not have the power to maintain armed forces, a perilous defect for a young nation in a dangerous world.

In May 1787 fifty-five delegates from twelve states (only Rhode Island's delegates did not attend, due to a dispute about trade) gathered in Philadelphia, Pennsylvania, at the Constitutional Convention, where the Constitution that is still in place today was created. The framers of the U.S. Constitution (those who conceived of and wrote it) felt that the best model of government for their nation was the democratic republic, a system in which the power of individual citizens is delegated or given to elected representatives. This model features a balance of power between federal and state governments and among the three government branches: legislative (lawmakers), executive (the president), and judicial (the legal system). Despite expanding the powers of the federal government, the concept of a limited government was continued. The Constitution was ratified in 1789, and three years later a set of ten amendments called the Bill of Rights was added. While protecting the rights of individuals, the Bill of Rights was intended to further limit the power of the federal government.

Two political parties emerge

The Constitution's framers hoped that the government would remain as unified as it had been when the first president of the United States, the unanimously elected George Washington (1732–1799; president 1789–93) took office. Nevertheless, differing ideas about the role of government in people's lives led to the emergence of two distinct political parties with different philosophies.

These differences of opinion had been expressed during the debates that came before the Constitution's ratification. Those who supported the Constitution—including statesman Alexander Hamilton (1757–1804), future president James Madison (1751–1836; see biographical entry), and future Supreme Court chief justice John Jay (1745–1829)—were called Federalists. They pushed for a strong central government and the growth of commerce and industry, attracting the support not only of wealthy merchants, lawyers, and owners of large plantations but of city dwellers. They believed that only a powerful national government could handle such tasks as controlling the settlement of the West, overseeing commerce and taxation, and establishing an army capable of fending off foreign invaders.

Opposed to the Federalists were small-scale farmers and others who worried that Congress would burden people

with high taxes, that the president had too much power, and that ordinary people's concerns would be overlooked in favor of the wealthy. At first those who shared these concerns were not part of any particular group, but eventually they come together as a political party known as Democratic-Republicans or just Republicans led by Thomas Jefferson (1743–1846; president 1801–09).

The nation's founders disapproved of political parties, which they believed existed only to promote the interests of members rather than the good of the whole country. Nevertheless, by the early 1790s it was clear that there were two such groups in the United States, the Federalists and the Republicans, each claiming that it had been forced into taking a party stance on various issues by the other side. The Federalists dominated the political scene through the 1790s. The last Federalist president, John Adams (1735–1826; president 1797–1801), worked to build the young nation's commercial interests along with its army and navy. The population of the

The delegates at the Constitutional Convention in May 1787 created the democratic form of government which is still in place in the United States. *Photograph courtesy of The Library of Congress.*

United States was growing, however, and the majority of its citizens were living on small farms. There was increasing resentment toward the growing military and taxes necessary to support the stronger federal government. More and more Americans were coming to see the Republican Party as the defender of common, working people. In 1801 Republican Party candidate Jefferson won the presidential election. Although Jefferson tried to downplay the division between the parties, claiming "We are all Republicans—we are all Federalists," it was clear that his own party had come to the forefront. Jefferson and Congress proceeded to cut the size of the United States's army and navy in order to cut expenses and reduce the national debt created by the previous Federalist administration, leaving the country in no position to go to war.

Important events, at home and abroad

While the young nation was struggling with its internal politics, during the first decade of the nineteenth century, several important events took place both at home and abroad that would change the course of American development and lead directly to the War of 1812. One was the war being fought in Europe between Great Britain and France, and the other was the Louisiana Purchase, which added a vast area of new territory to the United States. At the same time white settlers desire for lands traditionally inhabited by Native Americans would influence a war that was supposed to be about the freedom to roam the sea.

The Napoleonic Wars

In 1789 the French Revolution ended the reign of monarchs (kings and queens) in France. What followed was a period of great violence and chaos when the new government proved unstable. France was involved in a number of military conflicts in Europe and elsewhere, including the so-called Quasi War (1798–1800) with the United States, when the two countries fought an undeclared war over shipping rights, mostly in the Caribbean region. In 1799 a popular military commander named Napoleon Bonaparte (1769–1821) took over as leader of France, initially calling himself First Consul for Life but eventually taking on the title of Emperor Napoleon I.

Napoleon brought order and many positive changes to France, especially in the areas of law, education, and the economy. But he also carried on an aggressive, expensive, and finally disastrous campaign to conquer the rest of Europe.

Napoleon's armies gained victories in many parts of Europe, including Austria, Italy, and most of Germany, in the quest for a French empire. Nevertheless, France could not overcome the awesome strength of the British navy and thus was unable to invade Great Britain. The final blow came at the Battle of Trafalgar in October 1805, when Napoleon was soundly beaten by a British naval force under the command of Admiral Horatio Nelson (1758–1805), firmly establishing Great Britain as the "Mistress of the Seas." As long as Great Britain controlled the sea, Napoleon had no hope of conquering the British.

A trade battle at sea

Unable to defeat Great Britain through military action, Napoleon began a campaign to damage its trade with other countries. In 1806 and 1807 he issued the Berlin and Milan decrees, which ordered all nations to stop trading with Great Britain or face stern punishment (such as seizure of ships) from France. The British responded with laws called the Orders in Council, which required anyone intending to trade with France to stop first in England and purchase a license. This created a blockade of European ports, meaning that those who did not go along with the order could lose their ships if they were caught.

The United States was caught squarely in the middle of this economic battle. Before this, American merchants and shipping companies had made a lot of money through trade with both Great Britain and France, profiting especially from the needs of both countries for war materials. Now their ships could be seized by either country, even though the United States was officially neutral (not involved in the war). The United States had enjoyed a relatively good relationship with France (especially after the end of the Quasi War in 1800 and the election of Republican president Thomas Jefferson) but because the British ruled the seas, the United States had no real choice in the matter but to follow Great Britain's orders. Some ships did ignore the blockade. The profits were great, but so were the risks: between 1807 and 1812 France and Great Britain (along with their allies) seized about nine hundred American ships.

Impressment angers Americans more

At the same time, American resentment of Great Britain's rule of the high seas was being stirred up even more by a practice called impressment. The British navy was known as the best in the world, yet its sailors were among the world's unhappiest. They suffered from dismal working conditions and harsh discipline and were paid very low wages. Many deserted, often finding jobs on American merchant ships or even U.S. Navy ships. (In fact, it is estimated that about a quarter of the fifty thousand to one hundred thousand sailors who worked on American ships during this period were British.) Great Britain claimed the right to stop ships at sea and search them for deserters, who would then be impressed (forced) back into service with the British navy. Americans objected not only because they felt that no one had the right to stop their ships, but because U.S. sailors were sometimes impressed by mistake. Between 1803 and 1812 as many as six thousand Americans may have been impressed into the British navy. The British justified this by insisting that anyone born in Great Britain was a British citizen, even if he or she had since become an American citizen under U.S. law.

The *Chesapeake-Leopard* incident

The sparks of anti-British feeling were stirred into a blaze by an incident that occurred in June 1807. As it was sailing out of Chesapeake Bay (on the East Coast of the United States in the present-day states of Maryland and Virginia), the U.S. Navy frigate (a two-decked warship that could carry from twenty-five to fifty guns) *Chesapeake* was stopped by the British naval ship *Leopard*. The *Leopard*'s commander, Captain Salusbury Humphreys, demanded that several deserters who had sought refuge on the *Chesapeake* be returned to the *Leopard*. The *Chesapeake*'s commander, Commodore James Barron, denied that there were any British sailors on board and refused the British permission to search his ship. The *Leopard* responded by attacking the unsuspecting *Chesapeake* with a broadside (firing all the guns on one side of a warship at more or less the same time) that killed three sailors and injured eighteen. Unprepared for battle, the *Chesapeake* immediately surrendered. The British boarded and removed four sailors, one of whom was eventually hanged for desertion.

News of this incident was itself like a broadside, causing an explosion of anger among Americans. There were even calls for war against Great Britain, and some state militias (small armies made up of troops residing in a particular state; under certain circumstances they could be called into action by the federal government) began gearing up for a fight. Jefferson wanted to avoid war, but he did order all British warships out of U.S. ports. Four years later Great Britain would apologize for the incident, but by that time the damage was done...the insult had been felt too deeply.

Jefferson tries to punish Great Britain and France

Meanwhile Jefferson had already taken some steps to force Great Britain to change its damaging trade policies. In 1806 Congress passed the Non-Importation Act, which said that no British goods could be imported to the United States. Since the act actually took effect after the *Chesapeake-Leopard* incident had so angered Americans, Jefferson realized stronger measures were needed. So in December 1807 Jefferson, knowing the United States's military readiness was inadequate and in armed conflict the young nation would surely meet defeat, responded with the Embargo Act, which barred U.S. ships from sailing to any foreign ports and thus halted U.S. trade with other countries. Jefferson thought this act would punish Great Britain and France, but his plan backfired.

Although the effects of the Embargo Act were felt in Great Britain and France, it did the most damage in the United States. The act proved devastating to the merchants, shipowners, and sailors of the northeastern United States, who depended on overseas trade for their livelihoods. Southern planters, who had previously sold vast quantities of tobacco, rice, and cotton to Great Britain, also were hurt. Farm-

Public Opinion on the Embargo Act

The following newspaper editorial documents public sentiment on the matter of the Embargo Act. The act was passed in 1807 as a result to a series of restrictions on U.S. shipping and commerce by Great Britain and France. Controversial from the beginning, the act eliminated trade with other nations and was supposed to force Britain and France into respecting the neutral trading rights of the United States. Although the law inconvenienced England somewhat, it severely disrupted the U.S. economy, especially that of the New England States. As a result, the act was repealed by Congress in 1809.

"The Embargo Experiment Ended," *Baltimore Federal Republican,* March 1809

The embargo now ceases to be in force, and every merchant who can give a bond with good sureties to double the amount of vessel and cargo, is entitled to clear out for any port except in France or England or the dependency of either of them. After depriving government of its means of support for sixteen months, and preventing the people of the United States from pursuing a lawful and profitable commerce, and reducing the whole country to a state of wretchedness and poverty, our infatuated rulers, blinded by a corrupt predilection [preference] for France, have been forced to acknowledge their fatal error, and so far to retrace their steps. To the patriotism of the New England States is due the praise of our salvation. By their courage and virtue have we been saved from entanglements in a fatal alliance with France. The whole system of fraud and corruption has been exposed to the people, and those very men who were the first to cast off the yoke of England, have lived to save their country from falling under the command of a more cruel tyrant. The patriot who had the courage to encounter the fury of the political storm, who stepped forth in the hour of danger to give the first alarm to his country, we trust will one day be rewarded with the highest honors in the gift of a grateful people.

Source: Documents on the War of 1812. *[Online]* http://www.hillsdale.edu/dept/History/Documents/War/FR1812.htm (accessed on November 26, 2001).

ers couldn't sell their goods, ships sat idly in ports, and warehouses were empty. The measure's many opponents began referring to it as the "O-Grab-Me Act" (a name created by spelling embargo backwards).

After fourteen months, in 1809, the Embargo Act was replaced by the Non-Intercourse Act, which restored trade with all countries except Great Britain and France. It was followed by Macon's Bill Number 2 in 1810, which removed all trade restrictions but said that if either Great Britain or France would loosen its trade rules, the United States would put the non-intercourse law back in effect against the other country until it also agreed to change its rules. Eager to gain an advantage over England, Napoleon promised that he would lift the Berlin and Milan decrees, which had restricted trade with Great Britain. He had no intention of actually following through on this promise, but President James Madison (who had been elected in 1808) took him at his word and cut off all trade with Great Britain.

In 1809 the United States and Great Britain came close to resolving the problems through an agreement between Madison, when he was secretary of state under Jefferson, and George Erskine, Great Britain's minister to the United States. The Erskine Agreement, as it was called, said that Great Britain would drop its Orders in Council and the United States would drop its non-intercourse practices. But before the agreement could be signed, British foreign secretary George Canning (1770–1827), who was set on taking a much harder line toward the United States, called Erskine back to England. Both sides were disappointed by the failure of this diplomatic (related to international relations) effort.

By the summer of 1811, as efforts to resolve these disagreements continued to fail, it seemed that the United States was coming closer to war with Great Britain. More and more Americans suspected that England was up to its old tricks and hoping to turn the United States into a British colony again. In fact, the U.S. Congress was now dominated by a group of young lawmakers who felt this way and were eager for a fight would soon be granted.

The War Hawks dominate Congress

The 1808 election of James Madison as president of the United States extended the rule of the Republicans, the party of the previous president, Thomas Jefferson. In general, the Republicans were more anti-British and more inclined toward a war with Great Britain than the Federalists, who were afraid that a war would hurt America's shipping industry even more. But the influence of the Federalists was declining, and the congressional election of 1810 helped to push them farther down that slope. The new Congress was dominated by a group of aggressive, impatient young men whose enthusiasm for starting a new conflict with Great Britain led to their being nicknamed the War Hawks.

Most of the War Hawks were from the western and southern states, where people favored going to war with Great Britain, not only over shipping but also to secure their settlements on the frontier and possibly to acquire new land to settle. The very influential Speaker of the House (elected by all of the representatives to serve as their leader) was Henry Clay from Kentucky; other War Hawks included South Carolina's John Calhoun and Felix Grundy of Tennessee. Too young to remember the devastating toll that a war could take on a country (unlike the previous generation, which had lived through the American Revolution), these men argued that only all-out war would convince Great Britain to change its harmful policies on the seas. They also thought Great Britain was behind the Native American uprisings against the United States's western settlements.

Many Americans supported and represented by the War Hawks also wanted the United States to invade and conquer the large and valuable territory of Canada, which belonged to Great Britain. In addition, southerners were interested in expanding into the Spanish territory of Florida, then divided into East Florida and West Florida (covering what is now coastal Louisiana, Mississippi, and Alabama). This area was coveted because its easily navigated rivers would provide traders access to the Gulf of Mexico; it also served as a safe haven for runaway slaves and hostile Native Americans. The fact that Spain was an ally of Great Britain would provide an excuse for an invasion of the Spanish territory if the United States was at war with the British.

Americans eager to move west

Westward expansion (the movement of people westward past the first frontier, which had been defined by the western borders of the first thirteen colonies) had been an important issue even before the War Hawks and others began to covet Canada and Florida. Between 1790 and 1803 four new states had sprung into existence—Vermont, Kentucky, Tennessee, and Ohio—all of them carved out of what had been wilderness. Louisiana joined the union in 1812. The population of the United States was growing rapidly; in fact it would leap from three million in 1780 to eight million by 1815. Jefferson and other leaders believed that westward expansion was a necessary safety valve to keep cities from becoming overpopulated. Also, the failing shipping industry had caused high unemployment in the Northeast and it was hoped that the West would provide new economic opportunities.

In 1803 an agreement called the Louisiana Purchase made even more land available, fueling both Americans' enthusiasm for moving west and the government's need to make the frontier easier and safer to settle.

The Louisiana Purchase

Beyond the borders of the states that existed at the beginning of the nineteenth century was a huge land mass stretching to the Pacific Ocean, through which ranged the Native Americans who had lived there for thousands of years. Some white explorers and trappers also were there, many of them in search of valuable beaver pelts and other furs. From the early eighteenth century, a large portion of this land had been held by France; although it also had belonged to Great Britain and Spain for short periods, it was a French territory again by 1800.

This area covered more than eight hundred thousand square miles, including the present-day states of Arkansas, Missouri, Iowa, the part of Minnesota that is west of the Mississippi River, North Dakota, South Dakota, Nebraska, Oklahoma, most of Kansas, the parts of Montana, Wyoming, and Colorado that are east of the Rocky Mountains, and Louisiana west of the Mississippi but including the city of New Orleans.

The leader of France, Napoleon, dreamed of increasing his own and his country's fame and glory by establishing a great colonial empire in North America. But he was already waging an expensive war with England (see "The Napoleonic Wars" in this chapter). He was strapped for cash, so he decided to give up his dream of a New World empire and offer his North American territory to the United States. Although Jefferson and other leaders had no previous intention of acquiring France's land, Napoleon offered them an incredible bargain: this huge territory for only $15 million! The agreement between France and the United States, called the Louisiana Purchase, was signed in April 1803. The largest area ever added to the nation at one time, this purchase doubled the size of the United States, and it made westward expansion seem even more natural.

Native Americans resist white encroachment

Meanwhile, Americans were venturing into and beginning to settle what was called the Northwest Territory. It included the present-day states of Ohio (which in 1812 had about 250,000 white settlers), Indiana (which had 25,000), Illinois (13,000), and the still only sparsely populated Michigan. It was an area dense with forests, rivers, and lakes—including the five Great Lakes of Ontario, Erie, Huron, Michigan, and Superior—and home to the beaver and other animals whose pelts and furs were in great demand by fashion-conscious Europeans. The hunters and traders who had lived in the Northwest Territory for decades were now starting to give way to farmers and land speculators (people who buy land with the hope that they will be able to sell for a quick profit) knew they could make their fortunes selling land to settlers.

Between 1783 and 1815 the U.S. Congress passed a series of land acts that made it easier for ordinary people to buy land. Territory that had previously been inhabited by Native Americans was being opened up to white settlers, being acquired through purchase, treaties, or by just taking the land and driving the Native Americans away. This practice was justified by the American sense of what would come to be known as "manifest destiny," the idea that it was actually the duty of white people (who viewed their own culture as superior to those of native peoples), to conquer the continent.

Meanwhile, the many Native American tribes who lived in the wide-open expanses of the United States, existing as they had for thousands of years by hunting and small-scale farming and often warring with each other, did not share Eu-

ropean ideas about land ownership. The concept that one person could own a piece of earth was not understood by them. The result was that they were often cheated or tricked into signing away their rights to the land beneath their feet. Both white settlers and the Native Americans who had signed treaties often failed to honor them, and conflicts increased in number and intensity. The U.S. government let the Native Americans know that if they planned to settle down as farm-

A map of the Northwest Territory. During the late 1700s and early 1800s Americans began settling into the Northwest Territory, often displacing the Native Americans that were already living in the area. *Photograph reproduced by permission of the Granger Collection.*

ers and adapt themselves to the ways of white people they could remain in the region, otherwise they must leave their traditional hunting grounds and move farther west. The Native Americans saw white settlers arriving in greater and greater numbers, and their resentment led to violence.

Frequent and brutal attacks on white settlements by members of the Shawnee, Delaware, Miami, and Winnebago tribes who lived in the Northwest Territory struck fear in the hearts of those who were considering a move to that region. The United States government was encouraging its citizens to settle these territories (which were slated to become states eventually), and war veterans were even offered free land. The potential rewards were great, but there was a great risk of death at the hands of angry Native Americans. Contributing to these concerns was the widely held belief that the British, who carried on a great deal of fur trading in the territory, were actively encouraging the natives to attack settlers. It was even said—just as it had been during the Revolutionary War—that British agents paid Native Americans for white scalps. Claims like these were probably exaggerated, but the War Hawks made much of this rumored alliance between Great Britain and Native Americans because it helped to fuel their drive toward war. The Battle of Tippecanoe, a conflict between U.S. soldiers and Native Americans in what is now Indiana, provided a spark to ignite that fuel.

The Battle of Tippecanoe

Some historians consider the Battle of Tippecanoe (named for the river near which it took place) the first battle of the War of 1812, even though it took place about seven months before war was officially declared. In any case, it would prove to be one of the major confrontations between Native Americans and whites to take place east of the Mississippi River.

In the years just before the outbreak of the War of 1812, a Native American leader of great power and character emerged, and for a short time his existence seemed to pose the biggest threat to westward expansion. A member of the Shawnee tribe, Tecumseh (c.1768–1813; see biographical entry) was intelligent and courageous and had won the respect of his enemies as well as his allies. He believed that the only way Native Americans could hold on to their land—and thus to the lives they had known for so many centuries—was through organized, unified resistance against white encroachment (gradually taking over another person's property).

Convincing all of the different tribes, many of which had fought bitterly against each other in the past, to come together was no easy task. Aiding Tecumseh in his mission was his brother, Tenskwatawa (1775–1836; see box in Tecumseh biographical entry), a shaman or medicine man whom white people called the Prophet. Seven years younger than Tecumseh, Tenskwatawa had once been addicted (dependent on a habit-forming substance) to alcohol, but he had overcome his addiction and urged other Native Americans to put aside the bad habits they had learned from white people (especially drinking liquor, which had already done much damage among the Native American populations). While Tecumseh told Native Americans that their land was owned jointly by all of them and thus could not be signed away by any one person or tribe, his brother told them to hold on to traditional beliefs and customs. Together these brothers became an effective pair.

Tenskwatawa aided his brother Tecumseh in his mission to unify the Native American tribes to resist white settlement into Native American land. *Photograph reproduced by permission of Hulton/Archive.*

Tecumseh's followers gather at Prophet's Town

Tecumseh began traveling up and down the Mississippi River valley to gain support for his cause. Beginning in 1808 the followers he and Tenskwatawa had attracted began to gather at a village called Prophet's Town, located in northern Indiana near the present-day town of Lafayette. Meanwhile, the governor of Indiana, William Henry Harrison

(1773–1841; see biographical entry), was extremely worried about the increasing Native American resistance; furthermore, he believed that the British were helping the Native Americans in their cause. Harrison was strongly in favor of westward expansion and had pushed it along himself in 1809 by getting chiefs of the Potawatomi, Miami, and Delaware tribes to give up some of their lands. During the summer of 1810 Harrison met with Tecumseh, who told the governor that there could be no sale of Native Americans' land without the approval of all, and that he would severely punish the chiefs who had cooperated with Harrison.

The next summer Tecumseh again met with Harrison at Vincennes, Indiana. Although Harrison had asked him to come unarmed, Tecumseh showed up with several hundred battle-dressed warriors. Tecumseh told Harrison that the Native American alliance was simply imitating the example of the United States by banding together for their own good and protection. As he left Vincennes, Tecumseh informed Harrison that from there he would travel south to visit more Native American communities. Harrison realized that Tecumseh's absence from Prophet's Town made this a good time to stifle the trouble he believed was brewing there.

Gathering a force of one thousand men that included regular U.S. Army soldiers as well as members of Indiana's militia and some volunteers from Kentucky, Harrison headed toward the village. He intended to demand that the Native Americans there first hand over those responsible for some recent attacks on white settlers, then disperse. On November 6, as the group neared Prophet's Town, they received a message from Tenskwatawa proposing a meeting the next day. Harrison and his men stopped and set up camp for the night.

A bloody confrontation

Meanwhile, in Prophet's Town, Tenskwatawa (in Tecumseh's absence) was busy stirring the gathering of Native Americans from ten or more different tribes into a frenzy of anger and bloodthirstiness. He told them they should attack the white men's camp under the cover of darkness, and he promised them that his magical powers would turn the enemy

bullets into soft, harmless clumps of mud. The Native Americans attacked in the early morning hours of November 7, 1811.

At first it seemed that the Native Americans had the advantage, as the light from their burning campfires made Harrison's troops easy targets. In the first moments of the battle many of Harrison's men were killed, and Harrison himself had a narrow escape: in the confusion, he had been unable to find his white horse and had leapt onto a dark one instead, while the officer who mounted Harrison's horse was killed by Indians who thought they were slaying the general. After about two hours, however, the Indians retreated, leaving behind thirty-eight dead warriors. The Americans suffered about two hundred casualties, including about sixty-three men killed either during the battle or aboard the jolting wagons that carried the wounded away. The total casualties on Tenskwatawa's side were probably similar. Proclaiming a great victory for his own men—since the goal of chasing the Native

A scene from the Battle of Tippecanoe in which William Henry Harrison's troops defeated Tenskwatawa and his warriors. The battle began when Tenskwatawa disobeyed Tecumseh's orders and attacked Harrison's camp. *Photograph reproduced by permission of Corbis Corporation (Bellevue).*

Americans away from Prophet's Town had been met—Harrison ordered his troops to burn the now empty village.

Tenskwatawa's followers were furious, and the weak excuses he offered for why his magic had not protected them fell flat. Tecumseh returned to find Prophet's Town in ruins and his brother disgraced. He banished Tenskwatawa to keep him from causing further trouble. Believing that now his only option was an alliance with the British, who promised to protect Native Americans' rights to land if they won the war, Tecumseh finally joined those Native Americans who had agreed to fight alongside the British. In October 1813 he would lose his life at the Battle of the Thames (near present-day Chatham, Ontario, Canada).

The Battle of Tippecanoe had three major results: it helped bring an end to any prospect of an alliance among the Native American tribes, it helped Harrison win the 1840 presidential election—Harrison played on his reputation as a war hero, using as his campaign slogan "Tippecanoe and Tyler Too" (John Tyler [1790–1862] was the vice presidential candidate), and it fueled people's eagerness for war with Great Britain. Americans reacted to the news of the battle with anger and indignation, adding it to their list of complaints about the difficulties of settling in the West. When it was learned that British weapons had been found on the battlefield, anti-British sentiment also was inflamed. Only a few days after the Battle of Tippecanoe, Congress met to discuss the prospect of war with Great Britain. Seven months later this war would become a reality.

Where to Learn More

Books

Cleaves, Freeman. *Old Tippecanoe: William Henry Harrison and His Time.* New York: Charles Scribner's Sons, 1939.

Dowd, Gregory Evans. *A Spirited Resistance: The North American Indian Struggle for Unity, 1745–1815.* Baltimore: Johns Hopkins University Press, 1992.

Dudley, William S., and Michael S. Crawford, eds. *The Naval War of 1812: A Documentary History.* 2 vols. Washington, DC: Naval Historical Center, 1985–92.

Edmunds, R. David. *The Shawnee Prophet.* Lincoln: University of Nebraska Press, 1983.

Edmunds, R. David. *Tecumseh and the Quest for Indian Leadership.* Boston: Little, Brown, 1984.

Elting, John R. *Amateurs to Arms!: A Military History of the War of 1812.* 1991. Reprint. Cambridge, Mass.: Da Capo Press, 1995.

Heidler, David S., and Jeanne T. Heidler, eds. *Encyclopedia of the War of 1812.* Santa Barbara, Calif.: ABC-CLIO, 1997.

Hickey, Donald R. *The War of 1812: A Forgotten Conflict.* Urbana: University of Illinois Press, 1989.

Mahon, John K. *The War of 1812.* 1972. Reprint. Cambridge, Mass.: Da Capo Press, 1991.

Web sites

Discriminating Generals. [Online] http://www.militaryheritage.com/home.htm (accessed on November 26, 2001).

Documents on the War of 1812. [Online] http://www.hillsdale.edu/dept/History/Documents/War/FR1812.htm (accessed on November 26, 2001).

"War of 1812." *KidInfo.* [Online] http://www.kidinfo.com/American_History/warof1812.html (accessed on November 26, 2001).

"War of 1812." *Studyweb.* [Online] http://www.studyweb.com/links/388.html (accessed on November 26, 2001).

Thomas Warner Letters. [Online] http:www.haemo-sol.com/thomas/thomas.html (accessed on November 26, 2001).

War of 1812. [Online] http://www.galafilm.com/1812/e/index.html (accessed on November 26, 2001).

War of 1812–1814. [Online] http://www.members.tripod.com/~war1812/ (accessed on November 26, 2001).

War of 1812—Forgotten War. [Online] http://www.multied.com/1812/ (accessed on November 26, 2001).

An Unpromising Beginning

The War of 1812 between the United States and Great Britain was provoked by two major issues. The first was Britain's maritime policy of impressment in its war with France. This policy was where British officials often boarded U.S. ships to capture deserters from their own navy, often wrongfully taking American citizens in the process. The other issues that led to the war was Great Britain's overly friendly relations with Native Americans. Americans believed that the British were encouraging Native Americans to attack white settlers who were moving west. The Native Americans believed that the settlers were encroaching on (gradually taking over) their land. Although these two issues led to Americans being eager to fight a war with Britain, the United States was not necessarily ready to fight such a war. In fact the first year of the war was a disaster for the United States, generally, due to poor preparation, poor leadership, and poor strategy.

Congress debates and plans for war

The congressional election of 1810 had brought to the forefront a number of young lawmakers eager for war with Great Britain, earning them the nickname War Hawks. When U.S. President James Madison (1751–1836; see biographical entry) called Congress into a special session in November 1811 to discuss the possibility of war, the War Hawks led the debate on the "yes" side. The "no" side was voiced by the outnumbered Federalists (a political party favoring a strong central government), who made up only 25 percent in the House of Representatives and 18 percent in the Senate; most prominent among them were Josiah Quincy (1772–1864; see biographical entry) of Massachusetts and James A. Bayard (1767–1815) of Delaware.

It might seem like a contradiction that representatives of the northeastern states, where so many people depended on the shipping industry for their livelihoods, would oppose a war in which the nation's shipping rights were being defended. But the fact is that northeastern shipping companies and merchants had made a good living despite the trade restrictions imposed by Great Britain and France. They enjoyed especially strong commercial relations with Great Britain, and they believed that severing those relations would be financially disastrous. The Federalists in Congress argued that the nation's disputes with Great Britain could and should be resolved by other means. They recommended that trade restrictions be lifted and suggested that U.S. merchant ships be allowed to carry weapons and defend themselves against any illegal actions. The Federalists also viewed the prospect of invading Canada with scorn, asking Republicans why a conflict that was supposedly all about shipping and sailors' rights would be fought on land.

For the next seven months the debate continued, while at the same time Congress enacted a number of measures to prepare the nation for war, even though it was generally expected (and hoped, by some people, at least) that Great Britain would change its policies in time to avoid war. Legislation was passed that authorized the army to bring its enlistment up to the authorized number of ten thousand (from less than seven thousand) and also to recruit twenty-five thousand regular soldiers to serve for five years. The president also was authorized to call up one hundred thousand state militiamen (small armies made up of troops residing in a particular state) to serve for six months.

At this time, Congress was dominated by Republicans who were, for the most, against taxes. For this reason, Congress did not approve any war taxes, and instead, arranged for loans from the Bank of the United States (BUS)—a centralized, national bank created by Congress in 1799, over the protests of the Republicans. These loans proved a problem, however, because the twenty-year charter of the BUS had expired in 1810. Republicans opposed anything they saw as giving the federal government too much power and refused to renew the charter. That meant that the government had to borrow money from state banks with higher interest rates (the fees banks charge for the privilege of borrowing money). The war exposed this serious weakness of the U.S. economy, leading to a recharter of the national bank after the war.

The United States declares war

For a while Madison tried to use diplomacy (the art or practice of handling international relations, including negotiating treaties, alliances, and trade agreements) to resolve the problems with Great Britain and was expecting a breakthrough. As he awaited word from Britain, the War Hawks pressed their demands for war. On June 1, Madison relented and delivered to Congress a war message in which he stated that the British practices of impressing American seamen, interfering with U.S. trade, and urging and aiding Native Americans to commit acts of violence against Americans had made war necessary. Three days later, the House of Representatives approved the Declaration of War with a vote of seventy-nine to forty-nine; on June 17 the Senate voted in favor of the war by a margin of nineteen to thirteen. On June 18, Madison signed the formal war declaration. However, both vote tallies had revealed fairly substantial opposition to the war, especially in the northeastern states. From then on those who were against the war would scornfully refer to it as "Mr. Madison's War."

Meanwhile, in England, lawmakers had finally decided that a nation engaged in war with Napoleon (1769–1821; see "Napoleonic Wars" chapter 2) could not afford another conflict across the sea. But due to the slowness of communications between Europe and the United States, their decision came too late. Two days after Great Britain announced that it would repeal the Orders in Council, which required anyone intending

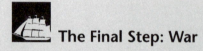

The Final Step: War

The following newspaper editorial from the *Washington National Intelligencer* supports the opinion that war should be declared against Great Britain. The author of the article believes that the United States has just cause for a war and will be successful defeating Britain.

Two months after this editorial was published the U.S. Congress did pass a declaration of war, and so began the War of 1812.

"War Should Be Declared," *Washington National Intelligencer*, April 14, 1812

But if the reports which we now hear are true, that with England all hope of honorable accommodation is at an end, and that with France our negotiations are in a forwardness encouraging expectations of a favorable result, where is the motive for longer delay? The final step ought to be taken, and that step is WAR. By what course of measures we have reached the present crisis, is not now a question for patriots and freemen to discuss. It exists: and it is by open and manly war only that we can get through it with honor and advantage to the country. Our wrongs have been great; our cause is just; and if we are decided and firm, success is inevitable.

Let war therefore be forthwith proclaimed against England. With her there can be no motive for delay. Any further discussion, any new attempt at negotiation, would be as fruitless as it would be dishonorable....

But is it said that we are not prepared for war, and ought therefore not to declare it. This is an idle objection, which can have weight with the timid and pusillanimous [cowardly] only. The fact is otherwise. Our preparations are adequate to

to trade with France to stop first in England and purchase a license, the United States (unaware of Great Britain's action) declared war against Great Britain.

The declaration of war had taken almost everybody by surprise, whether they were Republicans exhilarated by the news or Federalists who dreaded its effects on commerce. The vote in Congress had shown that a considerable number of Americans did not want to go to war. In the New England states, especially, many people were declaring their unwillingness to help with the war effort. Governor Caleb Strong (1745–1819) of Massachusetts even authorized a day of mourning in his state, when bells tolled and shops closed to

every essential object. Do we apprehend danger to ourselves? From what quarter will it assail us? From England, and by invasion? The idea is too absurd to merit a moment's consideration. Where are her troops? But lately she dreaded an invasion of her own dominions from her powerful and menacing neighbor [France]. That danger, it is true, has diminished, but it has not entirely and forever disappeared. The war in the Peninsula, which lingers, requires strong armies to support it. She maintains an army in Sicily; another in India; and a strong force in Ireland, and along her own coast, and in the West Indies. Can anyone believe that, under such circumstances, the British government could be so infatuated as to send troops here for the purpose of invasion? The experience and the fortune of our Revolution, when we were comparatively in an infant state, have doubtless taught her a useful lesson that she cannot have forgotten. Since that period our population has increased threefold, whilst hers has remained almost stationary. The condition of the civilized world, too, has changed. Although Great Britain has nothing to fear as to her independence, and her military operations are extensive and distant, the contest is evidently maintained by her rather for safety than for conquest. Have we cause to dread an attack from her neighboring provinces? That apprehension is still more groundless. Seven or eight millions of people have nothing to dread from 300,000. From the moment that war is declared, the British colonies will be put on the defensive, and soon after we get in motion must sink under the pressure.

Source: Documents on the War of 1812. [Online] http://www.hillsdale.edu/dept/History/Documents/War/FR1812.htm (accessed on November 26, 2001).

mark the beginning of what many citizens there viewed as a mistaken war. Massachusetts residents, like those in other New England states, were free to voice their opposition to the war. Those who took such a stance in the rough-and-tumble city of Baltimore, Maryland, however, paid a high price for speaking out.

The Baltimore Riots

In 1812 Baltimore was the fourth largest city in the United States, with a population of forty-one thousand. Located on the Chesapeake Bay, it was growing fast and was known as a rowdy place, especially around the neighborhood of Fells Point, close to the waterfront. It also happened to be a city with both a very high concentration of Republicans and an outspoken minority of war-opposing Federalists. Like members of their party in other cities, Baltimore's Republicans felt the time had come to support the war effort, no matter what differences of opinion had been expressed before war was declared. But the *Federal Republican,* a Baltimore newspaper that was considered the voice of the city's Federalists, disagreed. Under the spirited direction of its editor and co-owner, twenty-six-year-old Alexander Hanson (1786–1819), the newspaper came out passionately against Madison and the war. Other newspapers predicted that the *Federal Republican* would pay a high price for its stance, but Hanson refused to back down.

The Saturday, June 20 edition of the *Federal Republican* contained a strongly worded editorial condemning the war declaration, calling war completely "unnecessary," and suggesting that foreign nations (meaning France) were exerting too much influence on the U.S. government. The editorial stirred up Republican anger, and on the evening of Monday, June 22, a mob attacked and demolished the newspaper's offices. While city officials stood by, reluctant to become involved, the mob then marched to the waterfront, where they set on fire several Federalist-owned ships and other property.

Federalists everywhere were shocked and disgusted by this turn of events. For the next five weeks, the *Federal Republican* was published from a house near Washington, D.C. Then Hanson announced that the newspaper would soon begin publication from new offices in a house in Baltimore. War supporters immediately threatened to attack the *Federal Republican* again, and when city officials made no move to protect the newspaper, about twenty well-armed Federalists gathered to defend its offices. Among them were two well-known Revolutionary War (1775–83) veterans, General James Lingan and General Henry "Lighthorse Harry" Lee (1756–1818).

On June 27 the *Federal Republican* was published from its new Baltimore offices, featuring an editorial in which the previous violence against the newspaper was strongly condemned. That evening a crowd of angry war supporters gathered. At first they were content to throw stones at the house, but eventually they stormed its front door. The defenders inside opened fire, killing one man and injuring several others. The mob scattered, but later formed again. It was not until three o'clock in the morning that the city took action, and in this case it was not effective: two companies of militia and a cavalry unit were called out to restore order, but their commander, Brigadier General James Stricker (d. 1825), seemed not only unwilling to challenge the mob but actually sympathetic with them. By six o'clock the same morning, the crowd numbered between fifteen hundred and two thousand people. Finally, Baltimore mayor Edward Johnson and Stricker reached an agreement with those inside the newspaper office, guaranteeing them safe passage to the jail, where they would be charged with murder.

The price of dissent

Surrounded by militiamen, the *Federal Republican* defenders made their way to the jail, pelted constantly by rocks from the crowd, which remained outside the jail after the prisoners were safely inside. The newspaper's offices were quickly destroyed, and the militia made no attempt to intervene. Throughout the day, the crowd at the jail grew both in size and unruliness. By nightfall they had completely surrounded the jail, and finally they scared a guard into letting them enter. The terrified prisoners made a dash for the outside, hoping to mingle with the mob, but about half of them were caught. They were severely beaten and dumped in a heap on the front steps of the jail, where they remained exposed and subject to torture throughout the night.

Despite his pleas that his life be spared due to his age and war record, Lingan was killed, while Lee was crippled for the rest of his life. Hanson was severely injured and never fully recovered from his injuries; he died in 1819 at the age of thirty-three. A later investigation by the Maryland legislature found the city of Baltimore guilty of negligence in the incident, but city officials downplayed their role, and no one was ever punished for taking part in what came to be called the "Baltimore Massacre" or "Baltimore Riots." Federalists angrily denounced the incident, comparing it to the violent mob actions and excesses of the French Revolution (1789–1793), while Republicans called the *Federal Republican* a treasonous publication and excused the mob's actions as overzealous patriotism. Although outrage over the Baltimore Riots probably helped Federalist candidates win some subsequent elections in Maryland, New York, and New England, their legacy was generally one of fear as Federalists learned how much dissent could cost them.

Not enough troops to fight a war

Despite the steps Congress had taken to bolster the ranks of the U.S. Army, many more soldiers would be needed to fight Great Britain. However, a cornerstone of republican belief was that a large military was dangerous, as it might open the way for a military takeover of a democratically elected government (see "Two political parties emerge" in chapter 1). As soon as the Republican Party gained dominance by winning both the presidency and the majority in Congress in 1800, they began to cut the army's numbers substantially. By 1807 there were only about twenty-four hundred soldiers left, and very few good officers around to lead them. Notoriously low pay and a lack of adequate food, clothing, and medical supplies made a military career seem unattractive to many young men. These factors had combined to result in a woefully inadequate military.

Congress enacted a limited war program in early 1812 that was meant to prepare the nation for war. By the time war was declared, however, there were still less than seven thousand regular soldiers enlisted in the army. Most of the few available officers were either old enough to have fought in the Revolutionary War or had attained their rank through political connections, and in either case they often lacked the energy and skills necessary to lead men into modern warfare.

Neither was the U.S. Navy ready to go to war, especially against the Mistress of the Seas, as Great Britain was known. In 1812 the navy had less than twenty seagoing ships available. During the congressional debate, Secretary of the Navy Paul Hamilton (1762–1816) had even recommended having the U.S. Navy sit out the war, since it had no chance against Great Britain's superior navy. Congress had, nevertheless, authorized some funds to prepare what ships and seamen there were for battle. In addition, the United States would have to depend on privateers, private ships equipped with weapons and hired by the government, to fight the war on the high seas. The men on these ships risked death or imprisonment if they lost their sea battles, but if they won, they could gain great profits. Bringing in a captured enemy ship, referred to as a "prize," could earn thousands of dollars in profit to be shared among those responsible for its capture.

Depending on state militias

Clearly the United States would have to call on the individual state militias to fight the war. Congress had anticipated this need in legislation authorizing the president to bring one hundred thousand militiamen into the war. Although there were more than five hundred thousand militiamen available, relying on them brought its own set of problems. Militias tended to be poorly trained and often lacked adequate weapons. They usually considered themselves emergency, temporary forces that were to be used to defend against invasion by a foreign country, rather than to attack a foreign country. They were not required to lend their services to the federal government for more than three months per year, and some of them were not required to venture beyond their own state borders. Their officers were often men with political ambition but no practical military experience.

Although the militias of southern and western states—especially Kentucky and Tennessee—were generally cooperative and even enthusiastic about the prospect of conquering new frontiers, those of the Federalist-dominated northeastern states were decidedly reluctant to fight an all-out war. In some cases, state officials felt the same way: Rhode Island contributed no militiamen except those assigned to protect the city of Newport while Massachusetts, after initially complying with the federal government's order, finally ruled it unconstitutional and sent no more militiamen. Once the war was underway, even militia from states that were generally sympathetic to the war effort, such as New York, would prove (sometimes at crucial moments) reluctant to fight.

Great Britain not well prepared, either

The British were not much better prepared for the War of 1812. There were about ten thousand regular troops stationed in Canada, including both British and Canadian

Native Americans: Choosing Sides

Native Americans were intimately involved in the War of 1812. As white settlers moved farther west into the lands occupied by Native Americans for thousands of years, tension rose and more and more violent confrontations took place. The widespread American belief that the British were actually encouraging Native Americans to attack whites in the Northwest Territory was a contributing factor in the U.S. declaration of war against Great Britain.

Meanwhile, Native Americans were desperately searching for ways to preserve their lives and lands as they had always known them. Many thought their best chance of survival lay in alliance with the British, who promised to set aside Native American lands in exchange for help in fighting the United States. In the end, neither Great Britain nor the United States was truly interested in seeking justice for Native Americans, and as the nineteenth century progressed, their lands and rights would gradually be taken away from them.

Below is a list showing how Native American loyalties were divided during the War of 1812.

Great Britain	United States
Algonkian	Cayugas
Delawares	Mohawks
Iroquois	Oneidas
Kickapoos	Onondagas
Menominees	Senecas
Miamis	Tuscaroras
Misquakies (Foxes)	
Mississaugas	
Nanticokes	
Ojibways	
Potawatomis	
Sauks	
Shawnee	
Tutelos	
Weas	
Wyandots	

Estimated total:
< 3,000 warriors	1,050 warriors

Members of the Delaware, Algonkian, Shawnee, Wyandot, and Sandusky nations also fought on the side of the United States.

Source: War of 1812–1814: Native People. *[Online]* *http://www.members.tripod.com/~war1812/* *nativepeople.html (accessed on November 26, 2001).*

soldiers, but only about half of these could be counted on to be loyal to Great Britain. Although they were better trained than the U.S. fighting force, they were scattered from the colony's east coast to the Great Lakes. The British side also had militiamen—about eighty-six thousand of them—but they were not well organized or well armed, and their loyalty was often questionable. Whereas the United States had about seven-and-half million occupants at this period, the population of Canada was only five hundred thousand. Many Canadian citizens were transplanted Americans who lacked any strong loyalty to Great Britain. The Canadian geography (similar to that of the northern United States, but even more severe) was also a liability: there were few roads through the thick forests, the rivers were treacherous, and the winter weather was harsh.

The British forces in Canada could, however, count on help (especially after the Battle of Tippecanoe; see "The Battle of Tippecanoe" in chapter 2) from some of the western Native American nations, including the Sioux, Winnebago, Menominee, Kickapoo, and Shawnee. Their support had been cultivated before the war as British fur trappers and traders jostled for advantage in the Northwest Territory (an area of land that would become the states of Ohio, Michigan, Indiana, Illinois, and parts of Minnesota), and it became even more important after war was declared. The British believed that if they did not enlist Native Americans on their side early in the conflict, they instead would aid the Americans.

Great Britain, however, was too occupied with the war against France to offer much assistance to her colony in Canada. Responsibility for war strategy rested primarily with officials and military officers based in North America, especially Sir George Prevost (1767–1816), the governor of the Canadian territory, and Sir Isaac Brock (1769–1812; see biographical entry), a brilliant commander whose death in the opening stages of the war was a major loss for the British.

A three-pronged plan of attack

As the United States prepared for war with Great Britain, Madison, Secretary of War William Eustis (1753–1825), and Major General Henry Dearborn (1751–1829), a Revolutionary War veteran who had been assigned to command the troops in the northeastern region, worked out a three-pronged plan for the invasion of Canada. U.S. troops would cross into Canada at three important places: at Detroit in Michigan territory, located at the northern edge of the Northwest Territory; at the Niagara River, crossing from western New York about 200 miles northeast of Detroit; and about 250 miles farther northeast, crossing Lake Champlain from Plattsburg, New York. Meanwhile, the U.S. Navy was given the task not only of defending the American coast but of interfering as much as possible with British commercial and naval ships on the high seas. Former president Thomas Jefferson (1743–1846; president 1801–09) predicted that an American victory would be "a mere matter of marching." But Jefferson and others were headed for a big disappointment.

Hull leads attack from Detroit

In the summer of 1812, Detroit—then a town inhabited by about eight hundred people, many of them fur trappers and traders of French-Canadian origin—became the base of operations for the northwestern branch of the U.S. Army. General William Hull (1753–1825), a veteran of the Revolutionary War, was named to command them. Some historians claim that Hull accepted the assignment reluctantly, while others assert that he lobbied for it; most agree, however, that this fifty-nine-year-old grandfather in poor health turned out to be a bad choice for the job.

Hull began recruiting a force of regular soldiers, volunteers, and members of Ohio's militia, mustering (gathering together in preparation for war) them at Dayton, Ohio. From there Hull traveled north with about two thousand soldiers, arriving in Detroit on July 5. Incredibly, Hull had not yet been informed that war had been officially declared; the news had been sent to him through the regular mail system. To speed up his journey, Hull had sent some of his luggage, and most of the papers detailing plans for the invasion, on a ship across Lake Erie. The ship was captured by the British, and the papers were immediately delivered into the hands of General Isaac Brock, who was commanding the British troops in the region and whose superior officers had taken more care than Hull's to inform him that the war had begun. This was a worrisome beginning for Hull, and things would only get worse.

An unpopular retreat

Despite the eagerness of his men and officers to start their invasion, Hull waited for about a week until the slow-moving declaration of war finally arrived. Then he and his

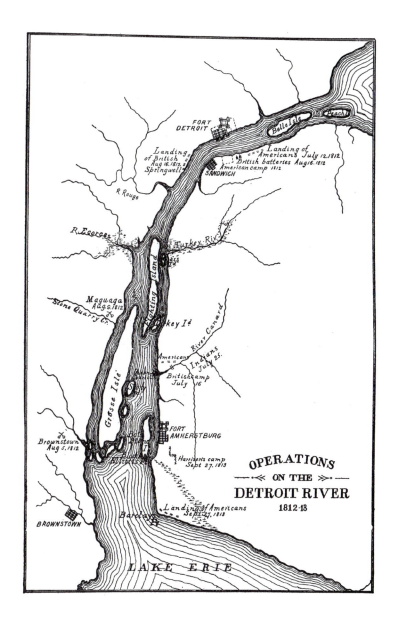

troops crossed the Detroit River and headed for Fort Malden (located near present-day Amherstburg, Ontario), where a British force about half the size of Hull's was stationed. The U.S. troops occupied Sandwich (now Windsor, Ontario) and Hull issued a proclamation informing the area's residents that they would be left alone unless they chose to oppose the invasion. Over the next few weeks, however, problems arose. Hull began to worry about the safety of his supply lines (which

Journal of an American Prisoner of War

The following journal excerpts are taken from *Journal of an American Prisoner at Fort Malden and Quebec in the War of 1812*, edited by George M. Fairchild and published in Quebec in 1909. They were written by James Reynolds, who was a surgeon's assistant on a British prison ship. The accounts give the reader an impression of life as a prisoner of war in the Northwest Territory during the first year of the war, enduring harsh weather, rampant disease, and the dispiriting news of the Surrender of Detroit.

Journal of an American Prisoner: Surgeon's Mate James Reynolds

16th - Sunday. Pleasant weather but unpleasant news we heard about noon that Hull had given up Detroit and the whole Michigan Territory. The Indians began to return about sunset well mounted and some with horses.... Who can express the feelings of a person who knows that Hull had men enough to have this place three times and gave up his post. Shame to him, shame to his country, shame to the world. When Hull first came to Detroit the 4th U.S. Regt. would have taken Malden and he with his great generalship has lost about 200 men and his Territory.

Can he be forgiven when he had command of an army of about 2500 men besides the Regulars and Militia of his Territory and given up to about 400 regular troops and Militia and about 700 Indians.

Oct. 1st - Thursday. Pleasant. Sergt. Maj. Huggins and two men all sick came on board our vessel and I sent (away) three well men in their room (place). The three men that came on board were very sick.

7th - Wednesday. Cold and squalls of snow. The guard came to bury Sergt. Stoner's child. I visited all the prison ships in the Harbor and gave medicine to the sick. We had some sugar, rice, and barley sent for the sick and some other refreshments was sent on board.

9th - Friday. Cold for the season. Corp. Berry's child died about three o'clock this morning. The men are something better. I visited all the prison ships in the harbor. Corp. Perry's child was buried this afternoon....

19th - Monday. Pleasant. Amos Ingalls died at 5 o'clock this morning. 6 men came from [ship] 406 and 4 returned. The men very sick many of them, 44 in our number of sick....

Source: Documents on the War of 1812. *[Online]* http://www.hillsdale.edu/dept/History/Documents/ War/FR1812.htm (accessed on November 26, 2001).

moved food and equipment along) and sent several detachments out to investigate. Both were attacked by hostile Native Americans. Then news of the British, joined by their Native

American allies, attack on Fort Michilimackinac (pronounced mi-shu-LEE-ma-ku-naw; located in northern Michigan territory; see "Fort Michilimackinac falls") on July 29 arrived. Apparently fearing this victory would bolster the Native Americans and the full fury of their aggression would roll southward like a tidal wave, Hull ordered his troops back to Detroit.

The retreat caused a great deal of unrest among Hull's officers and soldiers, many of whom were loudly questioning his competence to lead them. Meanwhile, across the Detroit River at Fort Malden, Brock had arrived with reinforcements. Letters from a captured U.S. mailbag revealed the disenchantment of the U.S. forces, and Brock decided to capitalize on this obviously poor morale. He put out a false message, making sure that it would be captured, in which he claimed to have many more Native American allies than he really did. Next Brock sent an officer to Detroit with a demand that Hull surrender. Hull waited two hours before refusing the demand, suggesting that he had seriously considered a surrender.

Strange behavior, and a flag of surrender

Meanwhile, Hull was irritating and worrying his men with his strange behavior. He would allow no preparations to be taken for Detroit's defense, and he stayed in his quarters or moved in a crouching walk as if afraid that bombs might fall at any moment. He spoke incoherently, and he stuffed wads of chewing tobacco in his mouth, ignoring spittle that dripped down his face. Many civilians had taken refuge in Detroit's fort, including Hull's own daughter and two grandchildren. It seems likely that he was overwhelmed by worry about what might happen to these innocent people during an attack, especially if Native Americans were involved. Hull had witnessed Indian attacks in the past and knew that even women and children were often subject to scalpings and other atrocities.

Brock now moved his troops into position, surrounding Detroit. On the afternoon of August 15, they began bombarding the fort, and the attack continued through the night and into the next day. Finally, without consulting any other officers, Hull sent up the white flag of surrender. The British took Hull and all the regular soldiers prisoner, sending the militiamen back to Ohio.

After the war, Hull was court-martialed (tried in a military court) for treason, cowardice, and neglecting his duty. He was convicted and sentenced to death (the only U.S. general ever to receive such a sentence), but Madison pardoned him because of his age and prior military service. Some historians have suggested that Hull was used as a scapegoat for the failings of others—most notably Henry Dearborn, who had failed to create a diversion or a distraction to occupy and thus weaken the British force as planned (see, "Montreal: the last target of the three-pronged invasion" later in this chapter).

The surrender of Detroit helped to crush U.S. hopes of a swift and glorious end to the war. The British now occupied an American fort in a very strategic place, and they would have the upper hand in the northwestern region for the next year. Two events that happened around the same time as the Detroit fiasco further dampened American hopes for victory.

Fort Michilimackinac falls

The surrender of Fort Michilimackinac, the news of which had struck so much fear in Hull's heart, was one of the events that led to the weakening of U.S. morale. Once a British possession, this fort located on an island in the strait between Lake Michigan and Lake Huron, had come under American control in 1794. On July 25 the fifty-four troops stationed at the fort—who were not yet aware that war had been declared—were surprised by an attack of British forces consisting of regular soldiers and volunteers, as well as about four hundred Native Americans. Completely unprepared and outnumbered, the Americans surrendered. The British would hold on to Fort Michilimackinac until the end of the war, fighting off a July 1814 attack by a much larger U.S. force.

A massacre at Fort Dearborn

Another disaster, for which Hull could be held partially responsible, occurred at Fort Dearborn (located near present-day Chicago, Illinois) on August 15. The fort was occupied by fifty-four soldiers and twelve militiamen commanded by Captain Nathan Heald. There also were nine women and eighteen children living at Fort Dearborn, which served more as a trad-

American general William Hull hands his sword to British general Isaac Brock after surrendering Detroit.
Photograph reproduced by permission of Hulton/Archive.

The Fort Dearborn Massacre

The following is an account of the Fort Dearborn Massacre written by Mrs. John Kinzie and Mrs. Linai Helm. On August 15, 1812, the fort was being evacuated in response to orders issued by General William Hull. As the group of occupants was leaving the fort under the watch of Captain William Wells and a small band of friendly Miami Native Americans, they were attacked by the Potawatomi and Winnebago. Of the ninety-three people living at the fort at the time of the attack only forty-one survived.

The Fort Dearborn Massacre by Mrs. John Kinzie and Mrs. Linai Helm

…the scene is best described in the words of an eyewitness and participator in the tragedy, Mrs. Helm, the wife of Captain (then Lieutenant) Helm, and stepdaughter of Mr. Kinzie…

The troops behaved most gallantly. They were but a handful, but they seemed resolved to sell their lives as dearly as possible. Our horses pranced and bounded, and could hardly be restrained as the balls whistled among them. I drew off a little, and gazed upon my husband and father, who were yet unharmed. I felt that my hour was come, and endeavored to forget those I loved, and prepare myself for my approaching fate.

While I was thus engaged, the surgeon, Dr. Van Voorhees, came up. He was badly wounded. His horse had been shot under him, and he had received a ball in his leg. Every muscle of his face was quivering with the agony of terror. He said to me, "Do you think they will take our lives? I am badly wounded, but I think not mortally. Perhaps we might purchase our lives by promising them a large reward. Do you think there is any chance?"

"Dr. Van Voorhees," said I, "do not let us waste the moments that yet remain to us in such vain hopes. Our fate is inevitable. In a few moments we must appear before the bar of God. Let us make what preparation is yet in our power."

"Oh, I cannot die!" exclaimed he, "I am not fit to die—if I had but a short time to prepare—death is awful!"

I pointed to Ensign Ronan, who, though mortally wounded and nearly down, was still fighting with desperation on one knee.

"Look at that man!" said I. "At least he dies like soldier."

"Yes," replied the unfortunate surgeon, with a convulsive gasp, "but he has no terrors of the future—he is an atheist."

At this moment a young Indian raised his tomahawk over me. Springing aside, I partially avoided the blow, which, intended for my skull, fell on my shoulder. I seized the Indian around the neck, and while exerting my utmost strength to get possession of his scalping-knife … I was dragged from his grasp by another and older Indian.

The latter bore me struggling and resisting towards the lake. Despite the rapidity with which I was hurried along, I recognized, as I passed, the lifeless remains of the unfortunate surgeon. Some murderous tomahawk had stretched him upon the very spot where I had last seen him.

I was immediately plunged into the water and held there with a forcible hand…. I soon perceived, however, that the object of my captor was not to drown me, for he held me firmly in such a position as to keep my head above water. This reassured me….

When the firing had nearly subsided, my preserver bore me from the water and conducted me up the sand banks. It was a burning August morning, and walking through the sand in my drenched condition was inexpressibly painful and fatiguing. I stooped and took off my shoes to free them from the sand with which they were nearly filled, when a squaw seized and carried them off, and I was obliged to proceed without them.

When we had gained the prairie, I was met by my father, who told me that my husband was safe and but slightly wounded. I was led gently back towards the Chicago River, along the southern bank of which was the Potowatomi encampment. Once I was placed upon a horse without a saddle, but, finding the motion insupportable, I sprang off. Assisted partly by my kind conductor … and partly by another Indian, Pee-so-tum….

The wife of Wau-bee-nee-mah, a chief from the Illinois River, was standing near. Seeing my exhausted condition, she seized a kettle, dipped up some water from a stream that flowed near, threw into it some maple sugar, and, stirring it with her hand, gave it to me to drink. This act of kindness, in the midst of so many horrors, touched me deeply. But my attention was soon diverted to other things.

The fort, since the troops marched out, had become a scene of plunder. The cattle had been shot as they ran at large, and lay about, dead or dying. This work of butchery had commenced just as we were leaving the fort. I vividly recalled a remark of Ensign Ronan, as the firing went on. "Such," turning to me, "is to be our fate to be shot down like brutes!"

Source: Documents on the War of 1812. *[Online]* *http://www.hillsdale.edu/dept/History/Documents/* *War/FR1812.htm (accessed on November 26, 2001).*

ing post than a military installation. Hearing of the British victory at Fort Michilimackinac and expecting further attacks, Hull ordered an evacuation of Fort Dearborn. Though warned that it would be suicidal to leave the fort due to the presence of hostile Native Americans, Heald went along with the order, destroying much of the fort's supplies before leading the soldiers and civilians out. Marching with them was a group of Potawatomi Indians who had supposedly agreed to protect them. As they left the fort, however, the Potawatomis melted away, joining a force of about four hundred Native Americans who attacked the evacuated group about a mile from the fort.

The ensuing fight was brutal: twenty-six of the soldiers, all of the militiamen, two of the women, and twelve of the children were killed. The fort was burned, and the survivors were handed over to a Native American chief named Blackbird; some eventually escaped, while others were later bought out of captivity by British officers.

The Battle of Queenston

The second part of the U.S. plan called for troops to cross the Niagara River into Canada. By the late summer and fall of 1812, a little more than six thousand American troops had gathered along the Niagara frontier. Command was divided between Major General Stephen Van Rensselaer (1764–1839), an officer in New York's militia, and Brigadier General Alexander Smyth (1765–1830), a regular army officer with no military experience. Van Rensselaer was supposed to be the overall commander of the region, but the pompous Smyth looked down on Van Rensselaer (because he was from the militia rather than the U.S. Army) and refused to cooperate with him. Smyth's arrogant attitude would contribute to the failure of this second phase of the plan, and he would eventually be expelled from the army.

Van Rensselaer planned to cross the Niagara River at Lewiston, New York, landing near the town of Queenston on the Canadian side. He wanted Smyth, who was stationed farther north on the river at Fort Niagara, to create a diversion by attacking Fort George (located across the river from Fort Niagara). Smyth refused to accept or acknowledge the messages from Van Rennselaer, who was forced to proceed without Smyth's help. Van Rensselaer put his more experienced relative, Colonel Solomon Van Rensselaer (1774–1852) in command of the attack; among the other officers also present was Lieutenant Colonel Winfield Scott (1786–1866; see biographical entry), who would gain great fame later in the war.

About four thousand U.S. troops assembled in the area, ready to take part in the attack; meanwhile, on the British side, Brock was expecting an attack on Fort George and had most of his troops stationed there. The invasion was set to begin before dawn on October 10. When the troops arrived at the river, however, they found that the boats that were to carry them across were missing their oars. The oars had disappeared downstream along with a young soldier; whether he took the oars intentionally or by accident is not known, for he was never seen again.

A lost opportunity for victory

After a three-day delay, the attack got underway. Since there were only thirteen boats to carry the troops across the river, they would have to be transported in shifts. The first group to land was to be made up of six hundred men. Solomon Van Rensselaer led three hundred militiamen, while Lieutenant Colonel John Chrystie (d.1813) commanded three hundred regular soldiers. Soon after entering the water, however, Chrystie's boat was carried downstream by the fast-moving current, and he would not arrive at the scene of the battle for several hours.

As the soldiers landed on the Canadian shore, they were fired upon by British troops stationed on rocks above the river, some towering as high as 345 feet (in fact, this is sometimes called the Battle of Queenston Heights). A fierce fight ensued as the Americans tried to scale the rocks. Soon Solomon Van Rensselaer was wounded, and had to be taken back to Lewiston. Since Chrystie had not yet appeared, command was transferred to Captain John Wool (1784–1869), who was only twenty-three years old and had never been in battle before.

Wool rose to the occasion admirably. Leading about 240 soldiers, he managed to find a fishermen's trail that led up the heights to the rear of the British position. Meanwhile, Brock had heard the sounds of the battle from Fort Niagara and had hurried to Queenston. He and his men had just arrived at the top of the heights when Wool's troops appeared, completely surprising the British, who made a hasty retreat back down. Assessing the situation from the bottom, Brock decided another quick attack would overcome the Americans now on the heights. He ordered another charge, which not only proved futile but led to his own death when he was shot by an American sharpshooter (an expert gun shooter).

Now about six hundred American reinforcements arrived, and command was passed to Scott. Sure that a victory was within reach, Stephen Van Rensselaer crossed back to the American side in order to bring the rest of the militiamen into the battle. By now, though, the troops waiting at Lewiston had seen the first wave of wounded U.S. soldiers return. They could also hear the cries of several hundred Iroquois Indians who were fighting alongside the British. The militiamen refused to cross the river, insisting that they were not required to enter foreign territory. Astonished and dismayed, Van Rensselaer rode back and forth among them trying to persuade them to rally, but nothing he could say would make them change their minds.

Some costly lessons learned

Back on the heights, the U.S. troops could look down and see the column of eight hundred British troops marching from Fort Niagara. They were not alarmed because they thought their own reinforcements would soon be arriving. But the remaining militiamen, of course, did not arrive, and the British were soon able to overwhelm the Americans. Their first attempt to surrender was ignored by the Iroquois warriors, so that Scott had to take a dangerous ride through thick hand-to-hand fighting—another officer's white neck scarf stuck to the end of his sword—in order to reach the British commander and offer the Americans' surrender. The American casualties were great: ninety were killed, one hundred wounded, and almost one thousand were captured. The British lost only fourteen soldiers, with eighty-four wounded and fifteen missing.

The Battle of Queenston lengthened the list of American defeats in the opening months of the War of 1812. But it also taught military leaders some valuable lessons: first, that militiamen might not be willing to fight a war that involved the invasion of a foreign country (rather than the defense of their own); and second, that an invasion undertaken for its own sake (rather than in response to some kind of provocation) could be a risky business. The only bright moments of

After hearing the sounds of the battle from Fort Niagara, General Isaac Brock road on horseback to Queenston to join the battle. *Reproduced by permission of The Granger Collection.*

the battle had been provided by those who had acted hero-ically despite the circumstances, especially Captain John Wool and Scott. For their part, the British had paid a very high price for their victory, for they had lost one of their most brilliant and promising generals and strategists, Brock.

Smyth's career comes to an end

Humiliated by the disaster at Queenston, Stephen Von Rensselaer soon resigned his position as brigadier general. The government then assigned command of the troops stationed along the Niagara River to Smyth, of whose failings they seemed unaware. Smyth spent the next month issuing proclamations written in very fancy language. Although they were meant to in-spire his men and the people of New York to embrace the war with gusto (saying, for example, that his soldiers would "con-quer or they will die"), they only brought ridicule to Smyth.

Meanwhile, Smyth continued building up the ranks of his army until it reached about four thousand, more than half of which were militiamen. In early November Smyth an-nounced his readiness to attack Fort Erie, located at the south-ern end of the Niagara River, close to Lake Erie. On November 28, he began loading his troops onto boats for the crossing to Canada, but he ordered them off again later in the day when it appeared they could not reach Canada before nightfall. Smyth tried to get the mission underway again on November 30, but this time many of the militiamen refused to get onto the boats, and the departure had to be delayed again. Now many of the soldiers and officers were frustrated and reacted with anger, some of them breaking their weapons in rage. A shot was fired into Smyth's tent, and he fought a duel with an officer who called him a coward (neither was hurt). Finally, the military ca-reer of Alexander Smyth came to an end as he was relieved of his position and slunk back to his home in Virginia.

Montreal: the last target of the three-pronged invasion

The remaining part of the planned three-pronged inva-sion involved an attack on the city of Montreal, located close to the southeastern coast of Canada. Major General Henry Dearborn, an overweight, slow-moving Revolutionary War veteran known to his troops as "Granny," was put in charge of this effort. After many delays Dearborn had gathered a force of six thousand regular soldiers and militiamen at Albany, New York. In early November, Dearborn and his troops moved to Plattsburg, on the banks of Lake Champlain, and began their advance on Canada. When they stopped at a small town about a mile from the Canadian border, about two-thirds of the militiamen refused to continue, invoking their right not to enter foreign territory. With the ranks of the regular soldiers much reduced by illness, Dearborn felt that his remaining force was not up to the task at hand. So the third stage of America's invasion plan ended in the same manner as the first two.

Surprising American victories on the high seas

At the same time that American troops on the ground were failing in their attempt to invade Canada, the U.S. Navy, on the other hand, was making some impressive gains on the high seas. This was contrary to everyone's expectations, for no one thought the fledgling U.S. Navy would pose any threat at all to the mighty British Navy.

When the War of 1812 began, the U.S. Navy had seventeen ships. Seven of these were frigates (fast, medium-sized sailing warships that carried from twenty-four to sixty guns); and three were heavy frigates or superfrigates, which were a little bigger and stronger but still fast. Unlike the army, the navy had many seasoned men in its ranks, including dynamic, capable officers like Stephen Decatur (1779–1820) and Oliver Hazard Perry (1785–1819; see biographical entry). Nevertheless, the navy was running short on sailors, as many young men found life aboard a military ship unrewarding—in terms of both working conditions and pay—especially compared with the rewards that could come from working on a privateer.

The *Constitution* defeats the *Guerriere*

Captain Isaac Hull (1773–1843) was a U.S. Navy officer who was eager to meet the British Navy in their own element,

"Old Ironsides": The USS Constitution

During the first year of the War of 1812, the flagging spirits of most Americans were lifted by the victories won by the USS *Constitution,* the nation's top warship. During her long and distinguished career, the *Constitution* was commanded by some of the Navy's most famous captains, including two from the War of 1812: Stephen Decatur and Thomas Macdonough.

In 1794 the U.S. Congress authorized the building of six new warships. The *Constitution* was one of the first three to be built. Constructed over a period of three years at Edmond Hartt's Shipyard in Boston at a total cost of $318,719, the vessel not only was bigger than most frigates (the second-largest type of warship, carrying 40 to 50 guns) but also faster. It took 1500 trees to build the *Constitution,* and her copper fittings were made by Boston silversmith (and famous Revolutionary War figure) Paul Revere. The *Constitution* was 204 feet long and could carry a crew of 475 officers and seamen.

The *Constitution* was launched on October 21, 1797, and put to sea the next year. Commanded by Captain Samuel Nicholson, she cruised through the West Indies, protecting U.S. merchant ships from French privateers. In 1803, the *Constitution* was sent to the Mediterranean region,

where the Barbary states—Tripoli (present-day Libya), Algeria, and Tunisia—were harassing U.S. ships by demanding payments before they could visit Mediterranean ports. Under the command of Captain Edward Preble, the *Constitution* led the bombing of Tripoli, and hosted the signing of a peace treaty between the three countries and the United States in 1805.

The *Constitution* returned to Boston and in 1809 was made the flagship (lead vessel, carrying the overall commander) of the navy's North Atlantic squadron. In 1810 Captain Isaac Hull was given command of the ship. About a month after the June 17, 1812, declaration of war between the United States and Great Britain, the *Constitution* was sailing from the Chesapeake Bay to New York when she ran into five British ships, which began to chase her. Through the crew's determination and ingenuity, the *Constitution* made an amazing escape.

On August 19, 1812, the *Constitution* was cruising about six hundred miles east of Boston when she encountered the British ship HMS *Guerriere.* During a fairly short battle, the *Constitution* shot down all of her opponent's masts, and the battle ended with an American victory. The *Guerriere* was so badly damaged that she had to be sunk. It was during this battle that one

the Atlantic Ocean. Assigned to command the USS *Constitution,* said to be the navy's finest frigate, Hull (a nephew of the ill-fated General William Hull of the U.S. Army) set out from

of the *Constitution*'s crew reportedly saw bullets bouncing harmlessly off the ship's side and exclaimed, "Huzzah! Her sides are made of iron!" From then on, the ship was affectionately known as "Old Ironsides."

The fame of the *Constitution* increased in December, when she defeated the HMS *Java* off the coast of Brazil. Although confined in port by the British blockade for much of the war, the *Constitution* managed eight captures altogether, and she served as both a morale booster to Americans and a wake-up call to the British, who had previously underestimated the strength and ability of the U.S. Navy. In her final clash of the War of 1812, the *Constitution* took on two British ships— the *Cyane* and the *Levant*—near Madeira (off the coast of West Africa) and beat them both.

After the war, the *Constitution* was docked at Boston Harbor until 1821 when she became the flagship of the navy's Mediterranean squadron. In 1830 the navy began researching the cost of refurbishing the *Constitution,* and word got out that she was headed for the scrap heap. Inspired by the poem titled "Old Ironsides" by Oliver Wendell Holmes, the U.S. public came to the defense of the *Constitution,* and the navy agreed to rehaul her.

In 1844 the *Constitution* made an around-the-world voyage that took her 52,279 miles in 495 days. From 1853 to 1855 the *Constitution* patrolled the coast of West Africa, looking for ships involved in the illegal slave trade. In 1860, she became a training ship for the U.S. Naval Academy, a job she performed for almost twenty years.

After more years as a training and barracks ship, the *Constitution* was brought back to Boston in time for her one hundredth birthday, after which she was turned into a naval museum. Between 1925 and 1930, the ship was completely restored, and in 1930 she made a tour of the Atlantic, Gulf, and Pacific coasts of the United States. She was boarded by 4.5 million visitors.

The *Constitution* returned to Boston in 1934 and has remained there ever since. In 1998 Boston Harbor hosted a bicentennial celebration for the *Constitution.*

Sources: "Old Ironsides": A Grand Old Lady of the Fleet. *[Online] http://www.geocities.com/CapitolHill/ 9703/constitution.html (accessed on November 26, 2001); Ramsdell, Lorraine. "USS Constitution: The History."* Naval Reserve Office of Information. *[Online] http://www.chinfo.navy.mil/navpalib/ships/ misc/constitution/sail200b.html (accessed on November 26, 2001);* USS Constitution History Timeline. *[Online] http://www.navy.mil/homepages/ constitution (accessed on November 26, 2001).*

Boston in early August and headed toward the West Indies, where he intended to catch British ships sailing home to Great Britain. About six hundred miles east of Boston, the *Constitu-*

tion encountered the HMS *Guerriere,* under the command of Captain James R. Dacres (1788–1853).

The two ships soon began a late-afternoon battle that lasted less than an hour. Lucky shots from the *Constitution* severely damaged the *Guerriere*'s three main masts early in the fight, rendering her defenseless. The ships came close enough to collide, causing damage to both, but especially to the *Guerriere*. Sailors from both sides tried to board the others' ship, but the rain of bullets was too heavy. The *Guerriere* surrendered at sunset. A member of the *Constitution*'s elated crew is supposed to have cried, after seeing a shot bounce off the ship's side, "Huzza, her sides are made of iron!" and from then on, the *Constitution* was known as Old Ironsides.

The British are shocked

The *Constitution,* which carried a crew of 456 sailors and 44 guns, had suffered only 14 casualties in the encounter (7 killed, 7 wounded), while the *Guerriere,* with a crew of 272 and 38 guns, had 23 men killed and 56 wounded. News of the battle caused reactions on both sides of the ocean, as might have been expected: Americans were pumped up with pride, while British military leaders (the British public was not informed of the *Guerriere*'s defeat, for fear there would be an uproar and more resistance to an already unpopular war) were shocked. How could this upstart U.S. Navy have pulled off such a feat against the Mistress of the Seas? They were forced to admit that the United States had at least one very strong, very well-made ship and the talent to handle her well.

More American victories

Americans went on to win several more victories at sea during the fall of 1812. On October 15 the frigate *United States,* commanded by Decatur, defeated the HMS *Macedonian* south of the Azore Islands (off the coast of Africa). The *Macedonian* became the first vessel captured by the United States to be brought to an American port when it was hauled to New York, and the crew of the *United States* earned the largest prize of the war: $200 thousand which was shared among them. Several days later, the eighteen-gun American sloop (a small warship with guns on only one deck) *Wasp,* commanded by Master Commandant John Jacob, beat the HMS *Frolic.* The battle resulted in British casualties that were about four times those of the Americans; 80 percent of the *Frolic*'s crew was either killed or wounded. The fact that the *Wasp* was captured the very next day by the British ship *Poictiers* did not make her earlier victory any less painful for Great Britain.

Near the end of December, the *Constitution,* now under the command of Commodore William Bainbridge (1774–1833), met the HMS *Java* in waters off the coast of Brazil. In the ensuing battle, the *Java*'s commander, Captain Henry Lambert (1772–1847), was killed and the ship so damaged that it had to be destroyed at sea. After this defeat, Great Britain ordered that from then on the U.S. superfrigates should only be taken on in battle by two or more British ships.

None of these battles made much difference in the overall course of the war, but they did give a big boost to American morale, especially in the wake of the losses being suffered by the army all along the Canadian border. Americans took great pride in defeating the Mistress of the Seas. In a speech delivered to Congress on December 16, 1812, U.S. Representative Lemuel Sawyer (1777–1852) declared that "the bully has been disgraced by an infant." For the moment, Americans could bask in the glory of these unexpected triumphs. The coming year would bring challenges and moments of despair to tarnish that glory, as well as some victories to set it glowing again.

Stephen Decatur was commander of the frigate *United States* when it defeated the HMS *Macedonian.* The *Macedonian* became the first vessel captured by the United States to be brought to an American port.

For More Information

Books

Elting, John R. *Amateurs to Arms!: A Military History of the War of 1812.* Cambridge, Mass.: Da Capo Press, 1995. Reprint. Originally published by Algonquin Press, Chapel Hill, NC, 1991.

Heidler, David S., and Jeanne T. Heidler, eds. *Encyclopedia of the War of 1812.* Santa Barbara, Calif.: ABC-CLIO, Inc., 1997.

Hickey, Donald R. *The War of 1812: A Forgotten Conflict.* Urbana: University of Illinois Press, 1989.

Mahon, John K. *The War of 1812.* Cambridge, Mass.: Da Capo Press, 1991. Reprint. Originally published by University of Florida Press, Gainesville, Fla., 1972.

Hitsman, Jay McKay. *The Incredible War of 1812: A Military History.* Toronto: University of Toronto Press, 1972.

Hollon, W. Eugene. *The Lost Pathfinder: Zebulon Montgomery Pike.* Norman: University of Oklahoma Press, 1949.

Maloney, Linda M. *The Captain from Connecticut: The Life and Naval Times of Isaac Hull.* Boston: Northeastern University Press, 1986.

Schroeder, John H. "Stephen Decatur: Heroic Ideal of the Young Navy." *Command Under Sail: Makers of the American Naval Tradition,* ed. James C. Bradford. Annapolis, Md.: Naval Institute Press, 1985.

Terrell, John Upton. *Zebulon Pike: The Life and Times of an Adventurer.* New York: Weybright and Talley, 1968.

Web sites

Discriminating Generals. [Online] http://www.militaryheritage.com/home.htm (accessed on November 26, 2001).

Documents on the War of 1812. [Online] http://www.hillsdale.edu/dept/History/Documents/War/FR1812.htm (accessed on November 26, 2001).

Thomas Warner Letters. [Online] http://www.haemo-sol.com/thomas/thomas.html (accessed on November 26, 2001)

War of 1812. [Online] http://www.galafilm.com/1812/e/index.html (accessed on November 26, 2001).

"War of 1812." *KidInfo.* [Online] http://www.kidinfo.com/American_History/warof1812.html (accessed on November 26, 2001)

"War of 1812." *Studyweb.* [Online] http://www.studyweb.com/links/388.html (accessed on November 26, 2001)

War of 1812–1814. [Online] http://www.members.tripod.com/~war1812/ (accessed on November 26, 2001).

War of 1812—Forgotten War. [Online] http://www.multied.com/1812/ (accessed on November 26, 2001).

Gains and Losses for Both Sides

4

The War of 1812 between the United States and Great Britain was provoked by two major issues. The first was Britain's maritime policy of impressment in its war with France. This policy was where British officials often boarded U.S. ships to capture deserters from their own navy, often wrongfully taking American citizens in the process. The other issue that led to the war was Great Britain's overly friendly relations with Native Americans. Americans believed that the British were encouraging Native Americans to attack white settlers who were moving west. The Native Americans believed that the settlers were encroaching on (gradually taking over) their land. Although these two issues led to Americans being eager to fight a war with Britain, the United States was not necessarily ready to fight such a war. Except for a few memorable victories at sea, the War of 1812 had not gotten off to a good start for the United States, generally, due to poor preparation, poor leadership, and poor strategy.

Hearing of defeats on the battlefield and the failure of U.S. troops to successfully invade Canada, more Americans began to wonder if this war was a good idea after all. Some felt that President James Madison (1751–1836; see biographical entry) was mismanaging the war—including some Republicans, who switched their support from Madison to New York statesman DeWitt Clinton (1769–1828) when it came time to vote in the November 1812 presidential election. Madison won the election, but just barely, and the Republicans also lost some ground in Congress: even though the Republicans were still a majority, more Federalists won seats in both the House of Representatives and the Senate. (Members of the Federalist Party favored a strong central government and did not support the war with Britain.)

Congress boosts the war effort

Addressing Congress in November after winning the presidential election of 1812, Madison avoided speaking of battles lost, focusing instead on the economic boom the country was enjoying as the government spent a lot of money running the war. Both Republicans and Federalists entered a series of long-winded debates on the merits of the war. More important in the long run were the measures Congress enacted to help with the war effort. They took steps to upgrade the army, which would be increased by twenty-two thousand regular soldiers to bring the total number to fifty-seven thousand. Soldiers' pay was boosted from five dollars a month (less than the wage a young man could earn as a common laborer) to eight dollars a month, and bounties (one-time sums of money paid as rewards for enlisting) and other incentives (such as free land) were offered to both short- and long-term recruits. Measures also were taken to improve the efficiency of the army.

Congress also endorsed an expansion of the navy, authorizing the construction of four ships-of-the-line (the biggest warship, carrying seventy-four guns), six heavy frigates (between twenty-four and sixty guns), six sloops (between ten and twenty-four guns) and other vessels. Despite their general opposition to the war, Federalists were in favor of strengthening the navy, because they felt that having a powerful navy roaming the seas increased the chances that trade could be carried on with less problems. Astonishing many observers, the Congress in office at the beginning of the war failed to enact any taxes to finance the war effort, leaving that unpopular task for the new Congress, which would meet in May.

Overall, as the year 1813 began, the United States did seem to be in a slightly better position as it faced another year of war. For one thing, leadership in Washington had improved dramatically when Secretary of War William Eustis (1753–1825), who almost everybody considered too militarily inexperienced (he had been a surgeon and congressman), was replaced with Revolutionary War (1775–83) veteran John Armstrong (1758–1843). And Secretary of the Navy Paul Hamilton (1762–1816), after an episode of public drunkenness, was replaced with William Jones (1760–1831), a Philadelphia merchant and former congressman with much more military experience and energy than his predecessor.

Under Armstrong's more able direction, talented army officers began to emerge, brought up from the lower ranks to positions of greater responsibility. Among them were William Henry Harrison (1773–1841; see biographical entry), who took over William Hull's (1753–1825) job as commander of U.S. forces in the Northwest Territory, and Andrew Jackson (1767–1845; see biographical entry), who was put in command of the southwestern troops. Younger but promising officers like Winfield Scott (1786–1866; see biographical entry) and Zebulon Pike (1779–1813; see biographical entry) also were being more quickly promoted.

The higher pay authorized by Congress did make military service more attractive, so that by spring, the army's numbers had climbed to thirty thousand (more than twice what it had been at the beginning of the war). In general, the army was running more efficiently and benefiting from lessons learned during the past year.

The Battle of Frenchtown and the Raisin River Massacre

As the year 1813 dawned, the U.S. government was eager to win back control of the Northwest, which had been lost with the surrender of Detroit and defeats at forts Michilimackinac (located in northern Michigan territory) and Dearborn (present-day Chicago, Illinois). Recovering Detroit from its British captors was a high priority, but the advent of winter made that a difficult goal for the time being. (Since most of the events of the War of 1812 occurred in the northern part of the United States, cold weather limited the campaign season—the time when military action could take place—to the spring, summer, and fall months.)

When Harrison took over command of the northwestern forces, he immediately went to work building up his army and purchasing the huge quantities of food, clothing, and equipment he needed to support that army. Despite the adverse weather, Harrison was determined to press on with a winter campaign and proceeded to make plans to retake Detroit. He split his troops in two, leading one force himself to Sandusky, Ohio, while another, under the command of Brigadier General James Winchester (1752–1826), moved farther west into the Michigan Territory. Winchester's troops stopped at Frenchtown (present-day Monroe, Michigan) on the Raisin River and chased away a small British force that had invaded the town.

When British colonel Henry Procter (1763–1822), who was in the area, heard of this event, he headed for Frenchtown with about twelve hundred troops as well as Native American allies. On January 21, Procter's men attacked the U.S. force (numbering about nine hundred), which quickly surrendered. Several hundred Americans were killed, but the worst loss occurred after the battle had ended. Procter withdrew from the town, taking with him the American soldiers his troops had captured as well as some of the wounded Americans; the rest of the wounded were left in the care of the Native American warriors who had fought with the British. In what came to be known as the Raisin River Massacre, the warriors killed many of the wounded men, thus violating a standard of European warfare regarding treatment of prisoners. "Remember the River Raisin!" would become a rallying cry in many subsequent battles of the War of 1812 and for recruiting fresh soldiers—especially among volunteers from Kentucky, for many of those killed had been Kentucky natives.

His plans for an attack on Detroit now scuttled, Harrison began building a fort on the banks of the Maumee River in Ohio. Located near the present-day town of Perrysburg,

Fort Meigs would, in May, become the site of a significant battle. For now, however, let's turn to examining the strategies being developed on the Great Lakes and in the Northeast.

A plan to gain control of the Great Lakes

As the warmth of the approaching spring began to thaw the snow and ice that blanketed the northeastern United States and the parts of Canada it borders, U.S. strategists began to make plans for the campaign of 1813. Armstrong and Major General Henry Dearborn (1751–1829), the commander of all troops in the northeastern region, agreed that they would gain the most from an attack on the large, important cities of Montreal and Quebec, but these were too well protected. Instead, they mapped out a plan to capture first Kingston and then York, both of which were naval bases and shipbuilding centers. Then the United States would try to gain control of Fort George, located at the northern, Lake Ontario end of the Niagara River (which connects lakes Erie and Ontario), and Fort Niagara, located on the southern, Lake Erie end.

Another crucial objective was to dominate the Great Lakes, especially Lakes Ontario and Erie. Dense surrounding wilderness and a lack of good roads made the lakes the best route for moving men, supplies, and equipment, and whoever controlled these large bodies of water would have the upper hand in this region. During the first year of the war, the British had maintained control of both lakes, with six ships anchored on Lake Ontario and six on Lake Erie, whereas the United States had only one ship on each lake. British general Isaac Brock (1769–1812; see biographical entry) had used the lakes to his advantage as he maneuvered into position for his successful attack on Detroit, underlining for the Americans the lakes' importance.

In September 1812 the U.S. government had wisely put a capable, experienced, forty-one-year-old officer in charge of its naval forces on Lakes Ontario and Erie. There was already a U.S. naval base on Lake Ontario, located at Sacket's Harbor, New York, and Captain Isaac Chauncey (1772–1840) quickly chose Presque Isle (now Erie), Pennsylvania, as the place to build a new base on Lake Erie. Then he began to put into action his plan to buy merchant ships and turn them into warships, while also building new vessels.

Meanwhile, the British understood very well that they must not allow the Americans to gain the upper hand on the Great Lakes, especially in view of the great distance between the source of much of their supplies and equipment (Great Britain) and the difficulties of transport if a water route was not available. In March 1813 James Yeo (1782–1818), a competent captain of the Royal Navy, was put in charge of Great Lakes operations. During the next year, under Yeo, the British held on to control of Lake Erie.

Both Chauncey and Yeo were cautious men, unwilling to needlessly squander the precious resources of sailors and ships unless the prospects for victory were bright. Yet both knew they must destroy or damage the other's naval bases to stop shipbuilding and prevent the other side from putting more ships and thus more power on the lakes.

The Battle of York

Although the original U.S. plan had been to attack Kingston first, Dearborn and Chauncey heard that Canada's governor-in-chief George Prevost (1767–1816) was waiting there with a huge force ready to attack Sacket's Harbor. This turned out to be untrue, but in the meantime the two officers had convinced Armstrong that the best plan would be to raid York (then the capital of upper Canada and a major shipping center) and destroy two ships that were being built there. From there, Dearborn would lead the army to the western end of Lake Ontario and attack Fort George. Armstrong agreed to the plan.

In 1813 York was defended by about eight hundred troops (a combination of regular soldiers, militiamen, and Native Americans) under the command of Major General Roger Hale Scheaffe (1763–1851), who had led Great Britain's victorious troops at the Battle of Queenston the previous year. Unsure where the American force would land or attack, Scheaffe had his soldiers dispersed throughout the town.

At dawn on April 27, 1813, about seventeen hundred U.S. soldiers under the command of Zebulon Pike crossed Lake Ontario and landed near York. Backed up by gun and cannon fire from Chauncey's ships on the lake, Pike's troops pushed the British back toward the fort. Seeing defeat was at hand, the Canadian militiamen (small armies made up of troops residing in a particular state) turned and fled the battle. Also preparing for a defeat, Scheaffe had the fort's magazine (ammunitions storehouse) blown up; the resulting huge explosion killed or wounded more than two hundred Americans. Pike was among those killed.

Scheaffe fled York with his remaining soldiers (150 had been killed or wounded and almost 300 captured) while the militiamen still in York were left to surrender to the Americans. Enraged by the deaths caused by the explosion and by the discovery of a scalp in a government office (for years it had been rumored that the British paid their Native American allies for American scalps), U.S. soldiers (along with some Canadian citizens) vandalized and destroyed public buildings. They also pillaged (took by force) property, which went against accepted rules of warfare. A little more than a year later, the pillaging would be used as an excuse for the British to burn Washington, D.C.

The costs of the Battle of York were high, for there had been a total of 320 casualties as well as the loss of the talented Pike, but the rewards were substantial too: the United States had gained a warship (one of those under construction at York; the other had been destroyed by the British), as well as a hefty amount of naval supplies that would later aid in the U.S. victory at the Battle of Lake Erie. Dearborn and Chauncey now returned to Sacket's Harbor to prepare for the planned attack on Fort George.

Success at Fort George, defeat at Beaver Dams

At the beginning of the War of 1812, Fort George had served as the main headquarters of General Isaac Brock. It was now defended by a force of one thousand under the command of Brigadier General John Vincent (1765–1848). In late May 1813, a combined U.S. Army and Navy force of twenty-five hundred under the command of Dearborn and Chauncey assembled across the Niagara River from Fort George. They began their attack on May 24 by opening fire on the upper-Canadian town of Newark (present-day Niagara), where many British soldiers were housed. Three days later the U.S. Navy provided a barrage of cannon and gun fire from the lake in front of the fort while the army attacked it from the rear. The British were forced to abandon the fort and flee; they had suffered 350 casualties to the Americans' 140.

The United States failed to follow up on this victory, for Vincent was able to regroup his troops at Burlington Heights (now Hamilton, Ontario). Finally the United States sent 2,600 troops under the command of two brigadier generals to chase Vincent. They made their camp at Stoney Creek, located about seven miles from the British camp. On June 6, a surprise attack on the U.S. troops by only 700 British soldiers (during which both American commanders were captured) forced the Americans to retreat. Later in the month, Dearborn tried to reestablish U.S. dominance by sending Lieutenant Colonel Charles Boerstler (b. 1778) and a force of 500 to attack a British outpost at Beaver Dams, where Lieutenant James Fitzgibbon (1780–1863) was stationed with a small band of soldiers and about 450 Native American warriors.

En route to Beaver Dams, Boerstler stopped for the night in Queenston, where a patriotic Canadian woman named Laura Secord (1775–1868) overheard the American officers discussing their plans. Secord walked twenty miles to warn Fitzgibbon, who arranged for his Native American allies to ambush Boerstler's troops as they came close to Beaver Dams. The Americans managed to fight off this attack pretty well, but then Fitzgibbon approached Boerstler with a truce flag and demanded a U.S. surrender. He told Boerstler that he had a much bigger force of soldiers and warriors ready to surround the U.S. troops, and he would not be able to restrain the Native Americans from brutally massacring the Americans. Boerstler agreed to the surrender, only to learn that Fitzgibbon had been lying.

News of the disaster at Beaver Dams did not sit well in Washington, D.C., where outraged Republicans called for Dearborn's dismissal. In July 1813 Dearborn was relieved of his command.

The British attack Sacket's Harbor

The United States wished to limit British naval strength by attacking naval and shipping centers, and Great

Britain had the same goal. Thus Prevost and Yeo decided, in May 1813, to attack the U.S. naval base at Sacket's Harbor, where the new frigate (a fast, medium-sized warship carrying between twenty-four and sixty guns) *General Pike* was under construction. On the night of May 27, Colonel Edward Baynes (d. 1829) set out across Lake Ontario with a squadron of ships carrying nine hundred soldiers. Their arrival at Sacket's Harbor was held up by winds that were blowing in the wrong direction—giving General Jacob Brown (1775–1828) of the New York militia time to call up more soldiers—but on the morning of May 29 they disembarked. Because of their unfamiliarity with the shallow waters in the area, the British did not want to risk sending their ships in too close to shore. That meant that the British soldiers faced fifteen hundred American defenders with no back-up from the Royal Navy.

Laura Secord meeting with British lieutenant James Fitzgibbon to warn him about lieutenant general Charles Boerstler's plan to attack the British outpost at Beaver Dams. *Photograph reproduced by permission of The Granger Collection.*

The outnumbered British troops put up a good fight, pushing through the first line of defense and scaring off some of the U.S. militiamen. Finally Prevost ordered Baynes to withdraw his force, but in the meantime they had managed to set two U.S. ships on fire (one of which the Americans would later be able to repair). A vast amount of naval supplies were destroyed by the Americans themselves, after someone told the young naval officer in charge of them that the British were going to win the battle (if defeat was at hand, it was common practice to destroy supplies and even ships to keep them from falling into enemy hands).

Throughout the fall and early winter, the British made raids on U.S. outposts—including Fort Schlosser and Black Rock—along the Niagara frontier, meant to exert pressure on the Americans to evacuate Fort George. Most of the fort's regular troops had already left to take part in action on the northeastern front. There were only about 250 defenders left at Fort George, and they were disgruntled about delays in

The Journals of Anne Prevost

Born January 1, 1795, Anne Prevost was the daughter of George Prevost, who served as governor in chief of Canada and commanded the British troops in North America from 1811 to 1815. Discovered in the mid-1990s among Prevost family papers, Anne's journals give the reader an idea of what life was like for the daughter of a government official and military officer living in Canada in the early nineteenth century. A teenager during the War of 1812, the journals reveal her loyalty to her father, who was faulted for his leadership during the ill-fated Battle of Plattsburg, as well as her crush on a British colonel. Prevost died before he could defend himself against the charges. Anne's mother soon also died, as did her brother and sister. She never married.

Declaration of War!

June 25th: I was summoned in the midst of my French lesson to hear some news that had arrived. It was indeed an important piece of intelligence:—"America has declared War against England...."

On this day I saw nothing before me but my Father's honour and glory. Although I knew how small a force we had to defend the Canadas, such was my confidence in his talents and fortune, that I did not feel the slightest apprehension.... I thought those abominable Yankees [Americans] deserved a good drubbing for having dared to think of going to War with England, and surely there was no harm in rejoicing that the War had happened during my Father's Administration, because I thought he was the person best calculated to inflict on the Yankees the punishment they deserved... Yet I must do myself the justice to say it was *pure fame* I longed my Father to win—I thought of *fame* more than of its accompaniments....

The attack on Sackett's Harbour; and Anne's "beau ideal"

June 3rd: We heard that an attack has been made on Sackett's Harbour. My Father was there, and as much exposed to danger as any common soldier. Thanks be to the Almighty he is safe! The attack was made with only 800 men, and the American prisoners say their force was 3000. We were not altogether unsuccessful—we drove the enemy to their block houses—blew up a magazine [ammunitions storehouse], caused them to set fire to some valuable stores—took ...150 prisoners, and then retreated to our ships....

Sunday 6th: The 89th Regiment commanded by Colonel Morrison ... arrived from Halifax. I took a great fancy to Colonel Morrison ... and I always admired his character exceedingly and considered him as agreeable as he was excellent. He afterwards became quite a hero, and I used very blushingly to declare him to be my beau ideal....

Summer of 1814; George Prevost arrives at Plattsburg

On the 30th August I made breakfast for my Father and his suite [soldiers]... previous to their departure.... I was most sanguine [hopeful] that something very brilliant would be achieved. I had often thought with regret that my Father had never yet been engaged in any bright affair—he had considered it necessary to conduct the defence of the Canadas with much caution—defence, not conquest was necessarily his object. But now I thought the time had arrived when all murmurs would be silenced.... Precious as was my Father's life, still I was so true a Soldier's daughter, I valued his renown even more.... I looked forward to certain Victory....

Defeat at Plattsburg!

Monday 12th [1814], the mortifying news arrived that our Squadron was defeated, captured, and Captain Downie killed.... and when Mr. B. went on to say the Army is to retreat, it seemed to me I heard a death's knell [stroke of a bell] ringing in my ears. I never was given to shedding tears, far from it—but I now wept bitter tears—not for poor Captain Downie or his Squadron, but because the Army was to retreat without having first destroyed Plattsburg! I felt certain that however necessary this determination might be, it would bring the greatest odium [disgrace] on my Father—it would not be tolerated at a period especially when our troops were so perpetually victorious. That my Father acted from the purest motives, who can doubt. He must have known that not one individual in that Army could be blamed for the retreat but himself; he took upon himself all the odium which he knew would be exited by an unpopular measure, and acted as he thought best. As the fleet was lost, Plattsburg must have been abandoned as soon as captured.... The weather was very rainy and the difficulty of moving artillery, stores, etc., increased every hour.—But it is useless to dwell on this most painful subject. Military fame cannot be rescued by argument—like woman's honour it is sullied [dirtied] even by the breath of calumny [false and malicious accusation]. And I know too well that not even the gracious approval of my Father's services, which George IV granted to his family, is sufficient to raise his memory to the estimation which it merits.

Source: War of 1812. *[Online]*
http://www.galafilm.com/1812/e/index.html
(accessed on November 26, 2001).

receiving their pay and by the prospect of inadequate housing for the winter.

Led by General George McClure (1770–1851), the U.S. troops evacuated the fort on December 10. They stopped at nearby British-controlled Newark and burned it to the ground, so as to deny shelter there to British forces; despite the bitterly cold weather, U.S. troops gave Newark's residents only twelve hours to vacate their homes. To retaliate, the British attacked Fort Niagara on December 18, completely surprising its defenders, inflicting 80 casualties and taking 350 prisoners. The British would keep control of Fort Niagara for the remainder of the war.

The same day as the attack on Fort Niagara, British troops under General Phineas Riall (1775–1850) crossed over the U.S. border and destroyed Lewiston, New York, and two other nearby towns. The Native American warriors who accompanied them slaughtered some of the town's residents. It was clear that more militia was needed to protect the area from these attacks, but most people were much more interested in taking care of their own farms, property, and families than in fighting a war with the British.

Nevertheless, General Amos Hall (McClure's replacement) did raise two thousand militiamen who took part in a battle at Black Rock in late December. The British came out on top, and they celebrated their victory by burning the towns of Black Rock and Buffalo. As 1813 drew to a close, the Niagara frontier was essentially in the hands of the British.

Meanwhile, back in Ohio…

At the beginning of 1813, Harrison had overseen the start of construction of a new fort in northern Ohio. Perched on a bluff overlooking the Maumee River rapids, Fort Meigs was finished by April. It enclosed an area of almost ten acres, and was exceptionally strong and well protected; it was surrounded by a barrier of picket logs (fixed upright with ends carved into points) as well as large mounds of dirt to make it harder for attackers to approach or damage it.

Lurking a little farther downriver that spring were two thousand British soldiers under the command of Henry Procter, as well as one thousand warriors under the great Shawnee leader Tecumseh (c. 1768–1813; see biographical entry). Knowing that if this force attacked, his troops would be outnumbered, Harrison called for help from General Green Clay (1757–1826) of the Kentucky militia. The British began bombarding Fort Meigs on May 1, but due to the strength of the fort, their cannonballs did little damage.

On May 5 Clay's twelve hundred militiamen arrived. They attacked the British with gusto, but not enough planning; Harrison said, as quoted in *Official Letters of the Military and Naval Officers of the United States, During the War with Great Britain in the Years 1812, 1813, 1814, and 1815* by John Brannan, that their "excessive ardour [energy]" turned out to be "scarcely less fatal than cowardice." After making some headway against the British, the Kentuckians became confused about what they were supposed to do next, with the result that they became caught in a crossfire. The U.S. casualties were great, but still the British were unable to penetrate the fort.

Shawnee leader Tecumseh meeting with British colonel Henry Procter to discuss their joint attack on Fort Meigs. *Photograph reproduced by permission of Corbis Corporation (Bellevue).*

At this point most of Tecumseh's warriors left the battle, and the Canadian militiamen who were fighting also were eager to depart—they told Procter they needed to get home and plant their crops. Thus Procter withdrew his troops. He made another unsuccessful attack on Fort Meigs in July, and in August sent 400 of his soldiers to Fort Stephenson, located on Ohio's Sandusky River. There 160 soldiers under U.S. Major George Croghan (1791–1849), who was only twenty-one years old at the time, caused the British (and their Native American allies) to retreat. These were the last British offensives in the Northwest Territory, for in September the U.S. naval victory on Lake Erie would leave them with no way to transfer supplies from the east, and they would have to retreat from the region.

And in Washington, D.C. ...

Soon after the British attack on Fort Meigs, but in a different and—at least for the moment—more peaceful part of the country, the Thirteenth Congress was meeting. President James Madison's May 25, 1813, message to Congress expressed hope that an offer by the Russian government to mediate a peace treaty between Great Britain and the United States (submitted in March and accepted at that time by Madison) would be successful. He also discussed military and naval developments, criticized the British for using Native American allies to wage war, and recommended that Congress adopt a tax program.

Soon after Congress opened its session, Madison became seriously ill, probably with dysentery (a severe gastrointestinal disease), and he was bedridden for five weeks. During this period he was unable to take any part in the nation's affairs. His opponents in Congress, however, kept busy. They voted against approving Madison's nomination of Treasury Secretary Albert Gallatin (1761–1849) to the Russian peace commission (the group that would travel to Russia to work on a peace agreement; the other nominees were diplomat John Quincy Adams [1767–1848] and Senator James Bayard [1767–1815]). Those who opposed Gallatin resented him because he had previously urged an aggressive tax program but now, they felt, wanted to escape the heat such a program (which would have to be enacted soon) would bring.

Some of Madison's most vocal detractors were members of his own party, a group of senators known as the "Invisibles." Led by William Branch Giles (1762–1830) of Virginia and Samuel Smith (1752–1839) of Maryland, these Republicans often sided with the Federalists—not so much because they were opposed to the war, but because they disapproved of Madison's administration and how it had handled the war.

Since early 1813 the government had been kept afloat financially by a $16 million loan funded for the most part by three wealthy merchants, David Parish, Stephen Girard (1750–1831), and John Jacob Astor (1763–1848). It was obvious that taxing U.S. citizens would be necessary not only to continue to wage the expensive war against Great Britain, but just to run the government. After long avoiding the issue—for members of Congress did not want to tackle the unpopular issue of taxes—Congress finally did enact a tax program. It was to bring in $5,500,000 for the government, but it would not go into effect until the beginning of 1814. That delay showed how reluctantly Congress approached taxes.

A squadron takes shape

Toward the end of 1812, Chauncey—who had been put in charge of building up the U.S. position on the Great Lakes—gave command of all Lake Erie operations to twenty-seven-year-old Commander Oliver Hazard Perry (1785–1819; see biographical entry). An ambitious young officer, Perry had previously been in charge of a fleet of gunboats in Newport, and he was ready for a greater challenge. Assigning Perry to Lake Erie left Chauncey free to concentrate his own energies on Lake Ontario.

In March 1813, Perry arrived at the U.S. naval base at Presque Isle, where work was already underway to finish four ships under construction and to bring in five more from the Niagara River. One of these was the *Caledonia,* captured the previous fall from the British. Perry spent the rest of the spring and the summer supervising the building and equipping of the ships, as well as working on the always-difficult task of finding enough sailors to staff them. He was grievously short on sailors and complained bitterly—at one point he was so angry he threaten to resign—that Chauncey kept the most able seamen for himself. Harrison helped to ease the pressure somewhat by supplying Perry with a hundred soldiers from his own army.

The commander of Great Britain's Lake Erie squadron (a group of warships assigned to a special task) was Captain Robert H. Barclay (1786–1837), a one-armed veteran of the Battle of Trafalgar in the Napoleonic Wars. He, like Perry, lacked adequate numbers of sailors. Barclay also was short on guns and his food supply was running dangerously low. Adding to this dilemma was the fact that the British were feeding about fourteen thousand Native Americans—the warriors who had agreed to fight with the British, as well as their families—at Amherstberg, Ontario, where the Royal Navy was based.

By mid-August, Perry was ready to face the British with his nine warships. His squadron consisted of the USS

Lawrence (which Perry commanded) and the USS *Niagara* (under the command of Lieutenant Jesse Elliott; 1782–1845), each equipped with twenty guns; the *Caledonia* (three guns); the *Somers* (two guns); the *Trippe* (one gun); and the gunboats *Tigress, Porcupine, Scorpion,* and *Ariel,* each with one to four guns. Barclay's six-ship opposing squadron included the HMS *Detroit* (eleven guns), the HMS *Queen Charlotte* (seventeen guns), the *Lady Prevost* (thirteen guns), the *General Hunter* (ten guns), the *Little Belt* (three guns), and the *Chippeway* (one gun). The U.S. squadron carried a crew of 532, while the British had 440.

Perry took his fleet to Put-in-Bay, located on Bass Island in the western end of Lake Erie. From this position he planned to disrupt the British supply lines and engage them in battle if possible. But it was Barclay who, just before noon on September 10, sparked the battle by opening fire on the U.S. squadron. (Lack of adequate food for his troops, as well as money to pay them, had forced Barclay into action; beating the Americans would relieve these pressures by opening up the British supply route). Aboard the *Lawrence*—flying its dark blue flag printed with the last words of Captain James Lawrence (1781–1813) during an earlier sea battle, "Don't Give Up the Ship"—Perry gave the order to engage the enemy.

The British and U.S. ships quickly moved towards each other, except for the *Niagara* which held back for some unknown reason. They fought intensely for about two hours. All the ships were damaged, but especially the *Lawrence,* and casualties were extremely high: 80 percent of Perry's crew was killed or wounded, and some of the wounded were ordered to continue fighting.

The situation looked hopeless, but Perry refused to surrender. Instead he made a daring move that, miraculously, worked: he climbed into a small boat with four crewmen who rowed him safely through a hail of gunfire to the *Niagara.* The *Lawrence* surrendered to the British, but due to all the damage to their ships, they were not able to claim their prize. In the meantime, Perry returned to the battle aboard the *Niagara.*

Meanwhile, Barclay had been severely wounded, and many other British officers were either dead or wounded. With all of his ships badly damaged, and lacking the sailors and officers necessary to continue the fight, Barclay surrendered. In ac-

cordance with naval tradition, he offered his sword to Perry, but Perry told all the British officers to keep their swords in honor of their brave and honorable performance.

In *Amateurs to Arms! A Military History of the War of 1812*, John R. Elting states "No major sea battle was ever more sternly and valiantly fought." Perry was praised for making the best possible use of his limited resources and for his personal courage under fire. In a note to Harrison soon after the battle, Perry wrote, "We have met the enemy and they are ours...," as related by Elting. This memorable phrase added to Perry's fame, and has continued to be widely quoted and used, even by people who do not know its source!

In addition to making Perry famous, the Battle of Lake Erie turned out to be the most important battle fought on the Great Lakes. It shifted the balance of power in favor of the United States, and it seemed to make up for the disheartening losses of 1812. The victory also paved the way for Har-

General Oliver Hazard Perry being rowed through a hail of gunfire to continue a naval battle aboard the *Niagara* **after his ship, the** *Lawrence,* **was damaged and surrendered to the British.** *Photograph reproduced by permission of Corbis Corporation (Bellevue).*

rison to chase the British back along the Thames River, and to achieve another U.S. success at the Battle of the Thames.

Harrison's troops pursue the British

Following his troops' failure to take Fort Meigs, Procter marched his troops back to the British base at Amherstberg. But the U.S. victory on Lake Erie made it impossible for them to stay there, because their supply lines were now cut off. Procter prepared to withdraw his troops, moving east along the Thames River. This plan was met with strong protests from Tecumseh and his followers, who had been promised land in the event of British victories. Tecumseh already held a very low opinion of Procter, and now he compared him—as reported in the *Niles Register* (a newspaper published in Baltimore, Maryland) several months later—to "a fat animal, that carries its tail upon its back, but when affrighted…drops it between its legs and runs off."

Despite Tecumseh's scorn, Procter's troops retreated. At the same time, Harrison had been recruiting soldiers in northern Ohio. He convinced Kentucky governor Isaac Shelby (1750–1826), a veteran of the Revolutionary War (1775–83) and a hero in the state, to promise that he would fight alongside any Kentuckians who signed up. And 3,000 of them did, bringing Harrison's roster to 5,500 troops. In late September they gathered at the west end of Lake Erie. They quickly occupied Detroit and Malden, which had been abandoned by the British as they fled eastward. Although about 150 Pennsylvania militiamen refused to cross into Canada, but the Kentucky volunteers had no such qualms, and Harrison's troops began their pursuit of Procter's forces.

The Battle of the Thames

Held up by bad weather, poor roads, and the necessity of transporting a heavy load of supplies, Procter's troops moved slowly. They also neglected to burn the bridges they crossed. Both these factors allowed Harrison's men to overtake them. On October 5, near Moraviantown (located about fifty miles east of Detroit on the banks of the Thames), Procter's army turned to face its enemy. Procter had 430 soldiers and

600 Native American warriors under Tecumseh, while Harrison had 3,000 troops, including 1,500 cavalry (soldiers mounted on horseback) under the command of Congressman—and future vice president—Richard Johnson (1780–1850).

The battle was short, for the U.S. forces soon managed to surround the exhausted, hungry British soldiers and trap them in a crossfire. Even after the British had surrendered, the Native Americans were willing to keep fighting. Then the news spread that Tecumseh had been killed (possibly by Richard Johnson), and the warriors gave up. Although some American soldiers later claimed to have cut strips of skin from Tecumseh's body as souvenirs, other reports claimed that his corpse was carried away by his warriors and buried in a nearby swamp.

The victory at the Battle of the Thames (called the Battle of Moraviantown by the Canadians) was particularly sweet for the United States. Although casualties on both sides were relatively light, the Americans captured six hundred

Tecumseh's death during the Battle of the Thames.
Photograph reproduced by permission of Archive Photos, Inc.

British soldiers and a large amount of supplies and equipment, including a cannon that had been taken from the British during the Revolutionary War and lost at the surrender of Detroit in 1812. Most important, though, was that thirteen months of British control of the Northwest had been brought to an end. In addition, the confederacy of tribes that Tecumseh hoped could protect Native American interests had crumbled with his death; this defeat would lead to greater opportunities for white Americans to move west.

After the battle, Procter was publicly scolded for his poor leadership during the retreat from Amherstberg and at the battle itself. Despite his status as the victor at the Thames and his having a much better reputation in general than Procter, Harrison's career also took a downturn. His continuing disagreements about strategy with Secretary of War John Armstrong soon led to his resigning from the army. Nevertheless, Harrison's fame as a war leader was established, and would help him win the presidency in 1840.

The northeastern frontier: An ill-fated plan to capture Montreal

The original U.S. plan for the 1813 campaign did not specifically include an invasion of Montreal, which was considered too well protected. In October, however, Armstrong changed his mind and ordered an attack on the city. This strategy was ill fated from the beginning, for two major reasons. First, the British had already established a strong foothold in the region when, in June, they had taken control of Lake Champlain. Located between New York and Vermont, Lake Champlain provided the British access to several important rivers and thus served as an important water route for transporting troops and supplies around the region.

The second factor that weakened the U.S. position was poor leadership. After Dearborn was fired, General James Wilkinson (1757–1825) was put in charge of northeastern operations, despite the unfavorable reputation he had earned as commander of troops in the Southwest. As recorded in Charles W. Elliott's *Winfield Scott: The Soldier and the Man*, Scott had called Wilkinson an "unprincipled imbecile," and he was widely viewed as untrustworthy.

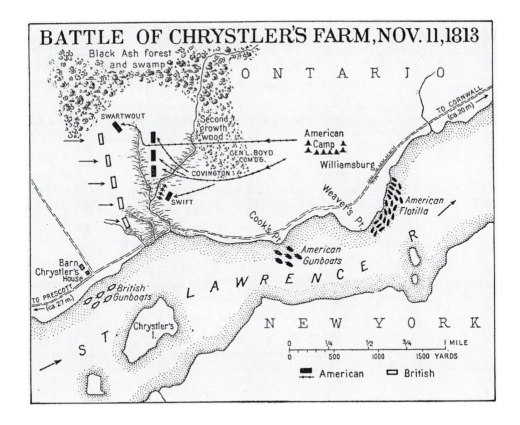

BATTLE OF CHRYSLER'S FARM, NOV. 11, 1813

A map showing the Battle of Chrysler's Farm.

Photograph reproduced by permission of The Granger Collection.

Wilkinson arrived at Sacket's Harbor in August and met with Armstrong. The plan called for Wilkinson to approach Montreal from the west, traveling down the St. Lawrence River with seven thousand men while General Wade Hampton (1751–1835), who was in charge of U.S. forces stationed at Plattsburg, New York, moved up from the south with forty-five hundred troops. The plan was clouded by two issues. The first was the vagueness of the orders issued to the two generals. The second was Hampton's resistance to following Wilkinson's command. Hamilton resented the fact that Wilkinson had been appointed to supercede Hamilton as senior officer.

Hampton waited through September and October for specific orders to begin the invasion. He finally decided to take his troops up the Chateauguay River, heading for the point where it meets the St. Lawrence River, not far from Montreal; here he would join up with Wilkinson's force. When it came time to enter Canada, however, Hampton's forty-five hundred militiamen refused to cross the border, and the four thousand regular soldiers who continued with him were neither well trained nor had any experience in battle.

On October 26, Hampton's troops faced British troops under Lieutenant Colonel Charles de Salaberry (1778–1829) at the Battle of Chateauguay. Though far outnumbered, the British troops made so much noise by shouting and blowing bugles that the Americans assumed they were fighting a force of five or six thousand, and they fell back after only two hours of fighting. After the battle, Hampton heard that Armstrong had ordered the construction of winter quarters on U.S. territory, which suggested to him that the top leaders already considered the attack on Montreal a lost cause. Discouraged, Hampton took his troops back to U.S. territory. He would resign in March 1814.

Meanwhile, Wilkinson didn't manage to get his own force on the river until November 5. They were immediately beset by a host of problems, including bad weather and Wilkinson's erratic behavior, caused at least partly by his taking laudanum (a medication containing the strong drug opium) and whiskey to combat illness. At Chrysler's Farm (located on the north bank overlooking the Saint Lawrence River) on November 11, they encountered eight hundred British troops under the command of Colonel Joseph Morrison (1783–1826). Too ill to command, Wilkinson sent his troops into battle under General John Boyd (1764–1830).

Although they were outnumbered, the British troops were better trained and more experienced, and they drove the Americans back, inflicting 340 casualties and capturing 100 soldiers (the British suffered only 180 casualties). Wilkinson now called off the campaign to invade Montreal, and he set up winter quarters at French Mills, New York. There his troops spent a miserable winter, suffering from frostbite brought on by inadequate shelter and clothing, beset by sickness, and deprived of pay.

Wilkinson would be relieved of his command about three months later. He was charged with neglect of duty, conduct unbecoming an officer (bad behavior by someone in a position of authority), drunkenness, and encouraging the disobedience of orders. Incredibly, Wilkinson was found innocent of these charges, and he returned to his New Orleans plantation.

Fighting Native Americans in the South

There also was fighting in the southeastern territories of the United States during 1813. Here, however, the enemy was not the British but the Creeks, a Native American people who occupied most of present-day Alabama as well as western Georgia. A civil war (conflict between two parties within a nation, rather than with an outside enemy) that broke out between different factions within the Creek nation led to brutalities against white settlers, requiring the U.S. government to take some kind of action. But U.S. leaders also thought the Creek War could provide an excuse to invade and conquer Spanish Florida—one of the underlying goals of American involvement in the War of 1812.

In 1810 the United States had taken control of much of western Florida (which was made up of what are now the states of Mississippi and Alabama), territory that the United States had a reasonable claim to anyway under the Louisiana Purchase. Eastern Florida (what is now the state of Florida) was still held by the Spanish. The United States was not at war with Spain, but Spain and Great Britain were allies in the wars being fought against Napoleon's French forces in Europe (see "Napoleonic Wars" in chapter 2). Spain had been weakened by the fighting at home and could spare few forces to defend its territory in North America.

Although the Creeks were initially fighting amongst themselves and not against the United States, the cause of their civil war had everything to do with white Americans and especially white American settlers. Guided by American Indian agent (a person assigned by the U.S. government to work with Native Americans) Benjamin Hawkins (1754–1816), a significant portion of the Creeks had adapted themselves to the ways of white people. Convinced that they must learn to fit in with white society or perish, they had learned to use white methods of agriculture (although many Creek men still considered farming women's work), they raised livestock, owned private property (instead of the joint ownership practiced in traditional Native American cultures), and had a tribal government.

Nevertheless, there were many Creeks who bitterly resented the encroachment of white settlers on native lands and the adoption of white culture. In 1811 the Shawnee leader Tecumseh, whom the Creeks considered one of their own because his mother was a Creek, had visited the area, preaching his message of solidarity among tribes and a return to traditional ways. The older Creek chiefs resisted this message, but many of the younger warriors were persuaded by Tecumseh's message to rebel against their elders. The group was called the Red Sticks, which referred to the Creek custom of sending bundles of sticks to indicate the number of days until an event would occur: if the sticks were red, the event was war.

The Battle of Burnt Corn Creek

The Red Sticks were eager to fight to defend their lands and traditions, and they were inspired by the news of victories the British, with Native Americans fighting alongside them, had been winning against the United States in the northwestern territories. In addition, they knew that Spanish officials in Florida stood ready to help them. In early 1813, a small group of Red Sticks who had traveled north took part in the Raisin River massacre. On their way home, these warriors paused at a white settlement near Nashville, Tennessee, and murdered several white people.

When news of the murders reached Creek territory, Hawkins told the chiefs he would bring those responsible to justice. The chiefs decided to take matters into their own hands, and they had the guilty warriors killed. This action sparked a full-fledged civil war among the Creeks, and the older chiefs were forced to seek refuge with Hawkins. Red Stick raids and attacks on whites increased. Several influential Red Stick leaders came to the forefront, especially Peter McQueen (c. 1780–1820) and William Weatherford (also known as Red Eagle; 1780–1824; see biographical entry), both of whom were of mixed Native American and white heritage.

In July 1813 a group of Red Sticks went to Pensacola, Florida, to pick up some weapons that Spanish officials had promised them. They were returning to their own territory and had traveled about eighty miles north from Pensacola when, on July 27, they were attacked at Burnt Corn Creek by a force of Mississippi militiamen led by Colonel James Caller. The Battle of Burnt Corn—considered the opening battle of the Creek War (1813–14)—ended with the Americans fleeing. Even though the U.S. soldiers escaped with all of the Red

Sticks's supplies, the Red Sticks felt they had won this confrontation, and news of the victory helped them recruit even more warriors.

The massacre at Fort Mims

The next major event of the Creek War took place on August 30 at Fort Mims, Alabama, about forty miles north of Mobile. Many families in the region were seeking protection at various forts and stockades, and there were about 300 people huddled at Fort Mims, including 120 militia under the command of Major Daniel Beasley. The major took a very relaxed approach to defense, and he and his men were completely surprised by the Red Stick attack; Beasley received a fatal wound while he was trying to close a gate that had been open so long that sand had drifted against it.

The attacking warriors killed about 250 people, including women and children who were slaughtered after the fort had already fallen to the Red Sticks. A few survivors were able to escape, and most of the African American slaves present were allowed to live, though they were then taken as slaves of the Red Sticks. All along the frontier, from the north to the south, news of the massacre at Fort Mims spread terror among the white settlers, and soon it became clear that the United States would have to counter the Native American violence.

A campaign against the Red Sticks

Secretary of War John Armstrong appointed Major General Thomas Pinckney (1750–1828) to coordinate the various state militias in a combined campaign against the Creeks. That annoyed Major General Thomas Flournoy (1775–1857), who was already commanding an army that occupied much of the Creek territory. Nevertheless, the expedition went ahead. Brigadier General Ferdinand L. Claiborne (1773–1815) of the Mississippi militia was to lead his troops to where the Coose and Tallapoosa rivers met, joining militia from eastern Tennessee (under Major General John Cocke; 1772–1854), western Tennessee (under Major General Andrew Jackson; 1767–1845) and Georgia (under Major General John Floyd; 1783–1837).

The Mississippi forces were closest to Creek territory, but their progress was held up when the still-angry Flournoy withdrew some of his troops from the campaign. They were late to arrive on the scene and didn't meet any Red Sticks until December, when they defeated a Red Stick force at a place called the Holy Ground. Floyd's progress was similarly slow, held up by a lack of food to sustain his forces and the fact that the enlistment terms of many of his militiamen ended before they even saw the action. Floyd's troops did attack the Red Stick town of Autosse on November 29, but the Red Sticks escaped, and the Georgians did little else in the remaining month of 1813.

Meanwhile, Tennesseans had responded most enthusiastically to the call for help in taming the Red Sticks, even though they were the most removed from the Creek territory. In the fall of 1813, twenty-five hundred Tennessee militiamen gathered to take part in the campaign, including two who were to become legendary frontier figures: Sam Houston (1793–1863; later the governor of Texas), and Davy Crockett (1786–1836; who became a champion of "settlers' rights" in the Congress). They were commanded by Jackson, whose legendary toughness had earned him the name "Old Hickory" and who was very experienced in fighting Native Americans.

The Battles of Tallushatchee and Talladega

Jackson's men were the first to arrive in Creek Territory, pausing on the banks of the Coosa River, about fifteen miles south of the town of Gadsden, to build Fort Strother as their base of action. On November 3, Jackson sent General John Coffee (1772–1833) and nine hundred cavalry to attack the Red Stick village of Tallushatchee. Coffee employed the time-honored military strategy of forming troops in a semicircle in front of the enemy, then closing the loop after the enemy attacks. The plan succeeded. Two hundred Red Sticks were killed, and eighty-four women and children were captured; on the Americans side only five were killed and forty-one wounded.

On November 9, Jackson himself led his troops in an attack on the village of Talladega, where Native Americans friendly to the United States had been besieged by hostile Red Sticks. The troublemakers escaped, but Jackson's troops inflicted such heavy casualties on the Red Sticks that the U.S. Army considered themselves victorious.

While Jackson was leading the attack on Talladega, fellow-Tennessean Cocke was stirring up trouble. Resentful because he was supposed to become subordinate to Jackson as soon as the two armies met, Cocke went off on his own and attacked some villages. Unaware that Jackson had previously made a peace agreement with these towns, Cocke's actions renewed hostilities.

During the remaining month of 1813, Jackson's supplies ran lower and lower. Adding to that problem was the fact that many of his militiamen were eager to return to their homes, as their terms of required service would soon expire. Jackson tried to keep his force intact, even resorting to threats if the men left, but finally he had to let them go. He was left at Fort Strother with less than 150 soldiers, and it would not be until early 1814 that the reinforcements necessary to continue the war against the Red Sticks would arrive.

The British bolster their naval forces

Although the inland war went better for the United States in 1813, the action on the high seas came almost to a standstill. That happened because the British finally realized that they had underestimated U.S. naval strength and were going to have to make more of an effort to oppose it. They increased their naval force in U.S. waters by one hundred ships of various sizes and used their naval power in three important ways: 1) through blockades of ports and harbors, which meant that U.S. ships that ventured out on the high seas would risk immediate attack; 2) through raids on towns along the East Coast; and 3) through actual battles at sea.

Experienced naval officer John Borlase Warren (1753–1822) was in charge of Royal Navy forces in the North Atlantic and Caribbean regions. His superiors had told him to put a quick end to the naval war. In the fall of 1812, Warren had established a blockade that extended from Charleston, South Carolina, to Florida, and with the arrival of a bigger fleet of ships in 1813 he was able to extend the blockade north to the Chesapeake and Delaware Bays as well as various other harbors and ports in the middle and southern states.

By November 1813, the whole Atlantic coast south of New England was blockaded. The British left New England alone due partly to that region's opposition to the war and partly because merchants there were sending goods to British troops in Canada and the West Indies. The blockade had a disastrous effect on the U.S. economy, causing a serious drop in foreign trade that deprived the government of the money it usually earned from taxes on imports. Domestic trade also was damaged, since merchants had to rely on overland transport of their goods, and bad roads made such transport difficult.

The blockades caused both over-supply and shortages of goods, resulting in some cases in ridiculously high prices; for example, a barrel of flour that cost $4.50 in Richmond, Virginia, cost $8.50 in New York and almost $12 in Boston. Because so few imported goods were being brought into the United States, people began panic-buying, and the prices of coffee, tea, sugar, salt, cotton, molasses, and spices doubled, tripled, and sometimes even quadrupled.

Cockburn harasses the Chesapeake Bay area

Warren assigned Admiral George Cockburn (1772–1853; pronounced coe-burn) the task of harassing the towns and cities along the East Coast of the United States, especially the Chesapeake Bay area. Cockburn's job was to destroy as many warships and as much government property as he could, while also disrupting trade along the coast. Another of his important aims was to show Americans firsthand the costs and perils of going to war with the Mistress of the Seas (Great Britain's nickname).

In late April 1813, Cockburn's forces attacked and burned Frenchtown, Maryland, and destroyed some ships in the harbor. They spent the next twelve days roaming freely through the region, raiding and burning other Maryland towns, including Havre de Grace, Principio, Georgetown, and Fredericktown. In mid-June, attracted by the prospect of capturing the USS *Constellation,* Cockburn directed an attack on Norfolk, Virginia, but the British were pushed back by the defending militia.

Cockburn's troops launched a more successful attack on Hampton, Virginia, on June 25, easily brushing aside the 450 militiamen who attempted to defend the town. The citizens of Hampton suffered greatly from the actions of the occupying troops, who were said to have pillaged the town, stealing and destroying private property as well as committing rape and murder. Cockburn would later claim that the evil deeds had all been done by Canadian chausseurs, deserters from the French army who had chosen to fight on the side of the British rather than go to jail.

"Don't give up the ship"

There were very few sea battles in 1813 because so few ships could get out of U.S. ports. The United States won only one major sea battle. Out of one of its defeats, however, came a phrase that was to serve as a rallying cry of sailors for the rest of the War of 1812 and even future conflicts.

In May 1813 Captain James Lawrence was given command of the USS *Chesapeake,* a frigate fitted with fifty guns that was considered an unlucky ship, perhaps due to its involvement in the *Chesapeake-Leopard* affair in 1807. Cruising off the coast of Boston on June 1, the *Chesapeake*—flying a flag printed with the motto of the U.S. Navy, "Free Trade and Sailors' Rights"—met up with the HMS *Shannon,* carrying fifty-two guns.

The two ships lined up side by side and exchanged broadsides (firing all guns on one side of a warship at more or less the same time), and after only fifteen minutes the *Shannon* emerged victorious. Attired in his colorful dress uniform, Lawrence had made a conspicuous target on the deck of the *Chesapeake,* and he had been mortally wounded. Before dying, he had told his men, "Don't give up the ship." They were, however, forced to surrender the *Chesapeake* to the British.

The British were thrilled with this victory, which was their first defeat of a U.S. frigate. Coming after a long string of sea victories for the United States, it was a great morale

Commander Oliver Hazard Perry on deck of his ship talking to a crew member before a naval battle.
Photograph reproduced by permission of Corbis Corporation (Bellevue).

booster to British at home and in North America. Meanwhile, Lawrence was given a hero's funeral, and his praises were sung by newspapers across the country. His dying words became the navy's new motto and the rallying cry of the War of 1812, and Commander Oliver Hazard Perry paid Lawrence a high tribute when he named his Lake Erie flagship after him.

Time is running out

Other naval actions at sea during 1813 included the defeat of the USS *Argus* (ten guns) by the *Pelican* (eleven guns) off the Irish coast on August 14. On September 5 the American ship *Enterprise* defeated the *Boxer* (both carrying fourteen guns) off the coast of Maine in a battle in which both ships' captains were killed. The frigate USS *Essex* (forty-six guns) cruised the Pacific doing a lot of damage to the British whaling industry, but in late 1813 it was virtually trapped at Valparaiso, Chile—a neutral harbor—by the British ships *Phoebe* and *Cherub*. In March 1814, the *Essex* would try to make a run for the open sea, but she would be caught and beaten by the British.

The blockades made the efforts of the privateers (private ships equipped with weapons and hired by a government to fight a war) even more valuable, but it was now more difficult for them to attack British merchant ships, which had started traveling in convoys (in groups, as a protection against attack). Privateers who stayed either in the West Indies or close to the British Isles had the best chances for success. The best example is probably the *True-Blooded American*, owned by an American living in Paris, France, which roamed British waters for more than a month. In that period the ships took twenty-seven prizes, occupied an Irish island for six days, and burned seven ships anchored in a Scottish harbor.

At the end of 1812, the United States had won some unexpected victories at sea and endured some unexpected defeats on land. A year later Great Britain reasserted its superiority on the sea (though not on the Great Lakes) while U.S. troops won some hard-fought battles on land. Yet the United States had not been able to take territory in Canada, and time was running out.

That was especially clear to anyone who kept an eye on events in Europe: in October Great Britain's allies had defeated forces led by French emperor and military general Napoleon I (1769–1821) at the Battle of Leipzig, and the British also had gained ground against Napoleon in Spain. Because Napoleon's fortunes had taken a turn for the worse, Great Britain could now begin to divert more soldiers and supplies to North America. Their approach had previously been defensive, but now they could afford to go on the offensive.

For More Information

Books

Brannan, John, ed. *Official Letters of the Military and Naval Officers of the United States, During the War with Great Britain in the Years 1812, 1813, 1814, and 1815.* Manchester, N.H.: Ayer Company Publishers, Inc.,1971.

Cleaves, Freeman. *Old Tippecanoe: William Henry Harrison and His Time.* New York: Charles Scribner's Sons, 1939.

Coles, Harry L. *The War of 1812*. Chicago: University of Chicago Press, 1965.

Dillon, Richard. *We Have Met the Enemy: Oliver Hazard Perry, Wilderness Commodore*. New York: McGraw-Hill, 1978.

Dowd, Gregory Evans. *A Spirited Resistance: The North American Indian Struggle for Unity, 1745-1815*. Baltimore: Johns Hopkins University Press, 1992.

Dudley, William S., and Michael S. Crawford, eds. *The Naval War of 1812: A Documentary History*. 2 vols. Washington, D.C.: Naval Historical Center, 1985 and 1992.

Elting, John R. *Amateurs to Arms!: A Military History of the War of 1812*. Chapel Hill, N.C.: Algonquin Press, 1991; Reprint, Cambridge, Mass.: Da Capo Press, 1995.

Heidler, David S., and Jeanne T. Heidler, eds. *Encyclopedia of the War of 1812*. Santa Barbara, Calif.: ABC-CLIO, 1997.

Heidler, David S., and Jeanne T. Heidler, eds. *Old Hickory's War: Andrew Jackson and the Quest for Empire*. Mechanicsburg, Penn.: Stackpole Books, 1996.

Hickey, Donald R. *The War of 1812: A Forgotten Conflict*. Urbana: University of Illinois Press, 1989.

Hollon, W. Eugene. *The Lost Pathfinder: Zebulon Montgomery Pike*. Norman: University of Oklahoma Press, 1949.

Moir, John. "An Early Record of Laura Secord's Walk." *Ontario History*. 51 (1959): 105-08.

Sugden, John. *Tecumseh's Last Stand*. Norman: University of Oklahoma Press, 1985.

Terrell, John Upton. *Zebulon Pike: The Life and Times of an Adventurer*. New York: Weybright and Talley, 1968.

Web sites

"The War of 1812 Website." *The Discriminating General*. [Online] http://www.militaryheritage.com/1812.htm (accessed on November 26, 2001).

"War of 1812." *Galafilm War of 1812 Website*. [Online] http://www.galafilm.com/1812/e/index.html (accessed on November 26, 2001).

War of 1812-1814. [Online] http://www.members.tripod.com/~war1812/ (accessed on November 26, 2001).

"War of 1812—Forgotten War." *History Central.com*. [Online] http://www.multied.com/1812/ (accessed on November 26, 2001).

Peace Is Promised, But War Continues

5

The War of 1812 between the United States and Great Britain was provoked by two major issues. The first was Britain's maritime policy of impressment in its war with France. This policy was where British officials often boarded U.S. ships to capture deserters from their own navy, often wrongfully taking American citizens in the process. The other issues that led to the war was Great Britain's overly friendly relations with Native Americans. Americans believed that the British were encouraging Native Americans to attack white settlers who were moving west. The Native Americans believed that the settlers were encroaching on (gradually taking over) their land. Although these two issues led to Americans being eager to fight a war with Britain, the United States was not necessarily ready to fight such a war. By the end of 1813, after almost eighteen months of war, the United States had little to show for their efforts. Although the United States had won some victories in the Northwest and elsewhere, the important planned invasion of Canada had failed. These failures were generally due to poor preparation, poor leadership, and poor strategy.

Albert Gallatin: Financial Expert and Skillful Negotiator

Much respected for both his intellect and his ability to forge compromises, Albert Gallatin was secretary of the treasury during President James Madison's administration. He also played a key role in the War of 1812 when he served on the five-member team sent to Ghent, Belgium, to negotiate a peace treaty to end the war.

The son of a wealthy merchant from an aristocratic, politically active family, Albert Gallatin was born in Geneva, Switzerland, on January 29, 1761. Orphaned as a child, he was raised by a relative. After graduating from the Academy of Geneva, the nineteen-year-old Gallatin sailed for the United States. Despite his aristocratic background, he had a liberal outlook and was inspired by the democratic ideals of the American Revolution and looked forward to becoming a citizen of the new nation.

Gallatin worked briefly as a merchant in Maine, then for several years as a French tutor at Harvard University in Cambridge, Massachusetts. In 1786 he bought a four-hundred-acre farm in western Pennsylvania. His neighbors were impressed by his intellect and broad worldview, and in 1788 they elected him as a delegate to a meeting to propose amendments to the U.S. Constitution. The next year, he was elected as a delegate to Pennsylvania's Constitutional Convention.

In 1790 Gallatin was elected to the Pennsylvania state legislature, where he served for two years and gained a reputation as a hard worker, a man of principle, and a good speaker. He also demonstrated a strong understanding of financial issues. Gallatin was elected to the U.S. Senate in 1793 as a Republican, but he served only three months because members of the opposing party, the Federalists, challenged his eligibility on the grounds that he had not been an American citizen long enough.

Returning to Pennsylvania, Gallatin was elected to the U.S. House of Representatives in 1795. There he worked especially hard on financial issues, proposing the creation of the Ways and Means Committee to oversee the government's finances. Gallatin became the Republican spokesman in the House in 1797. In this position he expressed strong opposition to the Quasi War (a brief conflict between the United States and France that took place in the Caribbean region and involved attacks on U.S. merchant ships) and to the Alien and

When Congress met on December 6 for its last session of 1813, a pessimistic mood prevailed. Despite its promising beginning, 1813 had not brought the United States any closer to the goals that it had set when it declared war on Great Britain: to secure its western settlements from Native Ameri-

Sedition Acts, which were intended to stifle criticism of the government.

Thomas Jefferson won the presidential election in 1800, and after taking office in 1801 he named Gallatin secretary of the treasury, a position he would hold until 1814. Gallatin pushed through a number of positive measures, including a plan to pay off the public debt, to promote manufacturing, and to devote federal money to the building of roads and canals.

When the War of 1812 began in June, it wreaked havoc on all of Gallatin's financial policies, for the federal government was not financially prepared to support the expenses of the conflict. Gallatin grew increasingly frustrated and unhappy in his position. When Russia offered to mediate peace negotiations between Great Britain and the United States, now-president James Madison gave Gallatin leave from his Treasury Department job to travel to Europe and assist with the negotiations. Before the talks could begin, however, Great Britain refused to participate.

By the time the British offered to hold peace talks in Ghent, Belgium, in August 1814, Gallatin had already been in Europe for many months. He was soon assigned by Madison to serve on the five-member team that would represent the United States in Ghent and played a major role in the negotiation. He not only crafted much of the final document, but he also helped the whole process to go smoothly through his calm presence and ability to compromise.

For most of the following decade, Gallatin was the U.S. diplomatic representative to France, a position he left in 1823. In 1826 he served as the U.S. minister to Great Britain. After his return to the United States, Gallatin settled in New York and in 1831 became the president of the National Bank, retiring in 1839. He spent his remaining years in active involvement with such cultural groups as the New York Historical Society and the American Ethnological Society.

Gallatin died in 1849, survived by Hannah, his wife of almost fifty-six years, and five children.

Sources: Encyclopedia of World Biography, *2nd ed., 17 vols. Gale Research, 1998; Heidler, David S., and Jeanne T. Heidler, eds.* Encyclopedia of the War of 1812. *Santa Barbara, Calif.: ABC-CLIO, Inc., 1997.*

can attacks, to stop Great Britain from disrupting trade and impressing U.S. sailors, and to expand its territory.

In his address to Congress, President James Madison (1751–1836) reported that Great Britain had rejected Russia's offer to help mediate a peace treaty; the British preferred to meet with the United States face to face. He focused on the U.S. victories that had taken place since Congress had last met and pointed out that war had stimulated the manufacturing and defense industries. Most importantly, Madison claimed, as recorded in the *Annals of Congress,* the war was showing that the United States was and would continue to be a "great, a flourishing, and a powerful nation."

On December 30 a British ship flying a flag of truce arrived in the United States. It carried news that Great Britain wanted to enter into direct peace negotiations. Madison accepted the offer, nominating almost the same team he had chosen for the proposed Russian-mediated negotiations: diplomat John Quincy Adams (1767–1848; president 1825–29), Senator James Bayard (1767–1815) from Delaware, and Speaker of the House Henry Clay (1777–1852) from Kentucky. Several months later, former secretary of the Treasury Albert Gallatin (1761–1849)—already in Europe because he had traveled there earlier in the year to take part in the proposed Russian-mediated talks—would also join the group in Ghent, Belgium. This time, Congress approved Madison's nominations. But fighting would continue for another year as each side tried to gain the upper hand and thus better their position in the peace talks.

More congressional debates about the war

Congress continued to debate the merits of the war, with the Federalists arguing for only defensive action and Republicans saying that the war was defensive but with inadequate resources, it could not be brought to a close. Raising the number of troops required to fight the war was still the Republicans' top priority. The number of new recruits had declined toward the end of 1813, and many soldiers who had enlisted before the war began or between 1812 and 1813 would soon be eligible for discharge. Again Congress raised the reward for new recruits and for those who re-enlisted; they also increased the length of the enlistment period. The authorized number of troops was raised to 62,500, and a new law was passed that gave the U.S. Army more power to force militiamen to obey orders. (Militiamen were members of small armies made up of troops residing in a particular state.) More money was allocated for naval operations, including funds for a steam-powered frigate (large warship) to be designed by inventor Robert Fulton (1765–1815), but the ship was completed too late to be used in the war. Learning that Great Britain had detained two thousand more prisoners of war than the United States and wishing to balance the scales, Congress also voted to increase the bounty (reward) paid for prisoners brought in by privateers (private citizens employed by the government to use their ships to disrupt enemy trade by attacking enemy ships and confiscating cargo).

Financially, the government was now teetering on the brink of bankruptcy (financial failure) as it struggled to meet both ordinary and war-related costs, even though additional taxes had been enacted in the previous session of Congress. Secretary of the Navy William Jones (1760–1831)—who also was serving as temporary treasury secretary until Gallatin's replacement could be named—recommended new taxes, but the Republicans, as usual, rejected this idea. Instead, they authorized a new $25 million loan and the issuance of $10 million in treasury notes or short-term bonds.

Stamping out trade with the enemy

Madison remained convinced that economic pressure would weaken Great Britain's position in the war. He also wanted to stamp out the trade that many Americans were carrying on with the British despite the war. Great Britain had made it clear that it would continue to trade with Americans who did not exhibit hostile behavior, and many merchants and traders had accepted their offer: in exchange for British textiles (fabrics), pottery, salt, and other products, U.S. citizens offered the food and supplies Great Britain needed to maintain its force in North America. Thus Americans were helping to feed and clothe the very soldiers who were fighting against U.S. troops.

In spite of the British blockade of American ports to the south of New England, sea trade also was taking place, most often by merchants whose ships (even though they were actually American or British) flew the flags of neutral countries. Smuggling (the buying and selling of illegally ob-

The Role of the Privateers

When the War of 1812 began, the United States Navy was not prepared to take on the Mistress of the Seas—the nickname Great Britain had earned through the prowess of her mighty navy. Fearful that a large military could pose a threat to a democratic nation, two successive Republican administrations had made sure that both the army and the navy decreased in size during the years that followed the Revolutionary War. The result was not only an ill-prepared army, but a tiny navy that lacked the ships and sailors it would need to fight Great Britain.

Fortunately for the United States, privateers were able to fill that gap. These were privately owned vessels licensed by "letters of marquee," documents that gave them official permission to attack, raid, and sink merchant ships sailing under the flag of the enemy country. While profitable for the owners and crew of the privateers themselves, this practice helped the United States by hurting Great Britain's economy and by keeping its own navy busy defending the commercial ships.

Privateering had been common in the United States since colonial days, and some of the naval officers who would gain fame during the War of 1812 (including Stephen Decatur and Joshua Barney) had gotten valuable early training by serving aboard privateers. Privateering featured a unique blend of patriotism and profit-seeking, and it was used with great success during the War of 1812. Privateers tended to be smaller and faster than war ships, making them hard for the British to catch. Eventually Great Britain did put a convoy system (by which ships would travel in groups, with warships guarding them) into effect, which cut down on their losses.

Privateers were much more numerous and better armed than the ships of the U.S. Navy, and they took more prizes (captured more British ships). For example, the U.S. Navy had 23 ships with 556 guns that had taken 254 prizes. In comparison, there were 517 privateer ships with 2,893 guns that had taken 1,345 prizes. Privateers inflicted 45.5 million dollars worth of dam-

tained goods) was a big problem. In New Orleans, pirates claiming to be privateers made a very good living bringing in goods stolen from ships they had attacked in the Gulf of Mexico. It was difficult to enforce the existing laws banning trading with the enemy, because too many people were making too much money from the practice.

Fed up with this situation, Madison presented Congress with a new system of restrictions: an embargo prohibit-

age to the British shipping industry, and captured 30,000 British prisoners.

The practice of privateering proved enormously enriching for many Americans, whose fortunes and social rank skyrocketed after several successful cruises (journeys made for the purpose of finding, fighting, and capturing or sinking enemy ships). Life aboard a privateer did involve danger and risk, however, and most of the U.S. prisoners of war in the main British prisons in Canada and England were privateer crew members captured at sea.

Several ships gained great fame for their daring and success as privateers. The *Yankee,* a ship out of Bristol, Rhode Island, that was equipped with 14 guns and a crew of 120, made six cruises, traveling to places as far apart as Nova Scotia in Canada, West Africa, and the English Channel. The *Yankee* took 40 prizes and seized an estimated $5,000,000 worth of property, making owner James De Wolfe one of the richest men in his state. Likewise, the Crowninshield family's *America,* based in

Salem, Massachusetts, had 20 guns and crew of 150. Despite its large size, this ship was one of the fastest. The *America* made four cruises and captured 21 enemy ships, earning more than $1,000,000.

One of the most famous U.S. privateer captains was Thomas Boyle of Baltimore. He commanded the *Comet,* which carried sixteen guns and made twenty-seven captures, as well as the *Chasseur,* with sixteen guns and fifty-three prizes to its credit. A ship distinguished by her sleek, low lines, the *Chasseur* became known as the Pride of Baltimore.

After the war, some of the privateers went on to take part in and profit from the revolutions that were springing up throughout Latin America. But in general, the War of 1812 was the last conflict in which privateering was used on such a large scale. The practice was outlawed in 1865.

Sources: Heidler, David S., and Jeanne T. Heidler, eds. Encyclopedia of the War of 1812. Santa Barbara, Calif.: ABC-CLIO, Inc., 1997.

ing American ships and goods from leaving port, a total ban on certain products produced in Great Britain or in its colonies (such as woolen and cotton goods and rum), and a ban on foreign ships entering U.S. ports unless three-quarters of their crew members were actually citizens of the country whose flag the ship flew.

The Federalists strongly protested, claiming that these new restrictions would severely damage commerce, agriculture, and government revenues. Nevertheless, the program was approved by Congress and signed into law by Madison before the end of 1813. However, the collapse of Napoleon's Continental System (restrictions on trade with the countries of Europe, which had helped bring about the War of 1812; See "The Napoleonic Wars" in chapter 2) meant that the British could trade with any country in Europe. Thus, the U.S. restrictions would not harm Britain much anymore, but they would hurt U.S. trade. Only four months after it had been signed, what has been referred to as the war's final embargo was repealed (officially done away with). Now Americans were barred only from direct trade with Great Britain.

Jackson's troops fight the Red Sticks

The first military action of 1814 was really a continuation of something that had been started, but not quite finished, in 1813. In the southwestern territories of Alabama, Mississippi, and West Florida, U.S. troops had been fighting Native Americans called the Red Sticks, a hostile faction of the Creek nation (see "Fighting Native Americans in the South" in chapter 4). In command of this effort was Andrew Jackson (1767–1845), known as "Old Hickory," a tenacious fighter who had only reluctantly let the majority of his troops return to their homes at the end of 1813 because they had reached the end of their enlistment terms.

In the early weeks of 1814, Jackson received one thousand reinforcements. He knew he had to act fast, because most of the men had enlisted for only a sixty-day period. The campaign began on January 22, when eight hundred of Jackson's troops— along with two hundred friendly Native American warriors (Cherokees and Creeks who had not sided with the Red Sticks)— marched from Fort Strother (in what is now central Alabama) to attack a Red Stick village on Emuckfau Creek. Although outnumbered, Jackson's troops sent their opponents fleeing. They fought another, somewhat shorter battle at Enitachopco Creek on January 24. Although neither of these confrontations was really conclusive, the Americans considered them victories.

Jackson now returned to Fort Strother to await the arrival of more troops and supplies. By February, he had command of four thousand additional soldiers from Tennessee

(six hundred were regular soldiers, the rest militia). Plagued by trouble with the militia, Jackson put a rigid disciplinary system into effect, even condemning to death an eighteen-year-old volunteer who had refused to obey orders. After that, Jackson had fewer problems with the militia.

Andrew Jackson and his troops defeating Creek Indians during the Battle of Emuckfau Creek. *Photograph reproduced by permission of The Granger Collection.*

The Battle of Horseshoe Bend

From his Native American allies, Jackson learned that hostile Creeks had camped on a peninsula called Horseshoe Bend that jutted into the Tallapoosa River. The Red Sticks had fortified the land approach to their camp, while placing their canoes on the river behind it for a quick escape. Jackson began his attack on the camp on March 27 by sending his Native American friends swimming across the river to steal the Red Stick canoes. Then some of Jackson's troops attacked the front of the camp while others, crossing the river in the stolen canoes, attacked from the rear.

The battle resulted in very heavy casualties, especially since most of the Red Sticks preferred to die fighting rather than surrender. Before the battle was over, 800 Creeks had died compared to only 200 Americans. In addition, 350 Creek women and children were captured, and some were killed during the course of the battle. Most of the few Red Sticks who managed to escape, as well as those who had not been present, lost heart for further fighting and fled south into Florida.

In April Jackson was surprised by a visit from William Weatherford (1780–1824), the Red Stick leader of mixed Creek and white heritage who was known among Native Americans as Red Eagle. Weatherford surrendered to Jackson, asking no favors for himself but requesting aid for the Creek women and children still hiding in the woods. Reportedly, Jackson was so struck by Weatherford's courage that he offered him a drink, shook his hand, and sent him home. Weatherford lived out his life as a successful Alabama plantation owner.

The Treaty of Fort Jackson

After the Battle of Horseshoe Bend, Jackson established a fort (named after himself) at the junction of the Coosa and Tallapoosa Rivers and fought a few more minor battles with the Red Sticks who remained in the area. By August the Red Sticks were conclusively beaten, and the United States government prepared to offer them a treaty. The U.S. goal was to cut the Creeks off from Spanish influence by limiting their access to Florida.

Jackson (recently appointed to the high rank of major general) was assigned to present the treaty. He had been chosen over several candidates who were thought to be too soft on Native Americans. The Creeks were given no opportunity to negotiate the Treaty of Fort Jackson, but were simply forced to sign it. Even though many Creeks had fought on the side of the Americans (in fact, only one Red Stick was even present at the signing—the other signers were all friendly Creeks), the entire Creek nation was punished. They were to give up their rights to more than twenty million acres of land, which made up more than half of their territory.

Thus the U.S. government's goal of protecting white settlers took precedence over any obligation it might have had to the friendly Creeks. Although the Treaty of Fort Jackson did improve security for white Americans who lived on the western frontier, it did not affect the outcome of the War of 1812 very much. And the United States would continue to have problems with the Creeks: a few years later, refugee Red Sticks in Florida would join with Seminoles in fighting the First Seminole War (1817–19).

Great Britain goes on the offensive

Great Britain's victories against French emperor Napoleon Bonaparte (1769–1821) at the Battle of Leipzig in Germany and in Spain in the fall of 1813 marked a turning point. In the opening months of 1814, Great Britain and its allies launched an invasion of France, and on March 31 they took over the French capital, Paris. Defeated, Napoleon was forced to abdicate (give up his position as emperor) and was exiled to the Mediterranean island of Elba. Europe was finally at peace. Now the British could devote more attention to the war in North America and better its position at the peace talks.

The British began sending more troops to North America—and these were not just any troops. They were seasoned veterans of the Napoleonic Wars, and there were a lot of them. By September 1814 thirteen thousand had arrived in Canada, bringing Great Britain's troop strength to thirty thousand; it would reach forty thousand by the end of the year.

As the United States took stock of its own position at the beginning of 1814 there were a few reasons for optimism. The U.S. Army was steadily improving in quality and quantity. The top ranks were now occupied by officers of more uniform skill and leadership ability, and the higher bounty authorized by Congress was attracting new recruits and re-enlistments. By the spring of 1814, the army was up to forty thousand troops—one-third more than it had been a year before—and by early 1815 it had risen to nearly forty-five thousand.

Also on the positive side, the Battle of Lake Erie and the Battle of the Thames had given the United States the upper hand in the Northwest. Goals for the 1814 campaign included holding on to that position while also gaining supremacy on the problematic Niagara frontier. Peace negotiations were already in the works, and the United States would be in a better position to bargain if its troops could gain some British-held territory before the talks got underway.

Back into Canada

On July 3, 1814, Major General Jacob Brown (1775–1828) led the next U.S. attempt to invade Canada, marching thirty-five hundred troops (plus six hundred Native American allies) into enemy territory. The plan was for the army to work its way up the Niagara River and capture the important shipping center of Kingston. The force was divided into two brigades, commanded by generals Winfield Scott (1786–1866) and Eleazer Ripley (1782–1839).

For several months, Scott had been intensively training his troops, subjecting them to at least seven hours of drilling per day but also making sure that they had good, plentiful food and hygienic conditions. They made an impressive, highly disciplined appearance, dressed in short gray jackets and white pants rather than the usual blue uniforms (due to a shortage of blue fabric). Some historians assert that this brigade's stellar performance on the battlefield led to the use of "cadet's gray" for students' uniforms at United States Military Academy at West Point, New York, but others claim there is no real evidence of this.

The British had occupied Fort Erie at the end of 1813, and the first task before Brown's force was to take it back. This was accomplished quite easily on July 3, when U.S. troops surrounded the fort with its small (only 137) band of British defenders inside. The British surrendered almost immediately. After securing Fort Erie, Brown pointed his troops north again, to search out the main British force.

"These are regulars, by God!"

Near the place where the Niagara and Chippewa rivers converge, advance troops (including militiamen as well as

friendly Iroquois warriors) led by Peter B. Porter (1773–1844) of the New York militia came under fire from hostile Native Americans. The U.S. troops drove them off, but fell back themselves when they encountered a much bigger British force. Scott soon arrived with fifteen hundred regular soldiers and engaged the British, who also numbered about fifteen hundred and who were commanded by General Phineas Riall (1775–1850).

When Riall saw the gray uniforms worn by Scott's men, he assumed they were militiamen and thus inferior troops. But the U.S. soldiers advanced in an impressively steady, orderly, and courageous manner, so that eventually Riall, as reported in *The War of 1812* by John K. Mahon, exclaimed, "These are regulars, by God!" (meaning regular soldiers). Suffering 500 casualties, Riall's troops were forced to retreat; the United States had 325 soldiers killed or wounded. Discipline and dedicated training paid off, and Americans felt proud of their troops' performance.

Major General Jacob Brown leading U.S. forces in an invasion of Canada.
Photograph reproduced by permission of Hulton/Archive.

Brown now began moving his troops north along the Chippewa River. He hoped to meet up with Commodore Isaac Chauncey's (1772–1840) Lake Ontario fleet, so that the navy could provide both supplies and back-up fire during battles as the army attacked British bases. Chauncey was ill, however, and this delayed his response to Brown's request. Finally Chauncey told Brown that his navy would not be available, as they were meant for higher purposes than just backing up the army. Brown's troops were on their own.

The Battle of Lundy's Lane

The next major battle of the campaign took place on July 25 when about one thousand troops under Scott engaged a British force of between sixteen hundred and eighteen hundred under Riall (reinforcements on both sides would bring their numbers up to twenty-one hundred and three thousand, respectively) at Lundy's Lane, located just west of Niagara Falls. The noise of the falls competed with that of the battle well into the night. It was an incredibly fierce fight that lasted five hours and included many moments of chaos and confusion; both sides, for example, experienced moments when soldiers were actually firing on their own troops. British soldiers who had arrived recently from fighting in the brutal Napoleonic Wars claimed the battle was as intense as any they had experienced.

The British had placed a battery (set of guns) of six big guns on top of a small hill, and the Americans succeeded in a daring assault to take it over. The charge was led by Colonel James Miller (1776–1851), who became famous for having calmly said, when told he must try to take the hill, "I'll try, sir," as quoted in Donald R. Hickey's *The War of 1812: A Forgotten Conflict*. The British made several attempts to recover the battery but the U.S. troops held on through mounting exhaustion and thirst. Each of the top four officers on the scene was wounded: on the American side, Brown and Scott (two horses had been killed under him during the battle, and his injuries sidelined him for the rest of the war), and on the British side, Riall and General Gordon Drummond (1772–1854).

Finally Brown ordered a retreat. The Americans managed to carry away only one of the guns for which this terri-

bly bloody battle had been waged. Casualties were very high on both sides: 81 British soldiers had been killed and 562 wounded; the Americans, 171 killed and 573 wounded. Afterward, the British expected the U.S. forces to attack again, but the attack never came. Instead, Brown pulled his troops back to Fort Erie. Although the U.S. forces had been the first to withdraw from the battlefield, they had done so while they were in a dominant position, also the casualties for each side were fairly close in number; therefore, the Battle of Lundy's Lane was considered a draw.

A scene of the fighting during the Battle of Lundy's Lane. Since U.S. forces withdrew while in a dominant position and both sides suffered similar casualties, the battle was considered a draw.
Photograph reproduced by The Granger Collection.

Successfully defending Fort Erie

As the summer of 1814 wore on, the British focused their attention on Fort Erie, now defended by twenty-one hundred soldiers under the command General Edmund P. Gaines (1777–1849) because Brown was in Buffalo, New York, recovering from his wounds. On August 13 the British showered the fort with artillery fire, and on August 15 they advanced with bayonets (daggerlike weapons that fit on the end of the muzzle of a rifle) drawn. One of their columns managed to break through the U.S. defenses and enter the fort, engaging its defenders in close combat for about two hours. During the battle a powder magazine (ammunitions storehouse) exploded, killing many British soldiers and sending the rest scurrying. Both of the British commanding officers had been killed, while 360 soldiers were killed or wounded and 540 were captured or missing. U.S. casualties numbered only 130, making this a major victory for the United States.

Rather than giving up on Fort Erie, the British began to bomb it from a position about five hundred yards away. Brown, who had returned to take command of his troops, was determined not to evacuate the fort. Instead, he made a plan to send a force out in a sortie (a quick raid) to destroy the cannons the British were using for the attack. On September 17 twelve hundred New York militiamen under the command of Miller and Porter headed out in the middle of a rainstorm, surprising the British and disabling two batteries of guns before withdrawing. Again, casualties were high: six hundred on the British side, five hundred on the American.

Brown was extremely pleased with the performance of the New York militia during the sortie, for throughout the war the various state militias had proved astoundingly uncooperative and often equally unskilled. Like the Battle of Lundy's Lane, this one had shown that American soldiers—and in this case, volunteers—could hold their own against the toughest British veterans. Despite this positive outcome, the Niagara campaign was now over, and it had brought the United States no real strategic gains. Meanwhile, other ups and downs had been occurring on the Chesapeake and Lake Champlain fronts.

Cochrane raids the Chesapeake Bay area

Having taken the offensive on the Niagara River, the British also were on the move along the mid-Atlantic coast. In August 1814, they had begun to launch raids on small towns around the Chesapeake Bay (which touches on the states of Virginia, Maryland, and Delaware), something similar to what they had done in 1813. Great Britain had several goals, the most important of which being to create a diversion that would relieve pressure on their troops fighting in the Northeast. They also wanted revenge for the burning and pillaging by American soldiers after the United States won the Battle of York.

Leading the naval part of this effort was Admiral Alexander Cochrane (1758–1832), who had succeeded John Borlase Warren (1753–1822; see "The British bolster their naval forces" in chapter 4) as commander of the British Navy in North America and who took up his task with enthusiasm. Meanwhile, Great Britain also sent a formidable land force to the area: twenty-five hundred soldiers, fresh from fighting Napoleon's troops in France, arrived in the Chesapeake Bay on August 15, commanded by Major General Robert Ross (1766–1814). The British now had a total of forty-five hundred troops in the region, and twenty warships.

Controlling the Chesapeake Bay gave Great Britain access not only to the many small towns situated along its coastline, but the important cities of Washington, D.C., and Baltimore, Maryland. An attack on the capital of the United States would deliver a severe blow to Americans' pride and morale, and Baltimore was a thriving, wealthy seaport and naval center. Considered a "nest of pirates," according to Elting, by the British, Baltimore was home base to many privateers and thus a source of potential prize money for those who captured privateer ships.

The British plan to attack Washington, D.C.

The British began their expedition by pursuing Joshua Barney (1759–1818), a privateer who had been assigned to protect the Chesapeake Bay with his flotilla (a small fleet or group) of ships but who had retreated up the Patuxent River when he spotted the large British fleet. The British ships proceeded about twenty-five miles up the Patuxent and landed at Benedict, which is located about sixty miles south of Washington, D.C. One of Cochrane's squadrons (several units of military organization) continued in pursuit of Barney, while Ross's army disembarked. On August 20, they began their march north, reaching Upper Marlboro, Maryland, two days later. Meanwhile, knowing he would soon be cornered, Barney managed to abandon and burn his ships before the British arrived.

Cochrane was convinced that the time was right for an attack on Washington, D.C., and Ross finally agreed with him. They decided that the least risky and less expected route into the city was through the town of Bladensburg, located just northeast of the city.

A shocking lack of preparation on the part of the U.S. leadership would soon prove that Cochrane's instincts were correct. As early as July 1, Madison had told Congress that he expected an attack on the capital. Secretary of War John Armstrong (1758–1843), however, was absolutely convinced that the British would never bother with Washington; their logical target, he maintained, was Baltimore, and he concentrated most of the available resources on the defense of that city.

Madison, nevertheless, did succeed in establishing the District of Columbia as a special military district. General William Winder (1775–1824), a Baltimore lawyer, was assigned to head up the defense of the nation's capital. Chosen primarily because the administration wanted to secure the support of his uncle, Levin Winder (1757–1819), who was the Governor of Maryland and a Federalist, William did not have much experience in commanding troops. There would be only about only five hundred regular soldiers available in the event of an attack, so the defense of the city would have to depend mostly on whatever militia could be rounded up. Winder, who did not arrive in Washington to set up his headquarters until August 1, wanted to call up four thousand militia right away, but Armstrong insisted that they could only be activated in the presence of imminent danger.

On August 18, the news of the British landing at Benedict, Maryland, arrived in Washington. Clearly the British were on their way, but was their destination Baltimore or the capital? Winder finally received word to call up the militia, and by August 20, he had gathered nine thousand (most of them from Maryland and Pennsylvania). Still unsure which city the British would attack, Winder sent five thousand troops to Baltimore, deploying the rest around the District of Columbia.

In an unusual move for a member of the president's cabinet, Secretary of State James Monroe (1758–1831) volunteered to serve as a scout, heading off on horseback toward Benedict to find out the number of British troops on the way. When Monroe neared Benedict, however, he was afraid to get any closer than three miles to the British, and he had forgotten his telescope. Thus, he concluded that they had six thousand troops; he overestimated the number by about fifteen hundred.

The Battle of Bladensburg

Since the Americans had failed to obstruct the roads or burn the bridges leading toward Washington, the British were able to make a fairly quick advance. Skirting Washington and arriving at Bladensburg to the north, they were met and engaged by the U.S. troops. But the U.S. forces were immediately at a disadvantage because Monroe mishandled the self-appointed task of how the troops should be arranged for battle. The fight did not go well for the hastily assembled, inexperienced U.S. soldiers, and many of the militiamen fled after only a few minutes of battle. The British use of very noisy—although not very harmful—Congreve rockets (a standard part of the ammunition of most British warships developed by Lieutenant William Congreve) proved especially terrifying to the Americans. After about three hours of fighting, and despite the late appearance of Joshua Barney's more seasoned troops, the British took control of Bladensburg, in spite of the fact that they had experienced more casualties than the Americans. After resting for two hours, Ross's troops set off for the capital, arriving at about eight o'clock in the evening.

The British began their plan to attack Washington, D.C., by pursuing privateer Joshua Barney who had been assigned to protect the Chesapeake Bay.
Photograph reproduced by permission of Corbis Corporation (Bellevue).

The capital city burns

Most of the city's residents, hearing of the American defeat at Bladensburg, had fled in a hurry. Madison was in

Virginia, and Winder had gone with his defeated troops to Frederick, Maryland. The President's wife Dolley Madison (1768–1849; see biographical entry) had left the White House with a wagon full of important documents and other official items, but most of her personal belongings had been left behind.

Finding no one with whom to negotiate the terms of Washington's surrender, Ross ordered the city's public buildings destroyed. A group of British officers entered the White House and found a table set for forty people; they ate a good dinner, complete with wine, before burning the White House to the ground. Also destroyed were the Capitol and the buildings housing the Congress, Treasury Department, and the War Department. The fires burned brightly all night. The next morning, the British departed from Washington and marched back to Benedict, where they reboarded their ships.

Meanwhile, a British force under Captain James Gordon (1782–1869) had sailed up the Potomac River to provide support for Ross's invasion. By August 27 (two days after Ross left Washington), Gordon had reached Fort Washington, about ten miles south of the capital. To the amazement of the British, the Americans there responded to the enemy's arrival by abandoning and burning the fort, leaving the way clear for the British to enter Alexandria, Virginia, located about six miles upriver.

The defenseless city immediately surrendered to the British, who began to load a huge quantity of goods—including flour, tobacco, cotton, sugar, and wine—into twenty-one ships. Upon leaving Alexandria, Gordon's troops were fired upon by Americans on the riverbanks, but they made it safely to Chesapeake Bay.

Madison and his cabinet members returned to Washington on August 27, where many citizens held him responsible for the humiliating invasion of the nation's capital. According to Walter Lord's book *The Dawn's Early Light*, someone had even scrawled on a wall of the destroyed Capitol, "George Washington founded this city after a seven years' war with England—James Madison lost it after a two years' war." Madison's lack of popularity was second only to that of Secretary of War John Armstrong (1758–1843), who soon re-

signed from his office. Madison then appointed Monroe to take over Armstrong's duties.

The British plan to attack Plattsburg

During the same month as Britain's successful invasion of Washington, D.C., about seventeen thousand battled-toughened veterans of the Napoleonic Wars arrived in the Quebec and Montreal areas of Canada, ready to assist in Great Britain's planned invasion of the United States in order to move closer to their food supplies and increase territorial gains. The first target of the invasion was Plattsburg, New York, since it exists along the Richeliew River-Lake Champlain line and is a natural gateway to the United States. The British intended to accomplish this invasion with the support of their fleet on Lake Champlain, a body of water that is sandwiched between Vermont and New York. Unfortunately for the U.S. side, Armstrong had earlier ordered that most of

Captain Daniel Pring Delivers Bad News

The following letter was written by Captain Daniel Pring to Commodore Sir James Yeo, commander of the British navy in the Great Lakes region, to inform him of the British defeat on Lake Champlain on September 10, 1814.

United States Ship SARATOGA, Plattsburg-Bay Lake Champlain, Sept 12, 1814

Sir,

The painful task of making you acquainted with the circumstances attending the capture of his Majesty's squadron yesterday, by that of the Americans under Commodore M'Donough, it grieves me to state, becomes my duty to perform, from the ever-to-be-lamented loss of that worthy and gallant officer, Captain Downie, who unfortunately fell early in the action....

From the light airs and the smoothness of the water, the fire on both sides proved very destructive from the commencement of the engagement, and with the exception of the brig [square-rigged sailing ship], that of the enemy seemed united against the CONFIANCE. After two hours severe conflict with our op-ponents she cut her cable, run down and took shelter between the ship and the schooner [a ship with two or more masts at its front and back ends], which enabled us to direct our fire against the division of the enemy gun-boats and ship, which had so long annoyed us during our close engagement with the brig without any return on our part; at this time the fire of the enemy ship slackened considerably, having several of her guns dismounted, when she cut her cable, and winded her larboard broadside to bear on the CONFIANCE, who, in vain, eneavoured to effect the same operation; at thirty-three minutes after two, I was much distressed to see that the CONFIANCE had struck her colours. The whole attention of the enemy force then became directed towards the LINNET, the shattered and disabled state of the masts, sails, rigging and yards, precluded the most distant hope of being able to effect an escape by cutting the cable; the result of doing so must, in a few minutes, have been her drifting alongside the enemy's vessels, close under our lee [side sheltered from the wind]; but in the hope that the flotilla of gun-boats, who had abandoned the object assigned them, would perceive our wants

the U.S. forces be moved from Plattsburg to Sacket's Harbor, New York. Left behind was General Alexander Macomb (1782–1841) with thirty-five hundred soldiers.

When Macomb learned of the British plan, he called for militia backup. New York and Vermont (which had previously

and come to our assistance, which would afford a reasonable prospect of being towed clear, I determined to resist the then destructive cannonading of the whole of the enemy's fleet, and at the same time, despatched Lieut. H. Drew to ascertain the state of the CONFIANCE. At forty-five minutes after ten I was appraised of the irreparable loss she had sustained by the death of her brave commander (whose merits it would be presumption in me to extol), as well as the great slaughter which had taken place on board, and observing from the manoeuvers of the flotilla, that I could enjoy no further expectation of relief, the situation of my noble comrades who had so nobly fought, and even now fast falling by my side, demanded the surrender of his Majesty's brig entrusted to my command to prevent a useless waste of valuable lives, and at the request of the surviving officers and men, I gave the painful orders for the colours to be struck....

...when it is taken into consideration that 16 days before the CONFIANCE was on the stocks, with an unorganized crew, composed of several drafts of men who had recently arrived from different ships at Quebec, many of whom only joined the day before and were totally unknown either to the officers or to each other, with the want of gun-locks as well as other necessary appointments not to be procured in this country, I trust you will feel satisfied of the decided advantage that the enemy possessed, exclusive of their great superiority in point of force....

I have much satisfaction in making you acquainted with the humane treatment the wounded have received from Commodore M'Donough. They were immediately removed to his own hospital on Crab Island, and were furnished with every requisite [necessity]. His generous and polite attention also to myself, the officers and men, will ever hereafter be gratefully remembered. Enclosed I beg leave to return you the return of killed and wounded.

I have the honour to be,

DAN. PRING

Source: "The War on Lake Champlain 2." Copies of Official Documents. [Online] http://www.cronab.demon.co.uk/lake2.htm (accessed on May 11, 2001).

not only taken a back seat in the war, but had provided large quantities of beef and timber to the British) responded with eight hundred and twenty-five hundred troops, respectively. On September 3, the U.S. Navy also heeded the call for help. thirty-year-old Lieutenant Thomas Macdonough (1783–1825) arrived commanding three warships: the *Saratoga* (twenty-six guns), the *Ticonderoga* (seventeen guns), and the *Preble* (seven guns), the *Eagle,* (a sloop with twenty guns), and ten gunboats. The gunboats, as well as a detachment of three hundred regular soldiers, harassed the British troops—about ten thousand of them—as they made their way toward Plattsburg.

Sir George Prevost (1767–1816), the governor-in-chief of Canada, was in command of the land invasion. The naval force on Lake Champlain was to begin an attack at the same time as that of the land forces. The ever cautious Prevost halted his troops across from the American position (three forts built on a peninsula between the lake and the Saranac River) to await the arrival of Captain George Downie's (d. 1814) fleet, which included the *Confiance* (thirty-seven guns), the *Linnet* (sixteen guns), the *Chubb* (eleven guns), and the *Finch* (eleven guns), along with twelve gunboats. The brand-new *Confiance* only had been completed just before the battle.

Fierce fighting on Lake Champlain

The British fleet arrived on September 9, and on September 11 they sailed into Plattsburg Bay to begin their attack. Because the U.S. Navy ships were equipped with more short-range than long-range guns, Macdonough also had moved his fleet into the bay to lure the British closer. The *Saratoga* and the *Confiance* were the first to do battle, and the *Saratoga* immediately took a broadside (in which a ship fires all of the guns on one side at the same time) that killed forty men. The crews' spirits plummeted, until a rooster that had escaped from its cage flew into the ship's sails. It gave a loud crow, and the men cheered and plunged back into the fight.

The battle lasted only an hour and a half, with each side repeatedly gaining and losing the upper hand. A big blow to British morale came in the first fifteen minutes of the battle, when Downie was killed. Macdonough was knocked down twice—once by the severed head of a soldier—but continued to direct the battle. Toward the end of the battle, the Americans surprised the British when Macdonough, having previously anchored the *Saratoga* so as to make it easier to maneuver, brought the damaged but still dangerous *Saratoga* around into position for a broadside on the *Confiance*. The other ship could not respond in kind and was soon forced to surrender.

Meanwhile, Prevost had waited until the naval battle was well underway before ordering the land forces into action. They had not made much progress when, hearing of the defeat of the British fleet on the lake and worried about his supply lines, Prevost ordered his men to retreat. The British generals under Prevost were stunned, for they knew their troops outnumbered the Americans; the U.S. generals also were amazed. Prevost was later accused of mismanaging the battle and court-martialed (called to trial before a military court) but died before he could present his case.

The British defeat at the Battle of Plattsburg crushed any remaining hopes they had of expanding their Canadian territory, while the victory put the United States in a stronger position at the Ghent negotiations. It also served as a morale booster that was much needed after the sacking of Washington, D.C. Macdonough became a nationally known hero and was showered with praise and rewards (including large plots of land in New York and Vermont).

The next British target: Baltimore

Also in early September 1814 Great Britain decided to follow up on its victory at Washington, D.C., with an attack on Baltimore. Home to forty-five thousand residents (making it the nation's third largest city), Baltimore was an attractive target to the British because it was not only an important commercial center and privateer base (its warehouses were loaded with merchandise taken from five hundred British merchant ships) but a hotbed of anti-British feeling.

Aware that the British would want to attack Baltimore, the city's leaders had established a Committee of Vigilance and Safety to oversee preparations for the defense of Baltimore. They asked Samuel Smith (1752–1839), a U.S. Senator and a major general in the Maryland militia, to lead this effort. Smith soon made it clear that every able-bodied male resident would either have to fight or pick up a shovel. By the middle of 1814, trenches and defensive breastworks (low walls put up to protect gunners) had been built around the city.

The British plan was for Ross's army troops to approach Baltimore on foot, while Cochrane's naval vessels attacked Fort McHenry south of the city. Ross landed forty-five hundred troops at North Point on September 12 and began marching them toward Baltimore, located about fourteen miles away. About halfway there, the British force met thirty-two hundred militiamen who had been sent out from Baltimore under the command of General John Stricker (d. 1825).

The battle that followed turned out to be a victory for the British, but it was costly: they had 340 casualties, while the Americans had 215. One of those killed was Ross himself, shot by an American sharpshooter as he rode his white horse to the front of his advancing troops to investigate a delay. Ross's body was shipped back to England in a barrel of rum, so that it would not decay during the long journey.

Colonel Arthur Brooke (1772–1843) took over command of the British troops and led them again toward Baltimore. As they approached the city, however, they found it heavily fortified. Unable to lure the Americans out from behind their defensive works, Brooke decided that the likelihood of overtaking the city by land was not enough to justify the number of casualties that an attempt would bring. He turned his troops back.

At the same time as Ross was moving toward Baltimore by land, Cochrane had brought his bomb and rocket ships up the Patapsco River toward Fort McHenry, which was defended by a thousand soldiers under the command of Major George Armistead (1780–1818). Cochrane's plan was to disable the fort's big guns, then bring in the lighter British ships to fire on and break through the line of American defenders.

"The rocket's red glare"

For twenty-four hours on September 13 and 14, the British kept up a continuous bombardment of Fort McHenry. But of the fifteen hundred rounds of ammunition they fired, only four hundred hit the fort, and these did very little damage. Only four Americans were killed, with twenty-four wounded. Because the Americans lacked the long-range weapons they would need to reach the British fleet, they could not respond to the attack, but that made little difference. The British were forced to give up.

Witnessing the "red glare" of the Congreve rockets that night was a Georgetown lawyer and militiaman named Francis Scott Key (1779–1843). Early in the confrontation, Key had boarded an American ship to help negotiate the release of a prisoner. Although he succeeded in this task, he was detained on the ship until the battle was over. Key kept watch through the night, and on the morning of September 14 he saw the oversized American flag still flying over Fort McHenry. The sight inspired him to write "The Star-Spangled Banner" to the tune of an old British drinking song. Immediately popular, the song became the national anthem of the United States in 1931. Relatively few Americans realize, however, that its author was aboard a British ship that was bombing the United States when it was written!

The fruitless Battle of Baltimore was the last in Great Britain's Chesapeake campaign, which had embittered Americans who had witnessed or heard about its excesses. In addition to its plundering of peaceful, sleepy

The death of General Robert Ross by a sharpshooter during the Battle of Baltimore. *Painting by Chappel. Photograph reproduced by permission of Hulton/Archive.*

A Flag So Big the British Couldn't Miss It

In June 1813, Major George Armistead was assigned to take command at Fort McHenry, which was the main source of defense for the city of Baltimore, Maryland. Any enemy who tried to enter Baltimore's harbor would first have to pass the fort. Soon after his arrival, Armistead told General Samuel Smith, the commander of Baltimore's militia, that his troops were ready to defend Baltimore but they still lacked a suitable flag to fly over the fort. Armistead requested a flag so big that the British would have no difficulty recognizing it from a distance.

Baltimore's leading flagmaker was Mary Young Pickersgill, whose sign advertised her expertise in creating "Silk Standards and Cavalry Colors, and other Colors of Every Description." Working out of her home on Baltimore's Albemarle Street, Pickersgill and her daughter Caroline Purdy fulfilled Armistead's request. On August 19, 1813, he received Fort McHenry's new flag, which was adorned with fifteen stars and fifteen stripes (representing the states then in existence) and measured forty-two feet by thirty feet.

No one knows whether this huge flag was flown before the British made their famous attack on Fort McHenry on September 14, 1814. But there is no doubt that it was flying when the British retreated after an unsuccessful bombardment. The sight of Pickersgill's gigantic flag still waving in the breeze the morning after the attack inspired Francis Scott Key to write the poem "The Star-Spangled Banner," which would eventually become the U.S. national anthem.

The flag last flew over Fort McHenry in 1824, in honor of the Marquis de Lafayette (a French general who had aided the United States during the Revolutionary War) when he was touring the nation. Armistead then kept the flag for himself, and after his death and that of his wife Louisa it became the property of his daughter Georgiana, who had been born at Fort McHenry in 1817. In 1907, the Armistead-Appleton family donated the flag to the Smithsonian Institute's National Museum of History in Washington, D.C., where it remains on display.

towns around the region, the British were accused of trying to start a slave rebellion. Although they had not really gone that far, Cochrane had issued a proclamation, recorded in Hickey's *The War of 1812*, that offered a "choice of either entering into His Majesty's Sea or Land Forces, or of being sent as FREE settlers to the British possessions in North America or the West Indies." About three hundred African American slaves took the British up on their offer and entered the British military service. When the British left the area, they took with them several thousand runaway slaves.

Almost a month before the Battle of Baltimore, representatives from the United States and Great Britain arrived in Ghent, Belgium, to begin negotiations for ending the war. This would be the last battle fought before the Christmas Eve signing of the agreement. Great Britain's failure to take the city of Baltimore and the defeat on Lake Champlain would weaken its position at the peace talks. By contrast, the U.S. victories would be the source of enormous pride for Americans across the country—especially after the humiliating invasion of Washington, D.C.

The Gulf campaign begins

In September 1814, with their Chesapeake Bay campaign finished, the British continued with the next phase of their plans: an invasion of the Gulf Coast of the United States (situated on the coast of the Gulf of Mexico and including the present-day states of Louisiana, Alabama, Mississippi, and Florida). Their ultimate goal was to attack New Orleans, a city of forty-five thousand people located about one hundred miles up the Mississippi River from the Gulf in what is now Louisiana. Control of New Orleans meant control of the mouth of the Mississippi River, the place where it meets the ocean and the place that provided a vital link to sea trade for Americans who lived west of the Appalachian mountains. The city would be a valuable possession for Great Britain in the peace negotiations.

About a month before the campaign actually began, the British set the groundwork for it by taking possession of Pensacola, a West Florida city that was held by the Spanish, along with adjoining Fort San Carlos de Barrancas. The Spanish reluctantly allowed the British to occupy the town since they feared an imminent invasion by the United States.

Meanwhile, two months after the Battle of Horseshoe Bend (which took place in March 1813; see "The Battle of Horseshoe Bend" in this chapter), Major General Andrew Jackson had been given command of an area that included the cities of Mobile (now part of Alabama) and New Orleans as well as the whole U.S. Army in the Southwest. Jackson was able to repel a British attack on Mobile in September at Fort Bowyer, which stood between the sea and the city.

From Pensacola to New Orleans

Jackson was firmly convinced that Pensacola was the key to dominating the Gulf Coast as well as eventually conquering all of West Florida, and he intended to take it from the British. Government leaders disagreed, fearing war with Spain might erupt over the issue. They sent word to Jackson that he was not to attack, but he had already left before the orders arrived. In early November, Jackson arrived at Pensacola with forty-one hundred regular soldiers, militia, and Native Americans to find the city deserted by the British (who had retreated into Fort Barrancas after their defeat at Mobile) and defended by only five hundred Spanish troops. The Spanish surrendered almost immediately.

The British now retreated, but as they left they blew up all the forts on Pensacola Bay. Pensacola posed no threat without its forts, so Jackson also left. Having heard that the British would soon attack New Orleans, he marched his troops there, arriving on December 1, 1814. New Orleans is situated in a terrain of swampy wetlands veined with bayous (small rivers or creeks running through the swamps) and canals, offering the British a wide variety of possible approaches. With his usual energy and aggressiveness, Jackson built up the city's defenses. Whereas a cloud of defeatism had previously hung over New Orleans's diverse population (which included French and Spanish people; African Americans; Native Americans; and Creoles, people of mixed heritage), almost everyone now pitched in to help.

Jackson quickly began making sure that all the water approaches from the Gulf to the city were blocked, and he set up batteries at strategic points along the way. Militia began arriving from nearby states. Jackson let it be known that free blacks (those who had managed to avoid or buy their way out of slavery) were welcome to enlist in his army, and he accepted the services of a special corps of black troops under the command of Colonel Jean Baptiste Savary.

The Baratarian pirates, who used the island of Barataria located on the mouth of the Mississippi River, were led by a dashing figure named Jean Lafitte (c.1780–c. 1826). They vol-

African American troops fighting at the Battle of New Orleans. Andrew Jackson encouraged free blacks to enlist in his army. *Photograph reproduced by permission of Hulton/Archive.*

unteered to serve in the U.S. military, mostly because they had been charged with violating trade laws and wanted to be pardoned. Even though Jackson had previously called them "hellish banditti," as reported in Hickey's *The War of 1812,* he had a desperate need for the Baratarians' guns and ammunition, so he accepted their offer. They would contribute a great deal to the Battle of New Orleans, because they were good shots and had a thorough knowledge of the local terrain. Lafitte even became a kind of unofficial aide to Jackson, and Madison did pardon him after the war; he later returned to pirating, however, and served as a spy for the Spanish.

The British begin their attack

The British were also preparing for their attack. After the unfortunate death of Robert Ross at the Battle of Baltimore, Major General Sir Edward Pakenham (1778–1815) had taken over command of the British troops. The British land

and naval forces (the latter still commanded by Cochrane), which numbered about ten thousand, met up in Jamaica, an island in the West Indies south of Cuba, and sailed for the Gulf of Mexico in late November. They arrived off the coast of Florida on December 5. Contemplating the various routes available for attacking New Orleans, they decided that the best was through Lake Borgne, east of the city.

On December 14, the British approached Lake Borgne, where they encountered a small force of U.S. troops (185 men on five gunboats) under Lieutenant Thomas ap Catesby Jones (1790–1858). Although they were not really prepared to fight, the Americans turned and faced the British assault force of forty boats and twelve hundred men commanded by Captain Nicholas Lockyer. Jones's troops were thoroughly beaten—forty were killed and the rest captured—but this skirmish delayed the British advance and gave Jackson a little more time to work on defenses.

The British force now advanced across Lake Borgne and proceeded via bayous and canals until, on December 23, they reached a plantation owned by Jacques Villeré, located about eight miles south of New Orleans on the Mississippi River. They took over Villeré's house and set up camp, but Villeré's son managed to slip away and went to warn Jackson of the enemy's location. Determined to catch the British before they were fully prepared, Jackson quickly hustled eighteen hundred troops to within a mile of the British position. Backing him up on the river were two U.S. ships, the *Carolina* (fourteen guns) and the *Louisiana* (twenty-two guns).

On the evening of December 23, the *Carolina* opened fire on the British, catching them by surprise. They were even more surprised when Jackson's army attacked. It was a chaotic, confusing battle with much hand-to-hand fighting and occasions when men fired at their own troops. When it was over and both armies withdrew, the British had suffered 275 casualties and the Americans, 215.

The next few days saw the arrival of British reinforcements as well as Pakenham, whose ship had made an especially slow crossing from England. Meanwhile, the U.S. troops had retreated and formed a new battle line about two miles from the British. Situated behind a canal, with a swamp on the east and the Mississippi River on the west, they began building breastworks (temporary fortifications).

On December 27 Pakenham took action against the two U.S. ships which had been constantly bombarding the British position. The British managed to blow up the *Carolina* but the *Louisiana* escaped. The next day Pakenham ordered his troops to advance on the American line, but the resulting barrage of fire was so great that the British were forced back. Another artillery duel took place on December 31, with the British again forced to retreat. As the negotiations for bring-

American and British warships firing on each other on the Mississippi River during the Battle of New Orleans. *Photograph reproduced by permission of Corbis Corporation (Bellevue).*

Naval Hero Stephen Decatur

One of the most celebrated heroes in U.S. naval history, Stephen Decatur first made a name for himself during the Tripolitan War in the first decade of the nineteenth century. He went on to become one of the most famous naval commanders of the War of 1812.

Born January 5, 1779, in Sinepuxent, Maryland, Decatur was the son of a merchant ship captain. After attending the University of Pennsylvania and working for a short period as a shipping company clerk in Philadelphia, Decatur received a commission as a midshipman (the lowest rank) in the U.S. Navy in 1798. He was sent to the Caribbean, where the navy was fighting against French privateers who had been attacking U.S. merchant ships.

Assigned to serve on the *Essex* and later the *Argus,* Decatur was next sent to the Mediterranean region, where the United States was involved in a conflict with the Barbary states (Tunisia, Algeria, and Tripoli), which were interfering with trade. Serving under Commodore Edward Preble,

Decatur took command of the twelve-gun ship *Enterprise.* On February 16, 1804, he led a daring expedition that managed to destroy the USS *Philadelphia,* which had earlier been captured by the enemy.

Praised for his bold, competent leadership, Decatur was promoted to captain and put in charge of a division of gunboats. While participating in the bombing of Tripoli, he captured two enemy gunboats. By the time he returned to the United States, the tall, handsome, curly-haired Decatur was already famous, and he received many honors. He spent the next few years performing the rather dull work of patrolling the U.S. coastline to enforce the Embargo Act, a measure that restricted U.S. ships from trading with other nations in an attempt to punish Great Britain and France for their own trade restrictions on the United States.

After the United States declared war against Great Britain in June 1812, Decatur was assigned to command a small squadron of ships based in Norfolk, Vir-

ing the war to a close were coming to a close in Ghent, Belgium, British and American forces positioned themselves for what would be the bloodiest conflict of the war—the Battle of New Orleans. (See "The Battle of New Orleans" in chapter 6.)

The war at sea

During the last year of the war, the British had continued to dominate the sea, especially through their use of

ginia. In this capacity Decatur would sail out to sea in search of enemy ships to fight. On October 25, 1812, he was commanding the USS *United States* when it met the British ship *Macedonian* near the island of Madeira (located off the coast of Morocco in North Africa). The battle ended in victory for the United States, and once again Decatur was greeted as a hero when he returned home. He also received a $30,000 cash prize.

Promoted to the high rank of commodore in 1813, Decatur spent most of that year and the next confined—due to the British blockade of much of the East Coast—to the harbor at New London, Connecticut. But toward the end of 1814, Decatur was assigned to command the *President* and ordered to take charge of New York's port defenses. In January 1815, in the middle of a snowstorm, he made a bid to slip through the British blockade. The attempt was unsuccessful, for the *President* got stuck on a sandbar and was detected and chased by the British ships enforcing the blockade. In a defeat that was both bitter and ultimately meaningless (the Treaty of Ghent, which ended the war, had been signed about three weeks earlier) Decatur had to surrender to the British.

After the war, Decatur returned to the Mediterranean in charge of an expedition that was successful in forcing the Barbary States to pay for damages the United States had incurred during the earlier conflict with those nations. For the third time in his career, Decatur was treated as a hero on his return to the United States.

From 1815 until his death, Decatur served on the Board of Navy Commissioners and advised the secretary of the navy. In March 1820, the hot temper and strong sense of honor that Decatur had always exhibited brought about his death when he was killed in a duel with another officer.

Sources: Heidler, David S., and Jeanne T. Heidler, eds. Encyclopedia of the War of 1812. *Santa Barbara, Calif.: ABC-CLIO, Inc., 1997;* Encyclopedia of World Biography, *2nd ed. 17 vols. Gale Research, 1998.*

the blockade. In April 1814 the blockade was extended to New England in an effort to prevent neutral countries from trading with the United States and to keep warships from using New England ports. American trade suffered even worse losses than before. For example, the value of exports (goods that are shipped to other countries) had been $61,300,000 in 1811 but fell to only $6,900,000 in 1814; while imports (goods that are shipped into a country) fell from $53,400,000 in 1811 to $13,000,000 in 1814. There were more oversupplies and shortages, just as there had been in 1813, and the shipping industry was especially hard hit.

The British stepped up their raids on coastal towns, and now New England also was affected. Coastal islands like Nantucket and Cape Cod (off the coast of Massachusetts) were cut off from the mainland and forced to declare neutrality or pay the British to avoid problems and receive supplies.

The British blockade meant that most U.S. warships were stuck in port, and those who tried to sneak out often paid a heavy price. A major loss to the U.S. fleet occurred after the peace treaty had been signed, but before the news reached the United States. In command of the heavy frigate *President* (fifty-two guns), Captain Stephen Decatur (1779–1820) decided to take advantage of a heavy, early January snowstorm to slip out of New York's harbor. The *President* was caught, however, by a squadron of British ships and defeated on January 15.

The famous ship *Constitution* fared better. Commanded by Captain Charles Stewart (1778–1869), the *Constitution* escaped from Boston harbor in December and subsequently defeated two British ships, the *Cyane* and the *Levant*. Also successful were three of the six new U.S. sloops, the *Hornet*, the *Peacock*, and the *Wasp*. These ships captured a number of British vessels, including the *Penguin*, the *Reindeer*, the *Avon*, and the *Epervier*. The other three U.S. sloops—the *Frolic*, the *Syren*, and the *Rattlesnake*—were defeated by the British, while the *Wasp* was lost at sea for unknown reasons.

Both warships and privateers kept up their harassment of British merchant ships. As in 1813, the British Isles was the best hunting ground, because there the merchant ships were not required to travel in convoys (small groups) for protection and consequently made easy targets. Two especially noteworthy privateers were the *Prince-de-Neufchatel*, which captured or destroyed one million dollars worth of British property in a single cruise, and the *Governor Tompkins*, which caught and destroyed fourteen ships in the English Channel (the body of water that lies between England and France).

The United States faces a crisis

The nature of the war had changed by the fall of 1814 as Napoleon's defeat in Europe allowed Great Britain to go on the offensive in North America. The U.S. envoys were at Ghent, Belgium, meeting with British officials. As yet there was no word of an agreement and if those peace negotiations failed, the United States would have to raise more troops to carry out a campaign in 1815. Currently there were about 40,000 soldiers enlisted in the army, well below the authorized level of 62,500. Without more soldiers, the United States would have to depend even more on state militias, which brought their own set of problems.

The government also continued to be plagued by financial problems. There was no doubt it would be short of funds for 1815, and the prospects of raising more money were bleak. Meanwhile, trade with the enemy had not only continued but increased, as the influx of troops from Great Britain had created a higher demand for provisions. It was hard for U.S. government officials to control smuggling, because they could not legally search every vehicle. In addition, the British had seized eastern Maine in September (terrain they coveted because it jutted into Canada between Nova Scotia and Quebec) and used the towns along the one hundred miles of coastline they controlled as ports of entry.

Economic conditions in the United States were divided, with some parts of the country suffering and others enjoying prosperity. In the South, which was dependent on the exports of agriculture, now prevented by the blockade, as well as in New England, where the important fishing and shipping industries also had been brought to a screeching halt, people were feeling the effects of a poor economy. Meanwhile, the middle and western states were benefiting from government contracts and manufacturing; Pennsylvania and New York, for example, sold huge quantities of war materials and agricultural products to the U.S. government. Military spending also helped Kentucky and Ohio, and such cities as Pittsburgh, Cincinnati, Lexington, Louisville, and St. Louis were booming.

Congress ponders the nation's problems

In the elections of 1814, voters in the New England states showed their discontent with Madison's administration by electing more Federalists than ever. However, there also was discontent within the Republican Party. Those who had supported New York statesman DeWitt Clinton (1769–1828) rather than Madison in the previous presidential election, as well as the group of Madison detractors known as the "Invisibles" kept up their complaints about how Madison was managing the war. There was increasing hostility in both parties to what was known as the "Virginia dynasty," the perceived dominance in national politics of men (like Thomas Jefferson, James Madison, and James Monroe) from Virginia. Madison's popularity plummeted even more when the British burned Washington, D.C.

Madison summoned the Thirteenth Congress for its third and last session on September 19, which was earlier than usual (normally the legislature would meet in November or December) but necessitated by the national crisis. Lawmakers and other officials were shocked to see the extent of the damage the British had inflicted on the capital, and everyone was scurrying to find suitable office space.

In his opening remarks to the Congress, Madison focused on American victories, leaving out any mention of Great Britain's gains. He admitted that there was a crisis at hand, but expressed optimism that the American people would find their way through it. Madison was not as optimistic about the prospects for peace, for he had heard from the U.S. representatives in Ghent that the British were making some extravagant demands, especially in their demand for a Native American homeland.

Among the issues debated during this session of Congress were the possibility of relocating the capital (Philadelphia was considered as a possible alternative, but eventually it was decided that Washington, D.C., would be rebuilt), how to raise more troops, and a controversial enlistment law. The administration wanted to call for seventy thousand more troops: forty thousand volunteers for local defense, and thirty thousand regular soldiers to fight in Canada. Congress would not accept the administration's plan to conscript (draft) soldiers, but eventually passed a law allowing state troops to be enlisted in federal service.

The enlistment law caused a controversy, especially in New England, because it said that minors between the ages of eighteen and twenty-one could enlist in the military without their parents' permission. Despite the controversy, the proposal became law. Congress also created a board of naval commissioners to make the navy more efficient, and authorized the construction of smaller ships that could—like privateers—make more of an impact on enemy commerce

New taxes and loans were authorized, but a proposal to establish a national bank was killed. Supporters of the idea claimed that the bank would serve as a source of national currency and government loans, make it easier to transfer funds across state lines, and in general streamline the financial system. But no one could agree on the details of how the bank should be designed, and Federalists (along with some Republicans) opposed it because they feared it would give the government too much control. Congress did pass a new enemy trade bill that made it legal for customs officials to search without a warrant any vehicles, ships, or people they suspected of involvement in illegal trade; this law was only two weeks old when its purpose was negated by the end of the war.

The final session of the Thirteenth Congress came to a close without accomplishing much in the opinion of many Americans. After all the talk about the nation's problems, hardly any solutions had been reached. The newspapers were full of criticisms of Congress and the administration, while in New England, opposition to the way things were going was addressed at the Hartford Convention.

The Hartford Convention

The strongest expression of Federalist opposition to the war, the Hartford Convention was a regional conference held in Hartford, Connecticut from December 15, 1814, to January 5, 1815. It was the product of discontent and frustration felt by the New England states over the war. In particular, they felt that the government had allotted a disproportionally small portion of money and soldiers for the defense of New England, forcing them to finance much of their own protection. Since the British had extended the blockade, the New England coast was more vulnerable to raids, and the costs of these raids had already proved high.

These and other complaints led Governor Caleb Strong (1745–1819) of Massachusetts to call a special session of the state legislature in the fall of 1814. There the legislature recommended that a convention be held to allow delegates to discuss the region's problems and try to come up with some solutions. Twelve delegates were chosen to represent Massachusetts. The legislatures of Connecticut and Rhode Island also endorsed this proposal, and sent seven and four delegates, respectively. Although New Hampshire and Vermont did not officially participate, two counties in each state chose delegates, three of whom attended the convention. Altogether, there were twenty-six delegates at the convention.

The New England press had been loud and extreme in its opposition to the Madison administration, even suggesting that the New England states secede (separate themselves) from the United States. By contrast, most of the delegates at the Hartford Convention were moderates with no intention of severing any ties with the United States (and aware of the danger of suggesting such a thing, in a time of war). Their deliberations were secret, and the only record kept was the very sketchy journal of convention secretary Theodore Dwight (1764–1846) from Massachusetts. Playing a prominent role was Massachusetts politician Harrison Gray Otis (1765–1848), who wrote most of the convention's final report.

The Hartford Convention's report

Released on January 6, 1815, the report focused partly on issues of the war, recommending that states use federal tax money collected within their borders to pay for local defense, and that states nullify (make nonexistent) the federal law authorizing minors to enlist in the military without their parents' consent and the proposals to begin drafting soldiers.

In addition, the convention proposed seven amendments to the U.S. Constitution, all of them attempts to address New England's grievances. One amendment would require a two-thirds vote in Congress to declare war, restrict trade, or admit new states to the union; others would limit embargoes to thirty days and require a two-thirds vote in both houses for the adoption of commercial nonintercourse (trade restrictions) acts. The law allowing states in which slavery was practiced to count each slave as three-quarters of a person (which gave southern states an advantage in terms of congressional and electoral college representatives, which were determined on the basis of population) would be repealed. To limit the influence of foreign-born individuals (such as the Madison administration's Swiss-born Albert Gallatin) as well as the Virginia dynasty, which is how some referred to the dominance of Virginia leaders (especially Jefferson, Madison, and Monroe) in national politics, proposed amendments would prevent naturalized citizens (those born in other countries) from holding federal office, limit presidents to one term of office, and prohibit presidents from the same state to be elected twice in succession.

The proposed amendments reflected all of New England's grievances during the last decade. Federalists hoped to help the New England states in practical, material ways while also increasing the region's influence in national politics. Except for the policy nullifying the enlistment laws, all of the convention's positions were moderately voiced, and no stronger solutions (such as secession) were proposed. The report stated that if these grievances were not addressed, another convention would simply be called in June 1815 or sooner.

The governments of Massachusetts and Connecticut approved the convention's report and endorsed the proposed amendments. They also both nullified the enlistment of minors law, although Massachusetts did not do so until the war was over and the law was no longer important. Just as emissaries (agents) were about to request that the federal government provide tax money for New England's defense, news of Jackson's victory at New Orleans arrived, followed soon by the news that the Treaty of Ghent had been signed. With the war over and the majority of Americans feeling that it had been both justified and successful, the Hartford Convention came to look like an occasion of disloyalty. Despite the delegates' desire to avoid the appearance of treasonous (attempting to overthrow the government of one's country) intentions, that's exactly what they—and, by extension, the whole Federalist Party—were suspected of having. In fact, memory of the Hartford Convention would contribute to the Federalists' downfall in the years following the war.

For More Information

Books

Altoff, Gerald. *Amongst My Best Men: African-Americans and the War of 1812.* Put-in-Bay, Ohio: The Perry Group, 1996.

Annals of Congress: Debates and Proceedings in the Congress of the United States, 1789–1824, 42 vols., Washington, D.C.: 1834–56.

Arthur, Stanley Clisby. *Jean Lafitte, Gentleman Rover.* New Orleans, La: Harmanson, 1952.

Brooks, Charles B. *The Siege of New Orleans.* Seattle: University of Washington Press, 1961.

Carter, Samuel. *Blaze of Glory: The Fight for New Orleans, 1814–1815.* London: Macmillan, 1971.

Coles, Harry L. *The War of 1812.* Chicago: University of Chicago Press, 1965.

Crane, Jay David, and Elaine Crane, eds. *The Black Soldier: From the American Revolution to Vietnam.* New York: William Morrow, 1971.

Elting, John R. *Amateurs to Arms!: A Military History of the War of 1812.* Da Capo Press, 1995. Reprint. Original published by Algonquin Press, Chapel Hill, N.C., 1991.

Furlong, William R., and Byron McCandless. *So Proudly We Hail: The History of the United States Flag.* Washington, D.C.: Smithsonian Institution Press, 1981.

Heidler, David S., and Jeanne T. Heidler, eds. *Encyclopedia of the War of 1812.* Santa Barbara, Calif.: ABC-CLIO, Inc., 1997.

Hickey, Donald R. *The War of 1812: A Forgotten Conflict.* Urbana: University of Illinois Press, 1989.

Kroll, Steven. *By the Dawn's Early Light: The Story of the Star-Spangled Banner.* New York: Scholastic, 2000.

Lord, Walter. *The Dawn's Early Light.* New York: W. W. Norton, 1972.

Lloyd, Alan. *The Scorching of Washington: The War of 1812.* Washington, D.C.: Robert B. Luce, 1974.

Mahon, John K. *The War of 1812.* Cambridge, Mass.: Da Capo Press, Inc. 1991.

Vogel, Robert C. "Jean Lafitte, the Baratarians, and the Historical Geography of Piracy in the Gulf of Mexico." *Gulf Coast Historical Review* 5 (1990): 63–77.

Web sites

Discriminating Generals. [Online] http://www.militaryheritage.com/home.htm (accessed on November 26, 2001).

Documents on the War of 1812. [Online] http://www.hillsdale.edu/dept/History/Documents/War/FR1812.htm (accessed on November 26, 2001).

Thomas Warner Letters. [Online] http://www.haemo-sol.com/thomas/thomas.html (accessed on November 26, 2001).

War of 1812. [Online] http://www.galafilm.com/1812/e/index.html (accessed on November 26, 2001).

"War of 1812." *KidInfo.* [Online] http://www.kidinfo.com/American_History/warof1812.html (accessed on November 26, 2001).

"War of 1812." *Studyweb*. [Online] http://www.studyweb.com/links/ 388.html (accessed on November 26, 2001).

War of 1812–1814. [Online] http://www.members.tripod.com/~war1812/ (accessed on November 26, 2001).

War of 1812—Forgotten War. Brief articles on battles. [Online] http://www.multied.com/1812/ (accessed on November 26, 2001).

A Proud Nation
Arrives at Peace

6

The War of 1812 between the United States and Great
Britain was provoked by two major issues. The first was
Britain's maritime policy of impressment in its war with
France. This policy was where British officials boarded U.S.
ships to capture deserters from their own navy, often wrongfully taking American citizens in the process. The other issue
that led to the war was Great Britain's overly friendly relations with Native Americans. Americans believed that the
British were encouraging Native Americans to attack white
settlers who were moving west. The Native Americans believed that the settlers were encroaching on (gradually taking
over) their land. Although these two issues led to Americans
being eager to fight a war with Britain, the United States was
not necessarily ready to fight such a war. As a result, almost as
soon as the war began, the effort to end it through diplomatic rather than military means also began.

War was declared in early June 1812, and later that
same month Jonathan Russell (1771–1832), the U.S. chargé
d'affaires (the top diplomat when there is no ambassador in
place) in London, told the British government that the Unit-

ed States would be willing to make peace if the British would discontinue the practice of impressment. In return, the United States would bar all British seamen from serving on U.S. ships. In October 1812 Great Britain offered an armistice (peace agreement) but would not agree to cease impressing American seamen. In March 1813 the Russian government offered to mediate, wanting Great Britain, its ally in the war against French emperor Napoleon Bonaparte (1769–1821), to focus all of its energies on the European conflict; in addition, Russia wanted to restore a normal trade relationship with the United States. The British turned down this offer, preferring to negotiate directly with U.S. representatives.

Negotiations begin in Ghent

When Great Britain and its allies defeated Napoleon in the spring of 1814, the British grew more interested in ending the conflict in North America, which was tapping their financial resources as well as proving to be more difficult to put to an end than expected. Everybody in Great Britain was tired of war. In the spring of 1814, U.S. president James Madison (1751–1836; see biographical entry) received an offer from Great Britain to begin peace talks, and he eagerly accepted. It was agreed that envoys (representatives) from both nations would meet in a neutral spot, Ghent, Belgium.

The men Madison appointed to serve as envoys represented a fairly wide spectrum of backgrounds and viewpoints. Two of them were men he had chosen for the proposed Russian-mediated talks: diplomat John Quincy Adams (1767–1848) and James Bayard (1767–1815), a Federalist senator known for his moderate views. (Federalists are members of a political party who favored a strong central government and disliked the idea of fighting a war with Britain.) In addition, Madison named Speaker of the House Henry Clay (1777–1852), who had been an avid advocate of going to war with Great Britain. When Madison learned that Albert Gallatin (1761–1849), former secretary of the treasury and a nominee (though he did not receive congressional approval) for the Russian talks, was still in Europe he added him to the list. Jonathan Russell was the fifth member of the team. This time, Congress had no problem with any of Madison's appointees.

The Americans arrived in Ghent in June, well ahead of the British. Because they wanted to allow their forces in North America more time to win battles and gain ground that could be used to bargain at the peace talks, the British took their time getting to Ghent. It is generally agreed that the British representatives were overshadowed by their U.S. counterparts. Great Britain's top diplomats were busy at the Congress of Vienna (the peace negotiations that followed Napoleon's downfall), so they had to send men with less skill and experience to Ghent. Their representatives included Admiralty lawyer William Adams; Lord Gambier of the Royal Navy, who was charged with looking after Great Britain's maritime rights; and Henry Goulburn, an undersecretary of the Colonial Office, who was supposed to protect Great Britain's Canadian interests.

The British make their first offer

The negotiations began on August 8. Although the United States soon decided to drop impressment as an issue (now that the Napoleonic Wars were over, Great Britain's need for sailors had dropped off, and the practice of impressment had stopped), it soon became clear that other issues divided the two nations. The U.S. envoys found the first terms offered by the British totally unacceptable. They wanted the Canadian-U.S. border to be adjusted in their favor (this applied to parts of Maine and Minnesota they had taken over), and they demanded that that the United States remove all its warships and forts from the Great Lakes and that Great Britain retain the right to navigate on the Mississippi River. Most troubling to the United States, the British wanted most of the Northwest Territory (including a third of Wisconsin, half of Minnesota, and almost all of Indiana, Illinois, and Michigan) to be returned to the Native Americans who had originally inhabited those areas.

The issue of a Native American homeland, which the British presented as non-negotiable, seemed to the Americans an insurmountable obstacle. Westward expansion was a major goal and driving force in the United States, and it would be seriously hampered by the loss of all that land; in addition, there were already one hundred thousand American settlers living there. The United States rejected the British offer and, with the talks seemingly deadlocked, sent a discouraging report home to Madison.

Actually, though, the British had simply been probing to find out how far they could go with the Americans. The Native American homeland was negotiable, as the U.S. envoys would eventually learn. In the meantime, throughout the fall of 1814, the war continued. At first the British were convinced that dragging out the peace talks could only benefit them, and the British capture and destruction of Washington, D.C. on August 28, 1814, seemed to confirm this. But following close on the heels of that glorious moment were two troubling defeats for the British: at the Battle of Plattsburg on September 11, and at the Battle of Baltimore, September 12 through 14.

The two sides come to an agreement

In October, Great Britain made a new offer: Each side would keep whatever territory it held at the end of the war. When the United States rejected this offer, the British were forced to consider whether or not they were willing to hold out for the territory they had won on the battlefield. Doing so would probably mean more fighting, and the next year's campaign might put them in a position worse than their current one. The great British military leader Arthur Wellesley, First Duke of Wellington (1769–1852) cautioned Great Britain's leaders not to push for more territory. That answered the question for the British, and they gave up their territorial demands.

Now that the most difficult issues had been decided, the two sides could come up with a treaty relatively quickly. The final document was put together during the month before its December 24 signing. Significantly, the treaty made no mention of the maritime (related to the sea) issues (free trade and impressment) that had caused the war and simply restored conditions to their "status quo antebellum" (the way they were before the war began). The United States and Great Britain each agreed to vacate each other's territories. No enemy property was to be confiscated, and prisoners were to be returned to their home countries as soon as possible.

Each side was to make its own peace with the Native Americans, restoring the possessions and rights they had

held in 1811. (This clause would prove to be meaningless, for the Native Americans would continue to lose more land in the years to come, and they had never really had any rights to begin with.) The two nations also agreed to postpone the resolution of any boundary dispute until sometime in the future. Finally, the United States and Great Britain agreed that the war would end not with the envoys' signing of the treaty, but when the governments of both nations had ratified (approved) it.

The American and British delegates meeting in Ghent, Belgium, to discuss the provisions of the Treaty of Ghent, which ended the War of 1812. *Photograph reproduced by permission of The Granger Collection.*

The Battle of New Orleans

During the months of negotiations, the two sides had continued fighting the war, with gains and losses on both sides and many deaths. In fact the bloodiest confrontation of the whole war—the Battle of New Orleans—was fought two weeks after the treaty had been signed.

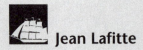

Jean Lafitte

Jean Lafitte is one of the most colorful and romantic outlaw figures in American history, and certainly among the most memorable characters of the War of 1812 period. A pirate who always claimed he was really a privateer (someone with a license from a government to plunder enemy ships), Lafitte and his followers joined the diverse force assembled by General Andrew Jackson to defend the city of New Orleans from British attack in late 1814 and early 1815. The U.S. victory in the famous Battle of New Orleans was at least partly due to their help.

Lafitte's earliest years are shrouded in mystery. He may have been born in Bayonne, France (other possible birthplaces include Haiti and Spain). The youngest of three boys, he may have been raised in the West Indies by his grandmother until he was fourteen. It also is possible that he attended a private school on the Caribbean island of Martinique and received military training on St. Christopher Island.

In 1800 Lafitt probably migrated with his brother Pierre to New Orleans, Louisiana, from Santo Domingo (now the capital city of the Dominican Republic, a Central American nation). It was at this time that he seems to have begun his career as a pirate, opening a blacksmith shop as a cover for his illegal activities.

A tall, handsome, well-educated (he is supposed to have spoken four languages) man with pleasant, diplomatic manners, Lafitte was an expert organizer and had a great ability to motivate people. Between 1807 and 1810 he became the leader of a large, successful network of pirates and smugglers (sellers of stolen goods) that was based on Grand Terre Island, located about fifty miles south of New Orleans, in a swampy region generally referred to as Barataria. By 1810 the operation included fifty ships, forty warehouses, and a force ranging from three thousand to five thousand men.

Lafitte's illegal business flourished because many people were willing to buy goods and slaves from him, and officials generally looked the other way. But in November 1812, the U.S. government finally took action against Lafitte. U.S. troops ambushed several of Lafitte's boats, and he was taken prisoner. Lafitte was soon released on bond, however, and no further action was taken against him until about a year later, when a federal agent was killed in another raid on Lafitte's operation. Louisiana governor William C. Claiborne offered a $500 reward for the capture of Lafitte, who in turn ridiculed the governor by offering his own reward of $1500 for Claiborne's capture.

Aware of the possible benefits of an alliance with the Baratarian pirates, in

September 1813 the British proposed that Lafitte and his men join their side in the war. Lafitte was offered $30,000 in cash, a pardon for his crimes, and the position of captain in the British army. Lafitte immediately informed the U.S. government of this offer, claiming that he preferred to offer his services to the American side, in exchange for a pardon. The offer was rejected, and in September 1814, several of his ships were captured, and eighty of Lafitte's followers were taken prisoner.

Despite the U.S. actions, Lafitte still refused to form an alliance with the British. Meanwhile, Jackson had been assigned to command the defense of New Orleans. Although he disliked the Baratarian pirates, Jackson now had a desperate need for both their weapons and their expertise (especially in navigating through the difficult surrounding terrain). Thus he offered a pardon to any pirate who would assist in the defense of New Orleans.

Lafitte's men responded with enthusiasm, and Lafitte offered to serve as Jackson's personal advisor and guide. Thus the Baratarian pirates made up an essential part, by all accounts, of the U.S. troops that defeated a much larger British force on January 8, 1815. Without the pirates, the impressive victory won by the United States might never have occurred.

In recognition of their contribution to the U.S. victory, President James Madison officially pardoned Lafitte and his followers in February 1815 for their crimes. Many of Lafitte's men then settled into legitimate pursuits, but the restless Lafitte was not able to mend his criminal ways. He eventually established another large, highly profitable pirating and smuggling operation, this one at Galveston, Texas. In 1819 eighteen of his followers were captured by the U.S. Navy, tried and publicly hanged in New Orleans. The next year, Galveston officials ran Lafitte out of town.

How Lafitte's life ended is almost as mysterious as its beginning. One story says that he moved to Mexico's Yucatan Peninsula in 1821, where he died of fever five years later. In another account, he changed his name to John Lafitte and ended up in the U.S. Midwest, dying in May 1851 in Illinois. Those who still live in Barataria, however, are sure that Lafitte is buried somewhere along the bayou that winds through that region.

Sources: Heidler, David S., and Jeanne T. Heidler, eds. Encyclopedia of the War of 1812. Santa Barbara, Calif.: ABC-CLIO, Inc., 1997; "Jean Lafitte: Gentleman Pirate of New Orleans." Dark Horse Multimedia. [Online] http://crimelibrary.com/americana/lafitte/main.htm (accessed on November 21, 2001); The New Orleans Tourism Marketing Corporation. "Jean Lafitte." Great Characters of New Orleans. [Online] http://dev.neworleansonline.com/culture/gcno-lafitte.shtml (accessed on November 27, 2000.

During December 1814 General Andrew Jackson (1767–1845; see biographical entry) had been preparing U.S. troops for a British attack on New Orleans. By early January 1814 British and U.S. troops at New Orleans had already met in skirmishes (small-scale battles), including confrontations at Lake Borgne and Villeré's plantation. The British had made two unsuccessful attacks on the U.S. line but had been driven back. But after the arrival of more troops, the British force was at its full strength of ten thousand and ready for a full-scale advance against the Americans.

The U.S. force numbered about five thousand and was made up of a colorful assortment of Baratarian pirates (pirates who volunteered to serve for the United States in exchange for them being pardoned for violating trade laws); Choctaw (Native American) warriors; militiamen (members of small armies made up of troops residing in a particular state) from Mississippi, Kentucky, and Tennessee; and U.S. Marines; sailors; and regular soldiers. On January 8 the British began their direct assault on the American line, moving across an expanse of open land called Chalmette's plain. At first their movement was covered by fog, but when the fog lifted they were completely exposed.

What followed was one of the most disastrous battles in British military history. When the British troops were five hundred yards away, the Americans fired their cannons. When they were three hundred yards away, the riflemen went to work, and at one hundred yards the muskets (long-barreled guns that had been used more before rifles were invented) were employed. The rain of fire and bullets was devastating to the British. Vast numbers of them were mowed down, while others fled the battle or laid down on the battlefield pretending to be dead until after it was over. Mounted on a white horse as he rode around desperately trying to rally his troops, Major General Edward Pakenham (1778–1815) made an easy target and was killed.

General John Lambert (1772–1847) took over command for Pakenham and soon stopped the battle, the major part of which had lasted only an hour and a half. The British asked to be allowed to bury their dead, and they piled the bodies into a mass grave (Pakenham's corpse was sent back to England in a cask of rum to preserve it).

The Battle of New Orleans was the most lopsided conflict of the war, if not of all time. The British lost about two thousand men (including three hundred dead and five hundred captured) while the Americans lost only seventy (including only about a dozen dead). Many battle-hardened British veterans of the Napoleonic War claimed that this was the worst fight they had ever experienced.

Despite their defeat at New Orleans, the British stayed in the area for another ten days, taking part in a few minor skirmishes and making an unsuccessful attack on Fort Saint Philip, located sixty miles downriver from New Orleans. They also made another try at taking Mobile, Alabama, and on February 11 they managed to forcibly gain Fort Bowyer from U.S. control. Before they could move on Mobile, however, they received the news that the war had ended.

Jackson stayed in New Orleans after the battle, where—to the great annoyance of its citizens—he ruled with

British general Edward Pakenham being supported by soldiers after he was hit by a cannonball during the Battle of New Orleans. He died a short time later.
Photograph reproduced by permission of Hulton/Archive.

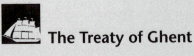

The Treaty of Ghent

The Treaty of Ghent was signed on December 24, 1814 by representatives of the United States and Great Britain, who had gathered at Ghent, Belgium, four months earlier to begin negotiations. Below are excerpts from each article contained in the treaty.

Treaty of Peace and Amity between His Britannic Majesty and the United States of America.

Article the First.

There shall be a firm and universal Peace between His Britannic Majesty and the United States.... All hostilities both by sea and land shall cease as soon as this Treaty shall have been ratified by both parties.... All territory, places, and possessions whatsoever taken by either party from the other during the war, or which may be taken after the signing of this Treaty, excepting only the Islands hereinafter mentioned, shall be restored without delay....

Article the Second.

Immediately after the ratifications of this Treaty by both parties as hereinafter mentioned, orders shall be sent to the Armies, Squadrons, Officers, Subjects, and Citizens of the two Powers to cease from all hostilities....

Article the Third.

All Prisoners of war taken on either side as well by land as by sea shall be restored as soon as practicable....

Article the Fourth.

...the boundary of the United States should comprehend all Islands within twenty leagues of any part of the shores of the United States and lying between lines to be drawn due East from the points where the aforesaid boundaries between Nova Scotia on the one part and East Florida.... In order therefore finally to decide upon these claims it is agreed that they shall be referred to two Commissioners to be appointed in the following manner: One Commissioner shall be appointed by His Britannic Majesty and one by the President of the United States ... and the said two Commissioners so appointed shall be sworn impartially to examine and decide upon the said claims according to such evidence as shall be laid before them....

Article the Fifth.

...The said Commissioners shall have power to ascertain and determine the points above mentioned ... and shall cause the boundary aforesaid ... to be surveyed and marked according to the said provisions. The said Commissioners shall make a map of the said boundary ... certifying it to be the true Map of the said boundary.... And both parties agree to consider such map ... fixing the said boundary....

Article the Sixth.

...The said Commissioners shall ... designate the boundary through the said River, Lakes, and water communications, and decide to which of the two Contracting parties the several Islands lying within the said Rivers, Lakes, and water communications, do respectively belong.... And both parties agree to consider such designation and decision as final and conclusive....

Article the Seventh.

It is further agreed that the ... Commissioners after they shall have executed the duties assigned to them ... shall be, and they are hereby, authorized upon their oaths impartially to fix and determine ... that part of the boundary between the dominions of the two Powers, which extends from the water communication between Lake Huron and Lake Superior to the most North Western point of the Lake of the Woods;—to decide to which of the two Parties the several Islands lying in the Lakes, water communications, and Rivers forming the said boundary do respectively belong ... and to cause such parts of the said boundary as require it to be surveyed and marked. The said Commissioners shall ... designate the boundary aforesaid....

Article the Eighth.

The ... two Commissioners ... shall respectively have power to appoint a Secretary, and to employ such Surveyors or other persons as they shall judge necessary.... The said Commissioners shall be respectively paid in such manner as shall be agreed between the two contracting parties.... And all other expenses ... shall be defrayed equally by the two parties....

Article the Ninth.

The United States ... engage to put an end immediately after the Ratification of the present Treaty to hostilities with all the Tribes or Nations of Indians with whom they may be at war at the time of such Ratification, and forthwith to restore to such Tribes or Nations respectively all the possessions ... and privileges which they may have ... been entitled to ... previous to such hostilities. Provided ... that such Tribes or Nations shall agree to desist from all hostilities ... upon the Ratification of the present Treaty.... And His Britannic Majesty engages on his part to put an end immediately after the Ratification of the present Treaty to hostilities with all the Tribes or Nations of Indians with whom He may be at war at the time of such Ratification, and forthwith to restore to such Tribes or Nations respectively all the possessions ... and privileges, which they may have ... been entitled ... previous to such hostilities. Provided always that such Tribes or Nations shall agree to desist from all hostilities ... upon the Ratification of the present Treaty....

Article the Tenth.

Whereas the Traffic in Slaves is irreconcilable with the principles of humanity and Justice, and whereas both His Majesty and the United States are desirous of continuing their efforts to promote its entire abolition, it is hereby agreed that both the contracting parties shall use their best endeavours to accomplish so desirable an object.

Article the Eleventh.

This Treaty when the same shall have been ratified on both sides ... shall be binding on both parties....

an iron fist. He had declared martial law (rule by a military force or government in which civil rights are suspended) on December 16 and did not lift it until March 13, even though news of the Treaty of Ghent ending the war had arrived on February 19. When a journalist complained about Jackson's heavy-handedness in a newspaper article, Jackson threw him in prison, and he also jailed the judge who ordered the journalist released. Jackson also dealt severely with his own troops. A group of Tennessee militiamen decided that they were only required to serve for three months instead of six and headed home. Jackson charged them with desertion and had the six leaders of the groups executed by firing squad.

News of peace brings joy

People in the twenty-first century, who are used to instant communication, find it hard to imagine a time when news traveling from Great Britain to the United States could only travel as fast as it took a ship to cross the ocean, which could take several months. Thus Americans heard no word of the Treaty of Ghent, which was signed on December 25, until the news arrived aboard the HMS *Favorite* in New York harbor on February 11, 1814. In the meantime, a significant number of Americans as well as British suffered death or injury in a conflict that had already been resolved.

Noisy celebrations soon erupted in New York, then in Boston, and eventually all over the United States. Madison submitted the treaty to Congress on February 15, 1815, and Congress ratified it the next day (Great Britain had ratified the treaty on December 28, 1814). The war officially ended at 11 P.M. on February 17. Most Americans felt that their side had won the war, no matter what the actual terms of the treaty might say. The United States had fought the most powerful nation in the world and emerged, if not quite victorious, then at least on equal footing. People felt that by signing the Treaty of Ghent, Great Britain was acknowledging that the United States truly was an independent nation.

Members of both the Republican and Federalist parties found reasons for pleasure in the news of peace. Federalists felt that in its notable lack of any mention of the original war-causing issues, the treaty proved that they had been right all along in saying that there was no reason to go to war against Great Britain. Republicans, however, interpreted the treaty as an American victory, and their speechmakers and writers soon went to work proclaiming it as such. In a special message to Congress, Madison noted that the war had been full of "most brilliant successes." He praised "the wisdom of the Legislative councils, ... the patriotism of the people, ... the public spirit of the militia, and ... the valor of the military and naval forces of the country," as recorded in the *Annals of Congress.*

On the other side of the ocean, British leaders and citizens also welcomed peace, for with the treaty came the easing of what had become an unwelcome burden. There were some in Great Britain, however, who felt that the United States should have been more severely punished. The London *Times,* on December 27 and December 30, 1814, expressed regrets that the United States had not received a "sound flogging [good beating with a whip]."

The War of 1812 has often been called the Second War of Independence, and it did involve many of the same issues and ideas of the American Revolution (1775–83), especially that of the fitness of the United States of America to be an independent nation. But some critics have noted that the War of 1812 was never really about independence, except in the minds of a few particularly passionate Republicans. Certainly the British—embroiled as they were in their own troubles with Napoleon, much closer to home—did not see it as a conflict of such grandiose consequence. For them, according to historian John R. Elting, it was "a minor colonial squabble, something to be mopped up as soon as possible to free ships and men for whatever new crises Europe might develop."

Costs and consequences

The War of 1812 lasted for two years and eight months. Official reports (which were often inaccurate) said that 528,274 troops had participated in it, including 57,000 regular soldiers, 10,000 volunteers, 3,000 rangers, and 458,000 militia. Another 20,000 served in the navy and marines. Casualty records showed 2,260 soldiers killed in battle and 4,505 wounded.

There are no figures available, however, for the number of troops who died from sickness, and historians agree

Camp Life at Point Henry, Kingston, May 1813

This account first appeared in 1895, when it was translated from the French and published as *Reminiscences of the War of 1812–14: Being Portions of the Diary of a Captain of the "Voltigeurs Canadiens" While in Garrison at Kingston, Etc.* The writer is Jacques Viger, who would go on to become Montreal's first mayor in 1833.

[We] were ordered by General Prevost on the 17th of May to cross over to Point Henry, where we now occupy tents which we again once more put up in a wilderness of stumps, fallen trees, boulders, and rocks of all sizes and shapes; sharing our blanket with reptiles of varied species; carrying out the precepts [commands] of the most self-sacrificing charity towards ten million insects and crawling abominations, the ones more voracious and disgusting than the others. Phlebotomized [opening veins] by the muskitoes, cut and dissected by gnats, blistered by the sand flies, on the point of being eaten alive by the hungry wood rats as soon as they shall have disposed of our provisions. Pray for us! Pray for us! ye pious souls.

Broken down with fatigue, drenched with rain, I enter my tent to find that the birds of the air have besmirched me with lime; I have no sooner sat on my only camp stool when a horrid toad springs on to my lap in a most familiar way; I cast my wearied limbs on to my couch, a slimy snake insists on sharing with me the folds of

that this number was huge due to unhygienic conditions in camp as well as inadequate treatment methods and supplies. Among the diseases that claimed thousands of soldiers' lives were dysentery, typhoid fever, pneumonia, malaria, measles, and smallpox. It has been estimated that there were about 17,000 non-battle-related deaths (in other words, deaths from illness or accidents) during the War of 1812. Adding in the numbers of soldiers executed (205 of them, mostly for desertion) and casualties among the privateer and civilian populations produces a grand total of about 20,000 casualties. The war took a high financial toll, too; the cost to the U.S. government was $158 million dollars.

The war leads to increased sectionalism

Besides the losses already discussed, the war had exposed many U.S. weaknesses, including a lack (at least during

my blanket, I hastily retire and leave him in possession. Let us have supper! The frying pan is produced to fry the ration of pork. Horror! A monstrous spider has selected it for his web; he holds the fort in a viciously threatening attitude in the centre of its rays, he defiantly seems to say, remove me if you dare! The flinty biscuit must be pounded and broken or one can't eat it, here again the beastly wood-bug must needs crawl under the masher, and in losing his life infect everything with his sickening odor. Oh! Captain, what can we do? exclaims my valet.... Light the candle, you blockhead, light the candle. Let us write to our distant friends the excess of our misery. O ye gods, what a place this is! The candle is lighted, it is the next moment surrounded by myriads of flying things. My table is littered with writhing abominations, June bugs hasten from all sides, they besiege the light, extinguish it under one's very nose, strike you in the eye, and as a parting shot stun you with a blow on the forehead. What a paradise this spot would be for an entomologist [person who studies insects]!

We remained in this inferno a whole fortnight, but thank heavens these very unpleasant experiences came to an end and were followed by better times....

Source: The War of 1812 Website. *[Online]* *http://www.militaryheritage.com/home.htm (accessed on November 26, 2001).*

the first year of the war) of competent leaders and officers, not enough troops, and an overdependence on militiamen, who tended to be inexperienced and inefficient and who would often flee a battle that got too hot or refuse to cross the U.S. border into Canada. The war also led to political discontent and to an increase in sectionalism, which is a narrow-minded concern for one section of the country over all others.

Divisions between the various areas of the United States had existed since colonial times, but they were expressed in strong terms during the War of 1812, and they would only intensify as the nineteenth century progressed. The United States was made up of three sections—the West, the South, and the Northeast—each of which had its own kind of economy, social life, and political ideas.

Westerners had left the security of the long-settled East Coast for the dangers and hardships of the frontier. They stressed the values of self-reliance, courage, initiative, and hard work and tended to judge people by these standards rather than by family connections or wealth. Eager not only to defend the honor of their country but to possibly expand its borders, westerners had by and large been in favor of war with Great Britain. The life of the South was dominated by large plantations on which cotton was grown with the aid of slave labor. The cultural focus was on social graces and social rank, factors that dated back to the English aristocracy (noble or privileged class) that many southerners idealized. Yet the trade restrictions imposed by Great Britain had hurt the southern economy, and most of them also had supported the war effort.

As many farmers moved west, the Northeast increasingly relied on shipbuilding, fishing, and trade with foreign countries for its economy. These activities were brought to a halt by the War of 1812, fueling New England's opposition to the war and to the Republican administration who favored it. At the same time, the war had sparked a trend toward domestic manufacturing that would grow throughout the rest of the century, especially as new inventions and processes were introduced, as cities grew, and as transportation improved.

As the nineteenth century progressed, these sectional differences became centered on one important issue: slavery. The northern and southern states came into strong opposition over this matter, with northerners either condemning slavery's inhumanity or resenting the economic advantage it gave the South, and with southerners defending their right to live as they chose. In the American Civil War, the violent conflict between the North and the South that erupted in 1861, the loyalties of the western states would be determined, generally, by their geographical location in either the northern or southern part of the country.

Who got the blame?

Congress took much of the blame for the nation's problems during the War of 1812, especially in failing to pass a tax program or establish a national bank, steps that many believed would put the country back on a solid financial footing. Criticized even more than Congress—at least while the war was still in progress—was President James Madison, who was faulted for weak leadership during a difficult period. A shy, cautious person who did not like to offend anyone, Madison treated his foes and enemies with fairness and humanity, but he also tolerated poor performances by his subordinates for far too long. He made, for example, several very bad cabinet choices (especially Secretary of War William Eustis and Secretary of the Navy Paul Hamilton) that probably had much to do with the disasters of the first year of the war.

Madison had been unable to inspire confidence in either Congress or the American people and thus contributed to the divisiveness that dominated the war years. Yet when the war was over, the perceived U.S. victory suddenly restored Madison's image, and he finished his term as a popular president. Faring far less favorable was the Federalist Party, which finally lost its long struggle for dominance over the Republican Party, and went into a steep decline after the war. The Federalists' loss of popularity had deeper roots (the country was changing, becoming both larger and more democratic, and the Federalist model of a compact nation ruled by a centralized, aristocratic elite no longer fit), but the war provided the final blow.

Opposition to the war may have been tolerated somewhat during the conflict, but after it had ended, that same opposition was considered traitorous. Federalists were seen as having wanted to prevent the United States from trouncing the British. The party's opponents cast the Hartford Convention, which had actually been dominated by moderation and no talk of seceding (separating) from the union, as the ultimate expression of Federalists' disloyalty. Although the Federalists claimed that they were being unfairly portrayed and unjustly criticized, their party continued to decline in popularity.

Another negative consequence of the War of 1812 was a heightening of the anti-British feeling that had prevailed in the United States since the days of the American Revolution. Americans especially resented the British use of Native American allies, attributing many atrocities to their presence in battles. Hatred for the British also had been stirred by the raids on the Chesapeake Bay region between 1813 and 1814, during which many Americans felt the British had been unnecessarily harsh and arrogant.

Adding to this hostile feeling was the treatment of the approximately twenty thousand Americans who were prisoners of war during the conflict. Two of the most notorious pris-

American Prisoners of War

Most U.S. soldiers and seamen who were captured by the British during the War of 1812 either were soon exchanged for British prisoners or sent to one of two prisons: Melville Island Prison in Halifax, Nova Scotia (located in northeastern Canada), or Dartmoor Prison in Devonshire, England.

Great Britain maintained the Melville Island military prison from 1803 until 1905. During the War of 1812, more than eight thousand American prisoners (some of them serving multiple terms) were housed there. About twelve hundred were army or militia soldiers, and a small number U.S. Navy sailors; the majority of prisoners were crew members from captured privateers (the privately armed ships that were authorized to attack enemy merchant ships). More than one hundred prisoners died at Melville, many of them succumbing to the diseases of smallpox or typhus.

Upon entering the prison, inmates would be issued the following supplies: a hammock, a blanket, a horse rug, a yellow jacket, pants, a vest, wooden shoes, and a cap. They also were also given a small amount of money so that they could buy food from local people who came into the prison to sell their products.

Used exclusively for prisoners captured on the high seas, Dartmoor Prison was even more notorious and dreaded than Melville Island. The first U.S. prisoners of war were brought there in April 1813, ons were located at Halifax in Canada and at Dartmoor in southwestern England. At Dartmoor Prison, about sixty-five hundred American prisoners suffered from the damp and very poor conditions and lack of adequate food. When the war ended, a dispute about who was responsible for getting the prisoners home caused a delay in releasing them. On April 6, 1815, the prisoners became unruly and their British guards opened fire on them, killing seven and injuring thirty-one. News of the "Dartmoor Massacre" sparked many anti-British editorials in U.S. newspapers.

The war brings some important changes

So the War of 1812 was expensive in many ways. What did the United States gain after paying such a high

and by April 1815 there were 5,542 Americans confined there. During this two-year period, 252 American prisoners died. Dartmoor Prison was a dark, damp, dismal place where disease was rampant. The prisoners were harshly disciplined, and food was scarce (though fairly nutritional); however, the medical care they received was relatively good. U.S. prisoners always were offered the chance to escape imprisonment by enlisting in the British navy, but only 75 of them did so.

Two months after the February 1815 ratification (official approval) of the Treaty of Ghent had ended the war, the U.S. prisoners had, because of an administrative mix-up, not yet been released. As a result, they staged a noisy demonstration on April 6 and were fired upon by their British guards, who killed seven prisoners and wounded thirty-one. British officials would later refer to the incident as an unfortunate accident and offer cash payments to the families of the dead and wounded. Even with this offer, anti-British sentiment in the United States was inflamed. The prisoners finally were released at the end of April.

Sources: "Dartmoor Prison." Dictionary of American History, 7 vols. Charles Scribner's Sons, 1976. Reproduced in History Resource Center. Farmington Hills, Mich.: Gale Group. http://www.galenet.com/servlet/HistRC/; Heidler, David S., and Jeanne T. Heidler, eds. Encyclopedia of the War of 1812. Santa Barbara, Calif.: ABC-CLIO, Inc., 1997; Shea, Iris. Melville Island. [Online] http://www.udata.com/users/hsbaker/melville.htm (accessed on November 27, 2001).

price? From a military perspective, the War of 1812 ended in a tie, with neither side showing clear dominance on either the land or sea. It accomplished nothing that it had set out to do, for the Orders in Council (British laws which required anyone intending to trade with France to stop first in England and purchase a license) had already been dropped when the war began and impressment had become a nonissue by the time it ended. In other ways, though, the war had some important consequences for the United States.

Despite its hopes of a successful invasion of Canada, the only land the United States acquired during the War of 1812 was part of West Florida, and that gain was connected more with the Creek War (see Chapter 4) than the war with Great Britain. But another important land issue *was* resolved by the war, for a wide expanse of U.S. territory in the northwest was made safer for white settlement. The death of the dynamic Shawnee war chief Tecumseh (c. 1768–1813; see biographical entry) at the Battle of the Thames signaled the end of a Native American alliance that had threatened the progress of westward expansion. Disheartened by the loss of their great leader, Native Americans gave up the dream of banding together to halt the tide of white encroachment (gradually taking) on Indian lands.

The failure of Great Britain to live up to its promises to establish a Native American homeland between the borders of Canada and the United States sealed the fate of those who had fought alongside the British. During the next century, the United States would continue to push Native Americans farther and farther west, into smaller and smaller spaces, with little regard for the rights and privileges mentioned in the Treaty of Ghent.

The War of 1812 resulted in some important changes in the U.S. military. The United States had been caught unprepared and without adequate troops too often during the war. In addition, the dangers of relying heavily on state militias had been well demonstrated. After the war, the troop level for the peacetime army was set at ten thousand, which was three times what it had been twelve years earlier. Congress also authorized the construction of twenty-one new ships and a program to fortify the U.S. coastline. Reforms in how the military was organized and run would be introduced during John C. Calhoun's term (1816–1819) as secretary of war. The war also had changed the face of the military, as older (and often problematic) men like James Wilkinson (1757–1825) and Henry Dearborn (1751–1829) gave way to more dynamic officers who had proven themselves in battle, like Jacob Brown (1775–1828), Andrew Jackson (1767–1845; see biographical entry), Oliver Hazard Perry (1785–1819; see biographical entry), and Thomas Macdonough (1783–1825; see biographical entry).

Other effects of the war

The war had a strong—though not entirely positive—effect on the U.S. economy. The New England and southern states suffered greatly due to the British blockade, which

brought the fishing and shipping industries to a standstill; by contrast, the middle and western states prospered, because their crops and other products were needed to sustain the U.S. troops. Manufacturing received a big boost during the war years, because the loss of imports (goods shipped from other countries) caused by the British blockade meant that more products had to be made in the United States. To keep these manufacturing gains alive, Madison pushed through Congress a two-year extension on duties (similar to a tax) on imports.

Another economic consequence of the War of 1812 involved the Bank of the United States. It had been chartered by the federal government in 1791, and by 1805 it had eight branches and served as the government's bank, while also accepting the deposits of private citizens and businesses. Even though the bank had served the government well and succeeded in establishing a sound currency, many leaders (including Madison) feared that it was too dangerous to have a

A Sioux camp in Upper Mississippi during the 1850s. After the War of 1812, Native Americans gave up the dream of banding together to halt the tide of white encroachment on Indian lands. *Photograph reproduced by permission of North Wind Picture Archives.*

financial institution with so much centralized power. Thus when the bank's charter expired in 1811, it was not renewed.

The War of 1812, however, exposed the need for a national bank, because in trying to finance the war, the government had to borrow money from the less reliable state banks, at higher interest rates. Alerted to this weakness, Madison and others changed their positions on the national bank, which would be rechartered in 1816. The second Bank of the United States would follow the same pattern as the first, functioning well before falling to political concerns in 1836, when President Andrew Jackson would veto its charter renewal.

Americans may have disliked the British more than they had before the war, but in Europe, the war led to increased admiration for the United States. Despite the mixed performance of U.S. troops in battle, their courage was noted and their accomplishments praised, even by some British observers. The War of 1812 also had established good reputations in the United States for some notable figures who later turned their wartime accomplishments into successful political careers. In addition to numerous governors, senators, congressmen, and other elected officials, the war helped to produce four presidents: James Monroe (1758–1831; see biographical entry), John Quincy Adams (1767–1848), Andrew Jackson(1767-1845; see biographical entry), and William Henry Harrison (1773–1841; see biographical entry).

One of these men, Monroe, would succeed Madison as president in 1818. He would run unopposed for the office, since the Federalist Party would by then have almost completely disappeared, and the one-party political system that George Washington and others had envisioned as the best possible for the U.S. (because it avoided the self-interested concerns of multiple parties or factions) would now prevail. Monroe would preside over the Era of Good Feelings (1817–23), a period so-called because it was free from the political bickering and bad feeling that had marked the war years.

Americans remember the war as glorious

News of the U.S. victory at the Battle of New Orleans reached most Americans only shortly before they heard about

A campaign poster for William Henry Harrison, who was elected president in 1840.

the Treaty of Ghent, and for them the two events were tied together. Even though it had been fought after the treaty was signed, the Battle of New Orleans was linked to the coming of peace in people's minds, almost as if the heroic actions of Jackson and his troops had actually brought about the peace. Americans were especially proud of having beaten not just Great Britain but the fabled British force that had fought Napoleon.

As time passed, most Americans seemed to forget about the negative aspects of the War of 1812—the blunders, the defeats, the goals unattained. They remembered it only as a glorious episode in American history, one in which the United States had proven that it could stand united against a powerful foe and win. The war did succeed in building U.S. confidence and determination, ushering in the all-too-short Era of Good Feelings. By the middle of the century, however, the unity and nationalistic pride that characterized this period would give way to disharmony as regional differences became more important and problematic. That disharmony would result in the American Civil War.

But for the moment, as the War of 1812 drew to a close, Americans felt for the most part unified, and they felt proud of themselves and their nation. Even before the terms of the Treaty of Ghent were widely known in the United States, Congressman Charles J. Ingersoll (1782–1862) said that it hardly mattered what was in the peace agreement, because it was enough for the United States to revel in its victory.

Where to Learn More

Books

Annals of Congress, February 16, 1815, pp. 13-3, 1156.

Coles, Harry L. *The War of 1812.* Chicago: University of Chicago Press, 1965.

Elting, John R. *Amateurs to Arms!: A Military History of the War of 1812.* Algonquin Press, Chapel Hill, N.C., 1991. Reprint, New York: Da Capo Press, 1995.

Heidler, David S., and Jeanne T. Heidler, eds. *Encyclopedia of the War of 1812.* Santa Barbara, Calif: ABC-CLIO, Inc., 1997.

Hickey, Donald R. *The War of 1812: A Forgotten Conflict.* Urbana: University of Illinois Press, 1989.

Hitsman, Jay McKay. *The Incredible War of 1812: A Military History.* Toronto: University of Toronto Press, 1972.

Mahon, John K. *The War of 1812*. Da Capo Press, 1991. Reprint. Originally published by University of Florida Press, Gainesville, FL, 1972.

Web sites

Discriminating Generals. [Online] http://www.militaryheritage.com/home.htm (accessed on November 26, 2001).

Documents on the War of 1812. [Online] http://www.hillsdale.edu/dept/History/Documents/War/FR1812.htm (accessed on November 26, 2001).

Thomas Warner Letters. [Online] http://www.haemo-sol.com/thomas/thomas.html (accessed on November 26, 2001).

War of 1812. [Online] http://www.galafilm.com/1812/e/index.html (accessed on November 26, 2001).

"War of 1812." *KidInfo.* [Online] http://www.kidinfo.com/American_History/warof1812.html (accessed on November 26, 2001).

"War of 1812." *Studyweb.* [Online] http://www.studyweb.com/links/388.html (accessed on November 26, 2001)

War of 1812–1814. [Online] http://www.members.tripod.com/~war1812/ (accessed on November 26, 2001).

War of 1812—Forgotten War. [Online] http://www.multied.com/1812/ (accessed on November 26, 2001).

Biographies

Isaac Brock

Born October 6, 1769
St. Peter Port, Guernsey, England

Died October 13, 1812
Queenston Heights, Canada

British general

D espite his death during the first year of the War of 1812, Isaac Brock was probably the most famous and respected general on the British side of the conflict. His military skill, knowledge of the Canadian terrain and people, and demanding but humane approach to his troops all made him an effective leader. Called the "hero of Upper Canada," Brock helped to show that Canada could be successfully defended against a U.S. invasion. He is credited with inspiring self-confidence not only in the troops who fought under his command but in the residents of Canada.

An ambitious young officer

Isaac Brock was born in St. Peter Port on Guernsey, one of the Channel Islands that lie off the coast of England. The eighth son of John Brock and Elizabeth DeLisle Brock, he decided as a teenager to follow three of his brothers into military service. When he was fifteen, Brock joined the Eighth (King's) Regiment of Foot (an infantry unit of the British army) as an ensign (the lowest rank).

Portrait: Isaac Brock.
Photograph reproduced by permission of Hulton/Archive.

163

Five years later, Brock was promoted to the rank of lieutenant. He was later transferred to the Forty-ninth Regiment and made a captain. He served in Barbados and Jamaica (two British colonies in the Caribbean region). In 1795 Brock became by purchase (a traditional practice in which officers paid a fee to receive a rank) a major and two years later became a lieutenant colonel by the same method.

By the end of 1797, when he was twenty-eight, Brock had been given command of the Forty-ninth Regiment. He participated in Great Britain's ongoing war against French forces under Emperor Napoleon I (1769–1821), and was wounded during a battle in Holland in 1799. Two years later he was aboard a ship in the fleet of the great naval commander, Horatio Nelson (1758–1805), when the British attacked Copenhagen, Denmark (the Danish had been aiding France).

Assigned to Canada

In 1802 Brock was ordered to take his regiment to Canada, Great Britain's vast, mostly undeveloped colony in North America. He viewed his time in Canada as a stepping stone that would carry him to more challenging places and assignments. Still, Brock did his work well, becoming a colonel in 1805 and a major general in 1811. He commanded the garrison (army outpost) at Quebec from 1805 to 1811 and then was put in charge of all the British troops in Canada. In addition, he became the head of the colony's civil government for a short time.

During his prewar years in Canada, Brock made many requests to be transferred to Europe. By the time his request was granted, though, Great Britain was on the verge of war with the United States. Disputes between the two countries over the right to free trade, impressment (the act of British officials boarding U.S. ships to capture deserters from the British navy, but often taking American soldiers instead), and westward expansion (Great Britain was suspected of encouraging Native Americans to attack white American settlers) seemed likely to erupt into a full-blown conflict. Knowing that he could play a key role if a war did start, Brock decided to stay in Canada.

Preparing for war

Even before the United States made its June 12, 1812, declaration of war against Great Britain—and despite the belief of some leaders, including the governor, George Prevost (1767–1816), that the United States would never actually take such a drastic step—Brock began preparing Canada to fend off any invasion attempts. At the beginning of 1812, there were fifty-two hundred regular British soldiers stationed in Canada, about twelve hundred of them serving with Brock in what was called Upper Canada (now Ontario). Another eleven thousand militia troops (temporary soldiers, usually called into service only in emergencies as a means of defense) were available, but Brock believed that only about four thousand of these could be considered completely loyal to Great Britain. Many residents of Canada had only recently arrived from the United States or other countries and were thought to still have divided loyalties.

Brock immediately called for more regular soldiers to be sent to Canada, and for training of militia to be stepped up. In February 1812 he enlisted the help of an influential fur trader named Robert Dickson (c. 1765–1823) who had some strong connections with Native Americans in the Northwest Territory (including a third of Wisconsin, half of Minnesota, and almost all of Indiana, Illinois, and Michigan) of the United States. Hostilities between Native Americans and white Americans had increased as large numbers of settlers moved farther and farther west. Brock felt it was important for Great Britain to form alliances with Native Americans and enlist their support in fighting the United States.

When the War of 1812 began, Prevost called for a restrained, nonaggressive approach, but Brock believed that Great Britain should go on the offensive from the beginning. Thus he ordered an attack on Fort Michilimackinac (pronounced mi-shu-LEE-ma-ku-naw), a U.S.-held outpost strategically located on the northern straits of Lake Michigan, in the northern part of what was then Michigan Territory. British troops surrounded the fort on July 17, 1812, and its small band of American defenders, taken by surprise and unprepared for a battle, offered no resistance. Just as Brock had hoped, the bloodless victory showed both the Americans and the Native Americans in the region (many of whom would join the British in future confrontations) that Great Britain would take this war seriously.

The surrender of Detroit

Meanwhile, U.S. troops under the command of General William Hull (1753–1825) launched an invasion of Canada from Detroit in Michigan Territory that began with the conquest of the town of Sandwich (now Windsor, Ontario), directly across the Detroit River from Detroit. Hull returned to Detroit, though, when news of the surrender of Fort Michilimackinac reached him. After meeting with Canada's legislature (law-making body) in early August, Brock headed out to challenge the U.S. invasion with a counterinvasion.

Brock arrived at Fort Malden, located near Amherstburg (in southern Ontario across from Detroit), on August 15. There he met the dynamic Native American leader Tecumseh (c. 1768–1813; see biographical entry), who had been rallying his fellow Shawnee and other Native American peoples to form an alliance to resist white encroachment on their lands. As quoted in a biographical essay of Brock by Alain Gauthier, Tecumseh was reportedly so impressed with the forceful Brock that he exclaimed, "Now here is a man!"

The next day Brock again demonstrated bold leadership when he decided to attack the fort at Detroit, even though he knew that his troops were outnumbered (Hull had about twenty-five hundred soldiers, whereas Brock had about thirteen hundred, plus six hundred Native American allies). Aware that morale among the American troops was low—a U.S. mailbag containing letters of complaint from U.S. soldiers had been captured—and that Hull's leadership was weak, Brock sent a message to Hull demanding that the United States surrender. He claimed that he had a large number of Native American warriors with him, and that he was not sure he could control them in battle.

A new hero for Upper Canada

Hull did not agree to Brock's order immediately, but after the British troops had crossed the Detroit River and

Hull's Proclamation to the Citizens of Canada

The following proclamation was issued by General William Hull after his troops had crossed the Detroit River into Canada in July 1812. This attempted invasion quickly proved a failure when Hull, worried that the British would soon unleash huge numbers of their Native American allies, retreated to Detroit.

Inhabitants of Canada

After thirty years of peace and prosperity, the United States have been driven to arms. The injuries and aggressions, the insults and indignities of Great Britain have once more left no alternative but manly resistance or unconditional submission. The army under my command has invaded your country. The standard of the union now waves over the territory of Canada. To the peaceful and unoffending inhabitants it brings neither danger nor difficulty. I come to find enemies, not to make them; I come to protect not to injure you ... I have a force which will break down all opposition, and that force is but the vanguard of a much greater. If, contrary to your own interest, and the just expectations of my country, you should take part in the approaching contest, you will be considered and treated as enemies, and the horrors and calamities of war will stalk you ...

Source: Documents on the War of 1812. *[Online]* http://www.hillsdale.edu/dept/History/Documents/War/FR1812.htm (accessed on November 26, 2001).

begun to bombard the fort, the U.S. troops did soon surrender. With this quick and easy victory, the main U.S. force in the region had been put out of commission, and the British were now in control of the Northwest and would remain so for another year. They had solidified the support of Native American allies, and captured a large number of much needed weapons and ammunition. Perhaps most significantly, though, was the victory's psychological effect on the people of Canada. They now believed that they could resist an American invasion. Brock was now considered "the hero of Upper Canada," and a knighthood was bestowed on him by King George III (1738–1820; ruled 1760–1820).

Brock now hurried back to the Niagara region, where the war's next major confrontations would take place. Major General Roger Sheaffe (1763–1851) was already there with his army, and more British reinforcements were on their way. Brock was determined to stomp out any chance for the United States to gain dominance on the Great Lakes, which were vitally important as routes for transporting troops and supplies. Thus he formulated a plan to attack Sacket's Harbor and

Buffalo, New York, both towns where the U.S. Navy was either building or harboring ships.

Meanwhile, Prevost had reached an armistice (peace agreement) with Major General Henry Dearborn (1751–1829), who was in charge of the American troops in the northeastern region. Although this peace was fragile, it gave the Americans more time to build their troops. Believing that the United States would attack either Fort Erie (at the southern end of the Niagara River, close to Lake Erie) or Fort George (at the northern end of the river, close to lake Ontario) Brock worked on bolstering defenses along the Niagara River.

A major loss for the British side

Brock was incorrect in his assumption about the place of attack. Instead on October 13, 1812, U.S. troops crossed the river from Lewiston, New York, to the Canadian shore near the town of Queenston (located just south of Fort George). The battle that followed centered on a battery of guns that the British had set up on the steep hill called Queenston Heights, with the two armies fighting for control of this position. Brock was awakened by the sound of the battle and hurried to Queenston, recruiting militia units he found along the road to join the fight.

Brock and his troops reached the scene of the battle and started moving up the hill toward the gun battery. Suddenly they saw that a regiment of Americans troops had just arrived at the top, so Brock's men scrambled back down again. They charged on the hill again with Brock in the lead. Six feet tall and dressed in the red jacket of the British army, Brock made an easy target for the American sharpshooters. One of them shot him in the chest, and he died almost instantly.

After Brock's death, command passed to Lieutenant Colonel John McDonnell, and then to Sheaffe when McDonnell also was killed. The British went on to win the battle, but the victory was tarnished by the loss of the dynamic Brock, who seems to have earned more respect and fondness from the troops than any other British commander in the War of 1812. Canada embraced him as one of its national heroes, and in 1824 a 130-foot stone memorial to Brock was placed on Queenston Heights. This monument was destroyed by an explosion in 1840, but another—this one fifty-two feet taller than the first—replaced it in 1856. The bodies of both Brock and McDonnell were interred in its base.

Where to Learn More

Books

Elting, John R. *Amateurs to Arms!: A Military History of the War of 1812.* Algonquin Press, Chapel Hill, N.C., 1991. Reprint, New York: Da Capo Press, 1995.

Heidler, David S., and Jeanne T. Heidler, eds. *Encyclopedia of the War of 1812.* Santa Barbara, Calif.: ABC-CLIO, 1997.

Hickey, Donald R. *The War of 1812: A Forgotten Conflict.* Urbana: University of Illinois Press, 1989.

Tupper, Ferdinand Brock. *The Life and Correspondence of Major-General Sir Isaac Brock.* 2nd ed. London: Simpkin, Marshall, 1847.

Web sites

Gauthier, Alain. "Biography of Isaac Brock." *The War of 1812 Website.* [Online] http://www.militaryheritage.com/brock.htm (accessed on November 26, 2001).

Monument to Sir Isaac Brock. Canadian History Image Gallery. [Online] http://canadahistory.about.com/aboutcanadahistory/library/b.../ b177-brockmonument.htm (accessed on November 26, 2001).

"War of 1812." [Online] http://www.galafilm.com/1812/e/index.html (accessed on November 26, 2001).

Henry Clay

Born April 12, 1777
Hanover County, Virginia

Died June 29, 1852
Washington, D.C.

Speaker of the House, politician

Henry Clay was one of the most important U.S. statesmen of the period between the Revolutionary War (1775–83) and the Civil War (1861–65). As a congressman from Kentucky, he served as Speaker of the House (the top leadership position in the House of Representatives) before and during the War of 1812, and was the leader of a group of legislators called the War Hawks. These men—most of them young and from the southern or western states—believed that the United States should go to war against Great Britain. Although he lacked the brilliance of men like Thomas Jefferson (1743–1826) and James Madison (1751–1836; see biographical entry), Clay was an effective speaker with a charming, persuasive personality. He gained enough of a following to run for president five times, but he never gained that office.

A boy from Virginia

Henry Clay was born in the middle of the American Revolution, the seventh of eight children of a Baptist minister named John Clay and his wife, Elizabeth Hudson Clay.

Portrait: Henry Clay.
Photograph courtesy of The Library of Congress.

The family lived in an area of Hanover Country, Virginia. His father died in 1781, when Clay was four years old.

Ten years after his father's death, Clay's mother married Henry Watkins, a resident of Richmond (now the capital of Virginia), who treated his stepchildren kindly and took a special interest in young Henry. The family moved to Richmond, where the fourteen-year-old Clay began working as store clerk. His stepfather felt he was qualified for more challenging work, and secured him a job as a clerk at the High Court of Chancery (a court of law during that period in Virginia). The bright young man came to the attention of George Wythe (1726–1806), chancellor (the top official) of the court, who made Clay his secretary.

A young Kentucky lawyer

Up to this point in his life, Clay had still not acquired much formal education, but Wythe encouraged him to use his library to augment his learning. In 1796 he began to study law under the attorney general of Virginia, Robert Brooke. During this period Clay lived in Brooke's home and had opportunities to meet many prominent people in Virginia politics. He was licensed as a lawyer at age twenty, and in November 1797 he moved to Lexington, Kentucky. At this period Lexington was an important, lively center of activity in the still-young west, and Clay's mother had already moved there.

Clay quickly established himself as the best defense lawyer in Kentucky, specializing in criminal cases. In 1798 he made a very well-received speech against the Alien and Sedition Acts, which Clay and others saw as intended to stifle criticism of the government. A year later, Clay was elected to Kentucky's Constitutional Convention (the meeting at which the state's constitution was written), and he offended some Kentuckians through his unsuccessful attempt to abolish (end) slavery in the state. Clay was himself a slaveholder, but he felt that slavery was wrong and should gradually be eliminated.

Also in 1799 Clay married Lucretia Hart, the daughter of a Kentucky businessman. The couple moved to a six-hundred-acre estate called Ashland where, during the next several decades, they would breed livestock and raise not only crops but a family of eleven children. Tall and slim with an expressive face and warm manner, Clay was gifted at making others feel at ease. Although he was not well-educated, he gained admirers through his personal charm, but he also made some enemies. Clay lived the somewhat rough-and-tumble life of the American frontier: he enjoyed drinking and gambling, and even fought in two duels (in 1809 and 1826).

Beginning a public service career

In 1803 Clay was elected to Kentucky's state legislature, where he established himself as a Democratic Republican like President Thomas Jefferson (1743–1826). Members of this political party (which eventually became simply the Republican party) believed that government should play a limited role in people's lives, and they tended to support the interests of farmers and plantation owners over merchants and city dwellers. During these years, the Napoleonic Wars (1803–15) in Europe between France and Great Britain (along with its other European allies) had created problems for U.S. trade. As a result, Clay advocated the development of domestic industries.

In 1806 and again in 1810, Clay served two short terms in the U.S. Senate, filling out terms that had been vacated before they expired. He often was involved in heated debates with another senator, Humphrey Marshall (1760–1841), with whom he fought a duel in 1809 (both men were injured but neither was killed). Elected to the U.S. House of Representatives in 1811, Clay settled in to the legislative role he enjoyed more than any other job he had held before or after.

A dedicated Speaker of the House

Soon after his arrival in Congress, Clay was elected Speaker of the House, which was an unusual honor for a first-term representative and proof of his personal charm and persuasiveness. During his long career in politics, Clay would be elected Speaker six times, and he helped to shape this into a position of true leadership rather than a fancy but empty title. He gained respect through his fairness and ability to forge compromises.

The War Hawks are eager for war

Clay soon became the leading member of a group that became known as the War Hawks. These men were mostly young, mostly western and southern legislators who favored war with Great Britain. They claimed that the honor of the United States had been insulted by British actions on the high seas (including trade restrictions and impressment, by which American citizens were forced into the British navy) and that the British also were encouraging Native Americans to attack white settlers in the western part of the United States. The War Hawks hoped to use the war to fulfill expansionist aims (such as possibly acquiring Spanish-held Florida or even British-held Canada). When the Twelfth Congress met in November 1811, the trade and impressment disputes between the United States and Great Britain were at their peak. In addition, the victory of U.S. troops against a Native American force at the Battle of Tippecanoe in early November would help to stir up the prowar spirit.

As Speaker of the House, Clay was able to appoint men who agreed with his views to important committee positions. He also pushed through legislation that would prepare the United States for war (such as an increase in taxes to help finance the war effort). He and the other War Hawks—who included John C. Calhoun (1782–1850) of South Carolina and Clay's fellow Kentuckian, Felix Grundy (1777–1840)—put a lot of pressure on President James Madison, who was not as enthusiastic about the idea of war as they were. While pushing the president along on the path toward war, they also tried to influence public opinion through confident talk; Clay, for example, announced proudly that the Kentucky militia (a military force that is made up of citizens rather than professional soldiers, and called out in times of emergency) alone could carry off a successful invasion of Canada.

In June 1812 Madison delivered a message to Congress in which he recommended war against Great Britain. The tensions between the two countries had finally met a breaking point. The two major issues were Britain's maritime policy of impressment (the act of British officials boarding U.S. ships to capture deserters from the British navy) during its war with France and the friendly relations between the British and the Native Americans. Americans believed that the British were encouraging Native Americans to attack white settlers who were moving west. The Native Americans believed that the settlers were encroaching (gradually taking over) their land. The declaration was passed by a vote that revealed a sizable amount of opposition, especially in the New England states. Many gave the persuasive Clay most of the credit (or the blame, if they disagreed with him) for getting the declaration passed.

Active in war and peace

During the less than two years that the War of 1812 lasted, Clay continued to work in Congress for measures that he thought would help the United States win. He was especially motivated by his belief that Madison was not capable of managing the war well on his own and that the nation needed especially strong leadership from others. Among Clay's efforts was helping to put U.S. troops in the crucial Northwest Territory (what would become the states of Ohio, Michigan, Indiana, Illinois, and parts of Minnesota) under the command of William Henry Harrison (1773–1841; see biographical entry), the governor of Indiana Territory and a skillful military leader. He also took an active role in defending the Madison administration and the war in general against attacks from Federalists (members of the opposition party, who had been opposed to the war from the beginning).

By the end of 1813, Clay felt that the conflict must come to an end soon. The nation was financing the war, which—despite a few impressive victories—had not gone as well as expected. Like other political leaders, Clay was relieved when, in December 1813, the British offered to begin peace negotiations. Madison appointed Clay to serve on the five-member commission that went to Ghent, Belgium, for the talks; the other members were diplomat John Quincy Adams (1767–1848); Federalist senator James Bayard (1767–1815), former secretary of the treasury Albert Gallatin (1761–1849), and Jonathan Russell (1771–1832), the top U.S. diplomat in London.

The representatives from the United States and Great Britain met at Ghent in August 1814, and their discussion continued during the next four months, ending with the signing of the Treaty of Ghent on Christmas Eve. The treaty resolved none of the issues that had brought about the war in the first place (for Great Britain had removed its trade restrictions soon after the war began, and impressment was no longer an issue now that Great Britain's war with France was over); rather, it stated that things would remain just as they had been before the conflict began. Nevertheless, most Americans chose to believe that their side had won, for they had taken on the mighty Great Britain and survived.

A distinguished legislator

Except for a short period as a private citizen (1821–23) Clay served in the House of Representatives from 1815 to 1825. During these years, he tried to encourage people in the eastern and western United States to work together to make the U.S. economy stronger. Clay also pushed for protective tariffs, which were duties or fees paid by those importing goods into the United States; he believed that these tariffs would benefit Americans who were producing goods and crops in competition with foreign traders.

Clay's skills as a negotiator were useful in 1819, when Missouri applied to join the union as a slave-holding state. By this time slavery had become a hotly contested issue, with many U.S. citizens (most of them in the northern part of the country) passionately opposed to it and others (most of them in the South, which depended on slave labor to grow cotton and other crops) upholding the rights of states to decide for themselves whether they would allow slavery. Missouri's admission as a slave state would tip the balance toward the slaveholders, since there would be one more slave state than free state, and that prospect ignited a controversy.

The Missouri Compromise

The congressional debate that followed Missouri's application highlighted the growing differences between the various parts of the United States (especially the North and the South), differences that would erupt into violence when the Civil War began four decades later. The initial debate resulted in what came to be known as the Missouri Compromise: Missouri would be admitted as a slave state and Maine as a free state (thus maintaining the balance), while slavery would be prohibited north of the Missouri border. Clay was not responsible for crafting that compromise, but he did resolve a subsequent conflict that came about when Missouri wanted to prohibit free blacks (those who had never been slaves or who had bought or been given their freedom) from entering the states. Clay got the Missouri legislature to agree that it would not restrict the privileges of anyone (black or white) who was a U.S. citizen.

In 1820 and 1822 Clay took time off from public service to attend to his private affairs as a Kentucky farmer and head of a large family. He was re-elected to Congress in 1823 and again elected Speaker of the House. One of four candidates for president in 1824, Clay had the lowest number of votes, so his name was not placed before the House of Representatives (which votes for the president if the Electoral College fails to determine a majority for any candidate).

As a representative, Clay cast his own vote for John Quincy Adams, even though most voters in his state favored Andrew Jackson (1767–1845; see biographical entry), who had been a popular general during the War of 1812. Clay was following his own convictions—he strongly believed that Jackson was simply a military leader and thus not qualified to serve as president—but his vote for Adams angered many Kentuckians. When Adams made Clay his secretary of state (a very important position that often led to the presidency), many suspected that Clay had made an under-the-table bargain with Adams (in other words, Clay had agreed to cast his vote for Adams in exchange for the appointment as secretary of state). Clay denied this, but the accusation continued to follow him throughout the rest of his career. Clay served as secretary of state for the next four years, but it was not a happy period for him. He missed his legislative work, and many of the efforts he led in his new position did not succeed.

Leaving and returning to politics

As the 1828 election approached, Jackson joined with John C. Calhoun (1782–1850) and others opposed to the Adams administration and the Republican Party, to form the

Democratic Party. Jackson won the election and, turning down Adams's offer to appoint him to the Supreme Court before he left office, Clay returned to Kentucky. Although he was tempted to settle into the life of a country gentleman, the acclaim he received from people as he toured his home state—added to his opposition to Jackson's policies—convinced him to return to politics.

In 1831 Clay was elected to the U.S. Senate, where he would serve for the next eleven years. He was nominated to run for president in 1832, but Jackson won again by a wide margin. Two years later Clay gained respect for working out a compromise on a tariff issue that had nearly caused South Carolina to nullify (cancel) a federal law, which might have led to the state's seceding (leaving) from the union.

The Whigs' nominee for president

Convinced that the Democratic Party candidate, Martin Van Buren (1782–1862), was unbeatable, Clay did not enter the 1837 presidential election. He became a leading member of the new Whig political party and expected its nomination in the 1840 election. Clay was bitterly disappointed, however, when the Whigs instead nominated William Henry Harrison. Nevertheless, Clay campaigned hard for Harrison, who won the election but died after only one month in office. His successor, John Tyler (1790–1862), opposed most of Clay's ideas, and Clay soon resigned from the Senate.

Clay was again the Whig Party's presidential candidate in 1844, but his shifting position on Texas independence—as he tried to balance the interests of southern and northern voters—cost him the election. The United States entered a war with Mexico when Texas seceded from Mexico and joined the union. Even though Clay opposed the war, he supported the government once it began, and one of his sons died on a Mexican battlefield.

The Compromise of 1850

Clay tried for the Whig nomination in the 1848 presidential election, but it went to Zachary Taylor (1784–1850), a general of the Mexican-American War (1846–1848). For the third time in his career, Clay had been passed over in favor of a candidate whose only qualification lay in his military heroism. Despite his disgust over this turn of events, Clay returned to the Senate in 1849, in time to take the lead on a series of compromises—collectively referred to as the Compromise of 1850, the year in which they were passed—that were all related to the slavery issue and that helped to postpone the coming crisis of sectionalism (divided interests and tension between regions of the country). For his role in resolving this crisis, Clay earned the title of "The Great Pacificator" (peacemaker).

As he neared the end of his life, Clay found himself so deeply in debt that he had to consider selling his beloved Ashland. Instead, his supporters around the nation took up a collection for him and raised $50,000, which was enough to cover his debts. After he died in Washington, D.C. (where he was still serving in the Senate) in 1852, Clay's remains were returned to Kentucky, with stops in Baltimore, Philadelphia, New York City, Albany, Buffalo, Cleveland, and Cincinnati for mourners to pay their respects. He was buried in a Lexington, Kentucky cemetery.

For More Information

Books

Colton, Calvin. *The Life and Times of Henry Clay.* New York: Garland Publishers, 1974.

Heidler, David S., and Jeanne T. Heidler, eds. *Encyclopedia of the War of 1812.* Santa Barbara, Calif.: ABC-CLIO, Inc., 1997.

Remini, Robert Vincent. *Henry Clay: Statesman for the Union.* New York: W. W. Norton, 1991.

Schurz, Carl. *Henry Clay.* New York: Chelsea House, 1980.

William Henry Harrison

Born February 9, 1773
Berkeley, Virginia

Died April 4, 1841
Washington, D.C.

General, president of the United States

In the years leading up to the War of 1812, William Henry Harrison, while serving as governor of Indiana Territory, negotiated a number of treaties through which Native Americans sold their traditional lands to the United States government. When Native Americans realized how much they had lost, they began attacking white settlers. In November 1811 U.S. troops under Harrison's command fought native warriors at the Battle of Tippecanoe. When the War of 1812 began, Harrison succeeded William Hull (1753–1825) as commander of all troops in the Northwest. Harrison's fame as a war hero propelled him to the presidency of the United States, but he died after only one month in office.

Choosing a military career

William Henry Harrison was born into a wealthy Virginia family who lived on the Berkeley plantation on the James River. His father, Benjamin Harrison (c. 1725 –1791), was a signer of the Declaration of Independence (the document drawn up by the founders of the American republic in

Portrait: William Henry Harrison. *Photograph reproduced by permission of Archive Photos, Inc.*

which they stated their reasons for seeking independence from Great Britain), and his mother, Elizabeth Bassett Harrison, was from a distinguished Virginia family.

Tutored at home through his teenage years, Harrison entered Hampton-Sydney College in the late 1780s. His father wanted him to become a doctor so he studied medicine in Richmond, Virginia, in 1790 and Philadelphia, Pennsylvania, in 1791. When his father died, Harrison turned to his own career choice, which was the military. He enlisted as an ensign (the lowest rank) in the First Regiment of Infantry in August 1791.

Harrison served in the northwestern army for the next seven years. He was an aide to General "Mad" Anthony Wayne (1745–1796; so called due to both his bravery and his hot temper) during the American Revolution (1775–83) and in August 1794 fought at the Battle of Fallen Timbers, a clash between U.S. forces and Native Americans that took place near what is now Toledo, Ohio. The resulting Treaty of Greenville, which Harrison witnessed and signed, opened much of Ohio for settlement by white people.

Governor of Indiana Territory

In November 1795 Harrison married Anna Symmes, the daughter of a wealthy judge and land speculator (someone who buys and sells land). The couple had ten children, and one of Harrison's grandsons, Benjamin Harrison (1833–1901), would become the twenty-third president of the United States. Three years after his marriage, Harrison retired from the army, having reached the rank of captain. He bought 160 acres of land at North Bend, situated about 14 miles down the Ohio River from Fort Washington.

About a month after his retirement, President John Adams (1735–1726; president 1797–1801) made Harrison the secretary of the Northwest Territory. The following year, he was elected as the territory's delegate to the U.S. Congress. As a delegate, he worked hard to protect the rights of those living in the northwest. He helped sponsor the Land Act of 1800, which allowed people to buy smaller pieces of land than had previously been available, and gave them five years to repay their debt. Harrison supported the 1800 division of the northwest into two parts, the Northwest Territory (what is now the state of Ohio) and the Indiana Territory (the states of Indiana, Illinois, Michigan, Wisconsin, and part of Minnesota).

Adams made Harrison governor of the new Indiana Territory, an office he would hold for twelve years. He moved his family to the territory's capital, Vincennes, and built a mansion on the Wabash River that he named Grouseland. His main task as governor was to continue, through treaties, to remove the Native Americans from their lands so that white U.S. citizens could settle on them. He also was supposed to encourage a friendly relationship with the Native Americans, a task that would prove impossible.

Harrison meets Tecumseh

In 1809 Harrison negotiated the Treaty of Fort Wayne with the Delaware, Potawatomi, and Eel tribes. This agreement called for the Native Americans to trade about three million acres of land for payments to each tribe that ranged from two to five hundred dollars. Resentment over this and other unfair arrangements grew among Native Americans, leading to violent attacks on white settlers. It also resulted in the rise of Tecumseh (c. 1768–1813; see biographical entry), a dynamic Shawnee war chief who began to rally Native Americans of many tribes to come together to fight off white encroachment (the gradual taking over of land). Tecumseh and his followers maintained that lands belonged to all Native Americans in common and could not be signed away by individual chiefs. Tecumseh was joined in this effort by his brother Tenskwatawa (1775–1836; see box in Tecumseh entry), known as the Prophet, who was believed to have magic powers.

Aware of Tecumseh's plans and of his influence over his followers, Harrison invited the Shawnee leader to Grouseland for a discussion on August 10, 1810. Tecumseh arrived with four hundred armed warriors, and the meeting was tense and unproductive. Attacks on whites continued, so Harrison arranged another meeting with Tecumseh in July 1811. He warned Harrison that he and his people would not honor the Treaty of Fort Wayne, which referred to land along the Wabash River. After this meeting Tecumseh traveled south to rally more Native Americans to his cause.

Harrison believed that Tecumseh's absence made this a good time for a military expedition against Prophet's Town, the village Tecumseh's followers had established on the Wabash River (near the present-day town of Lafayette, Indiana). At a site about a mile from Prophet's Town, Harrison and a force of about one thousand made their camp and sent a message to the Native Americans—who were now under Tenskwatawa's leadership—on November 6 that they would meet with them the next day.

The Battle of Tippecanoe

Early the next morning, the Americans were surprised by an attack led by Tenskwatawa; the Prophet had convinced his people that they would be immune from the bullets of the white soldiers. After several hours of hard fighting and many casualties (soldiers killed or wounded), the Native Americans scattered; the next day, Harrison's troops destroyed Prophet's Town.

Although this had not been a great victory for the United States, Harrison's reputation soared. He continued to warn the government about the Native American threat, and he put much of the blame for the violence on British agents, who he believed were helping to arm the Native Americans and encouraging them to attack white Americans. This suspicion was shared by others and was a contributing factor in the decision to declare war against Great Britain (other reasons included trade restrictions Americans felt were unfair, and the impressment or forcing of U.S. sailors into the British navy). Even before the June 1812 declaration of war, however, the government sent more soldiers to the Northwest. William Hull (1753–1825), the governor of Michigan Territory, was appointed to command them.

Command of the northwestern army

Only a few months after the war had begun, Hull surrendered Detroit in a defeat that made the United States look foolish to British general Isaac Brock (1769–1812; see biographical entry). Secretary of War William Eustis (1753–1825) had to replace Hull, and his first choice was Brigadier General James Winchester (1752–1826), who was unpopular with the militia

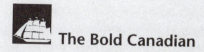

The Bold Canadian

The song below was probably sung by Canadian soldiers in the first few years of the war. It refers to the failed attempt by troops under General William Hull to invade Canada, and Hull's subsequent surrender of Detroit to British general Isaac Brock (who commanded a much smaller force than Hull's). The song suggests that Canadians took considerable pride in preventing the U.S. troops from invading their country.

Come all ye bold Canadians,
I'd have you lend an ear
Unto a short ditty [song]
Which will your spirits cheer,
Concerning an engagement
We had at Detroit town,
The pride of those Yankee [American] boys
So bravely we took down.

The Yankees did invade us,
To kill and to destroy,
And to distress our country,
Our peace for to annoy,
Our countrymen were filled
With sorrow, grief, and woe,
To think that they should fall
By such an unnatural foe.

Come all ye bold Canadians,
Enlisted in the cause,
To defend your country,
And to maintain your laws;
Being all united,
This is the song we'll sing:
Success onto Great Britain
And God save the King.

Source: Graves, Donald R. "Songs of the War of 1812." The War of 1812 Website. [Online] http://www.militaryheritage.com/home.htm (accessed on November 26, 2001).

in the area. (Militias were small armies made up of troops residing in a particular state.) Harrison, however, was popular, especially in the state of Kentucky. In order that he would have a higher rank than Winchester, the Kentucky militia made him a major general. As a result, the U.S. government finally bowed to this pressure, and on September 17, 1812, Harrison was given command of all forces in the Northwest.

Meanwhile, Harrison was already on the march with the Kentucky militia, raiding the villages of Native Americans who had attacked white settlers. Eager to start a campaign against Great Britain immediately, he divided his troops into two forces and sent them up to northern Ohio and southeastern Michigan, with the goal of eventually retaking Detroit. The division under Winchester (now Harrison's second-in-command) arrived first and proceeded to Frenchtown, located on the Raisin River near present-day Monroe, Michigan, where they chased away a small British force. On January 20 Winchester's troops were defeated by British troops under Henry Procter (1763–1822), commander of British troops in this region.

Battles at Fort Meigs and Lake Erie

Newly promoted to major general, Harrison was told that his role would be a purely defensive one for the time being, as the government had decided to concentrate its resources on the war's northern theatre (along the Niagara River, which divides New York state from Canada and connects Lake Erie and Lake Ontario). Harrison began building Fort Meigs on the Maumee River near the present-day town of Perrysburg, Ohio.

In May Procter's forces attacked the fort, but with help from General Green Clay (1757–1826) of the Kentucky militia, who arrived with timely reinforcements, Harrison's troops fought off the British. Later in the summer, Procter made another unsuccessful attempt to take Fort Meigs.

During the summer of 1813, Harrison spent a lot of time in Cleveland, Ohio, preparing to provide support for naval commander Oliver Hazard Perry (1785–1819; see biographical entry), who was building up U.S. naval strength with the goal of getting control of Lake Erie. Aware that dominance on Lake Erie would put his own troops in a better position for land victories (the Great Lakes were important routes for transporting men and supplies), Harrison loaned Perry—who was desperate for sailors—soldiers from his own army, especially those with some naval experience.

In pursuit of Procter

In September 1813 Perry's fleet defeated the British in an important battle on Lake Erie. With his supply lines now cut off, Procter had to make a quick retreat into Canada. Harrison, with reinforcements mainly coming from Kentucky led by Governor Isaac Shelby (1750–1826), began to pursue Procter's forces on October 2. Procter was accompanied by Tecumseh and his warriors, who had joined the British side after the Battle of Tippecanoe. Tecumseh insisted that Procter must turn and face the enemy, and on October 5 the two armies met near the small town of Moraviantown (located in southern Ontario, on the Thames River). During this clash—called the Battle of the Thames by Americans and the Battle of Moraviantown by Canadians—Tecumseh was killed, effectively crushing the Native American confederacy he had tried to build.

Returning to civilian life

Despite the fame and respect this victory earned him, Harrison was dissatisfied, primarily because he did not get along with John Armstrong (1758–1843), who had replaced William Eustis as secretary of war in early 1813. A Revolutionary War veteran with, perhaps, a very high opinion of his own military skill and judgment, Armstrong often overruled the orders of his field commanders or bypassed them by issuing his own orders to their subordinate (lower-ranking) officers. Frustrated by Armstrong's behavior and with very little military action promised in the Northwest for the immediate future, Harrison resigned from the army in the spring of 1814.

Returning to North Bend, Harrison continued to assist with negotiations between the U.S. government and Native Americans, working on treaties that completed the federal takeover of Native American lands in the northwest. From 1816 to 1819, Harrison represented his district in the U.S. Congress, serving as chair of the committee on militia. He served in the Ohio state senate (Ohio had become a state in 1803) from 1819 to 1821. Elected to the U.S. Senate in 1825, Harrison served for three years, chairing the committee on military affairs and the militia.

Despite his lack of experience as a diplomat (an official who represents a government in a foreign country), Harrison was appointed in 1828 by President John Quincy Adams (1767–1848; president 1825–29) to serve as minister to Colombia in South America. He arrived there in February 1829 but stayed only until September, when the new president, Andrew Jackson (1767–1845), appointed someone else because of his and Harrison's political differences. During his months in Colombia, Harrison offended that country's president, Simon Bolivar (1783–1830), who claimed that Harrison had openly sided with a group planning to rebel against the Colombian government (diplomats are not supposed to interfere in the internal affairs of foreign countries).

"Tippecanoe and Tyler, Too"

After he returned to the United States, Harrison found himself financially strapped. With a large family of children and grandchildren to support, he had to accept a position as clerk of the court of common pleas in Hamilton County, Ohio, a job that did not fit his background or prestige as a former military leader. The next year, however, he was nominated as one of the newly created Whig Party's presidential candidates in the 1836 U.S. elections. Harrison lost to Democratic Martin Van Buren (1782–1862) but was the most popular of the three Whig candidates. He and his supporters, however, soon began to plan for the 1840 election.

During the 1940 elections Van Buren was running for reelection, but hard economic times had hurt his reputation. His supporters tried to ridicule the sixty-seven-year-old Harrison as an elderly backwoods character who was most comfortable sitting on the porch of a log cabin (actually Harrison, of course, came from a wealthy, East Coast background). But Harrison's campaign embraced this image, casting him as the "log-cabin candidate" who was a man of the people, a westerner who had fought the Native Americans and helped to settle the frontier.

This campaign would be a historic one in American history, because it was the first truly modern presidential campaign in which the focus was on personal images rather than issues. The Whigs offered no platform (statement of their positions on issues) and Harrison was advised to say as little as possible, especially about the controversial issue of slavery. As a friendly gesture to the southern states, former Virginia senator John Tyler (1790–1862) was chosen to run as Harrison's vice presidential candidate. Harrison's speeches attracted so many attendees at his rallies that it was said they could be measured by the acre. His campaign slogan— "Tippecanoe and Tyler, Too"—reminded voters of his role in the War of 1812, with a nod to his running mate.

Voter turn-out was the highest of any election ever held in the United States, an increase of fifty percent over the previous election. Although Harrison won a popular majority of less than 150,000, he swept the Electoral College (the method used to elect U.S. presidents, in which each state has a certain number of Electoral College delegates, and whoever wins more votes in that state earns all of the delegates) by 234 to Van Buren's 60.

On March 4, 1841, Harrison delivered an inaugural speech that was noteworthy mostly for its length (one of the longest in U.S. history, taking more than one hour and forty minutes to deliver) and for its wealth of allusions to classical history and literature. He caught a cold at the ceremonies and by late March was diagnosed as pleurisy (pneumonia). On April 14 Harrison died. It was the first death of a U.S. president in office, which stunned the nation.

For More Information

Books

Cleves, Freeman. *Old Tippecanoe: William Henry Harrison and His Time.* New York: Charles Scribner's Sons, 1939.

Dowd, Gregory Evans. *A Spirited Resistance: The North American Indian Struggle for Unity, 1745–1815.* Baltimore: Johns Hopkins University Press, 1992.

Heidler, David S., and Jeanne T. Heidler, eds. *Encyclopedia of the War of 1812.* Santa Barbara, Calif.: ABC-CLIO, 1997.

Hickey, Donald R. *The War of 1812: A Forgotten Conflict.* Urbana: University of Illinois Press, 1989.

Peterson, Norman L. *The Presidencies of William Henry Harrison and John Tyler.* Lawrence: University Press of Kansas, 1989.

Web sites

The American Presidency: William Henry Harrison. [Online] http://www.grolier.com/presidents/ea/bios/09pharr.html (accessed on November 26, 2001).

War of 1812. [Online] http://www.galafilm.com/1812/e/index.html (accessed on November 26, 2001).

"William Henry Harrison." *Ohio History Central.* http://www.ohiokids.org/ohc/history/h_indian/people/whharris.html (accessed on November 26, 2001).

"William Henry Harrison." *White House Biography.* [Online] http://www. whitehouse.gov/history/presidents/wh9.html (accessed on November 26, 2001).

Andrew Jackson

Born March 15, 1767
Waxhaw Settlement, South Carolina

Died June 8, 1845
Nashville, Tennessee

Army general, president of the United States

The seventh president of the United States, Andrew Jackson gave his name to an era in which the idea of "democracy" came to be seen as something closely connected to ordinary, working people and not just the wealthy, educated citizens who had previously dominated U.S. politics. Jackson embodied the self-made, frontier man whose accomplishments resulted from his own courage and will, not his family connections or wealth. It was during the War of 1812 that Jackson established his reputation as a man of great strength and action by leading a diverse force to victory at the Battle of New Orleans.

A hot temper and a hatred for the British

Andrew Jackson's parents, Andrew and Elizabeth Hutchinson Jackson, emigrated (moved from another country) to the United States from Carrickfergus, Ireland, in 1765 with their two older sons, Hugh and Robert. They made their home in poor, isolated Waxhaw Settlement, located about 160 miles northwest of Charleston, South Carolina. The elder Andrew died at the age of 29, two months before the birth of his

Portrait: Andrew Jackson.
Photograph courtesy of the National Portrait Gallery.

191

namesake. Jackson's mother, a very religious woman, hoped young Andrew would grow up to be a Presbyterian minister.

Jackson attended several schools but never attained a love for learning. He grew into a tall, very slender teenager with a long, narrow face and intense blue eyes. He had a hot temper and was often involved in fistfights. At thirteen, Jackson became a helper and messenger for Colonel William Richardson of South Carolina's mounted militia (an army made up of ordinary citizens rather than professional soldiers, and called on in emergencies). He took part in several clashes, including the Battle of Hanging Rock.

Jackson's family was shattered by the Revolutionary War (1775–83) and this led to his deep hatred for the British. His brother Hugh was killed in battle, and he and his brother Robert were captured by the British and put into prison in Camden, South Carolina. When he refused to polish a British officer's boots, Jackson was struck with a sword and was left with permanent scars on his face and hand. Jackson's mother secured her sons' release after both had contracted smallpox (a highly contagious viral disease) in prison. Robert died of the disease, but Andrew survived. While nursing other prisoners, his mother also died of smallpox.

A rowdy but successful young lawyer

At fourteen, Jackson was an orphan. When the war ended he spent a short period learning how to make saddles, and another serving as a schoolteacher. When he inherited three hundred dollars from his grandfather, he went on a gambling spree in Charleston and had soon lost all of his money. Next Jackson decided to study law, which seemed like a good profession for a bright, energetic young man. At this time, lawyers trained for their professional not by attending school but by working and studying with established attorneys. Thus Jackson joined the office of Spruce Macay in Salisbury, North Carolina.

Jackson soon developed a reputation as a wild, rowdy prankster with a taste for gambling. Nevertheless, he passed the bar (the examination lawyers must pass in order to qualify to practice law) in 1787 and set up an office in McLeanville in Guilford Country, North Carolina. Eager for new challenges, Jackson stayed only a year before heading west with his friend John McNairy (1762–1837), who also was a lawyer. The two young men crossed the Cumberland Mountains and eventually reached Nashville, Tennessee, which was then a small frontier town and part of western North Carolina.

McNairy had connections in Nashville and managed to get himself appointed as judge of the superior court; he then made Jackson a public prosecutor (a lawyer who represents the state in criminal cases). Jackson soon made a name for himself, especially for the skill and energy with which he went after debtors (people who owe money to others), and he built up a thriving law practice.

Marriage and politics

While living in a boarding house owned by the widow of John Donelson, one of Nashville's founders, Jackson fell in love with the daughter of the house, Rachel Donelson Robards. Separated from her abusive husband, Rachel had dark hair and eyes, a lively personality, and very little education. Believing her husband had divorced her, she married Jackson in 1791. Two years later, the couple learned that the divorce had only just become official, so they went through another wedding ceremony.

In the late eighteenth century, a couple living together while not legally married was cause for scandal, and throughout the rest of his career Jackson's opponents would use this part of his past against him. The fiery-tempered Jackson also would take part in several duels, when he felt that his beloved wife's honor had been insulted. Although the two never had biological children, they adopted Rachel's infant nephew, naming him Andrew Jackson Jr.

In 1790 the westernmost section of North Carolina was made into a separate territory, and Jackson was appointed prosecuting attorney of the territory. In 1796 the territory became the state of Tennessee. Jackson was elected as a delegate to the state's constitutional convention, at which the structure of its government was established. He then became the state's sole delegate to the U.S. House of Representatives.

Jackson was homesick and unhappy in Philadelphia, however, which was then the nation's capital, and was noticed for his moodiness and fierce temper. After a year as a representative, Jackson was elected to serve out the term of a Tennessee senator who had left his office. He did so from September 1797 to April 1798, then retired and returned to Tennessee.

A militia general

The War of 1812 between the United States and Great Britain was provoked by two major issues. The first was Britain's maritime policy of impressment in its war with France. This policy was where British officials boarded U.S. ships to capture deserters from their own navy, often wrongfully taking American citizens in the process. The other issue that led to the war was Great Britain's overly friendly relations with Native Americans. Americans believed that the British were encouraging Native Americans to attack white settlers who were moving west. The Native Americans, however, believed that the settlers were encroaching (gradually taking over) their land.

Despite his lack of military experience, Jackson was elected major general of the Tennessee militia in 1802. He was elated when the War of 1812 began, for he believed the British had deeply insulted the United States through its practice of impressment on the high seas. He also was a strong expansionist (someone who believed the United States should increase its territory) and saw the war as an opportunity for the nation to acquire more territory. The government, however, turned down Jackson's offer to lead an invasion of Canada.

General James Wilkinson (1757–1825) had been put in command of all U.S. troops in the Southwest (what are now the states of Louisiana, Alabama, and Mississippi). In early 1813 Jackson was told to lead twenty-five hundred militiamen to Natchez, Mississippi to await further orders from Wilkinson. Jackson made the difficult journey, but found himself and his men stranded in Natchez without adequate food, supplies, and equipment. Ordered to disband his troops, Jackson instead kept them together and personally led them back to Tennessee, earning their respect and also the nickname "Old Hickory" in honor of his toughness.

The War of 1812 had aggravated tensions that already existed among the Creeks, a Native American people who lived in what are now Alabama and western Georgia. Although a large number of Creeks had accommodated themselves to the arrival of whites in their territory, even learning to live, farm, and dress like white people, others had resisted. Influenced by the great Shawnee chief Tecumseh (c. 1768–1813; see biographical entry), who had traveled through the region preaching his message of resistance, a faction of the Creeks called the Red Sticks had begun a series of raids and attacks on white settlers. Hopeful that a British victory could help them reach their own goals, the Red Sticks had allied themselves with Great Britain.

Fighting the Creeks in Alabama

In August 1813 Red Sticks had killed about 250 white settlers who had taken refuge at Fort Mims in Alabama. Militia in surrounding states, including Tennessee, were called out to revenge the massacre and put an end to the Red Stick attacks. Jackson was put in command of one of several armies to take part in the effort. He marched south with 2,000 poorly trained, inadequately supplied, and often unenthusiastic troops, keeping them on the move through the sheer force of his personality.

Reaching Mississippi Territory, Jackson's force took part in several inconclusive confrontations with the Red Sticks, including battles at Tallushatchee and Talledega. As 1813 drew to a close, supplies were dwindling and many of the men were at the end of their enlistment periods (militia usually only had to serve for a few months at a time). Despite his frustration and attempts to keep his troops intact, there was not much Jackson could do until reinforcements arrived.

Thus Jackson had to wait until early 1814 to restart his campaign against the Creeks. The final confrontation occurred on March 14 at Horseshoe Bend on the Tallapoosa River, when Jackson's troops managed to surround and wipe out a large force of Creek warriors. The battle was especially savage and bloody, with a number of Creek women and children being caught in the crossfire. Jackson lost only forty-nine soldiers, while the Creek death toll rose to eight hun-

Andrew Jackson's Plea to African Americans

In 1814 the War of 1812 was still being waged between the United States and Great Britain. Being desperate for soldiers to fight against the British in Louisiana, General Andrew Jackson made a plea to the free African Americans of Louisiana to serve in the U.S. Army. Besides needing soldiers, Jackson believed that the inclusion of African Americans in the military would counter British recruitment of blacks as spies and messengers. Although many African Americans responded to Jackson's address to serve in the military, after the War of 1812, they did not receive the compensation they were promised and many were reenslaved by the country that they had helped to defend.

General Andrew Jackson's Proclamation "To the Free Colored Inhabitants of Louisiana, Headquarters, Seventh Military District, Mobile, September 21, 1814"

Through a mistaken policy, you have been heretofore deprived of a participation in the glorious struggle for national rights in which our country is engaged. This no longer shall exist.

As sons of freedom, you are now called upon to defend our most inestimable blessing. As Americans, your country looks with confidence to her adopted children for a valorous [heroic] support, as a faithful return for the advantages enjoyed under her mild and equitable government.

dred. The few survivors who managed to escape scattered into the surrounding woods.

In August, Jackson gathered together thirty-five Creek chiefs, almost all of them representing Creeks who had remained friendly to the United States, and including some who had actually fought on the U.S. side against the Red Sticks. They were forced to sign the Treaty of Fort Jackson, which gave twenty-three million acres of Creek land (more than half of their total territory) to the United States.

In command of defending New Orleans

The U.S. government recognized Jackson's dynamic leadership during the battles with the Red Sticks (also known as the Creek Wars) when, in May 1814, he was made a major general in the regular army and given command of Tennessee, Mississippi, and Louisiana. At this time Great Britain

As fathers, husbands, and brothers, you are summoned to rally around the standard of the eagle [America's national symbol] to defend all which is dear in existence.

Your country, although calling for your exertions, does not wish you to engage in her cause without remunerating [compensating] you for the services rendered. Your intelligent minds are not to be led away by false representations. Your love of honor would cause you to despise the man who should attempt to deceive you. With the sincerity of a soldier and the language of truth I address you.

To every noble-hearted freeman of color volunteering to serve during the present contest with Great Britain, and no longer, there will be paid the same bounty, in money and lands, now received by the white soldiers of the United States....

Due regard will be paid to the feelings of freemen and soldiers. You will not, by being associated with white men in the same corps, be exposed to improper comparison or unjust sarcasm. As a distinct independent battalion or regiment, pursuing the path of glory, you will, undivided, receive the applause and gratitude of your countrymen.

Source: Althoff, Gerard T. Amongst My Best Men: African-Americans and the War of 1812, Put-in-Bay, Ohio: The Perry Group, 1996.

was expected to begin a campaign in the gulf region (the parts of the United States surrounding the Gulf of Mexico), and Jackson was ordered to New Orleans to prepare the city's defenses against a British attack.

When Jackson finally arrived in New Orleans in early December, he found the city not only poorly defended but dominated by a pessimistic mood. He immediately set to work bolstering the city's defenses and instituting martial law (military rule), enlisting the help of all of its citizens and managing to inspire them. Jackson also began putting together an unusually diverse fighting force that eventually numbered six thousand soldiers that included six hundred free blacks, friendly Native Americans, and people of Creole (mixed) heritage as well as militiamen from Tennessee and Kentucky.

Meanwhile, Great Britain had about ten thousand soldiers in the region, including seasoned veterans of the recently concluded, victorious war against French forces led by Emperor Napoleon Bonaparte(1769–1821). Commanded by the experienced and respected Lieutenant General Edward Pakenham (1778–1815), these troops arrived in the New Orleans area in mid-December and took part in several inconclusive skirmishes (minor battles) with parts of Jackson's army through the end of the year.

During the first week of 1814, Jackson gathered his troops at a location a few miles south of New Orleans, arranging them in a line behind a canal. On January 8 the British crossed a wide expanse called the Chalmette plain to attack the American line. Initially, they were protected by a mist, but when the mist lifted they were visible and exposed. The Americans used a merciless barrage of small-arms fire to mow down the British as they tried to approach. Pakenham himself was killed, and the battle was soon over. It had ended disastrously for the British, who suffered two thousand casualties (soldiers killed, wounded, or captured), but gloriously for the Americans, whose casualties numbered only seventy (including only about a dozen killed).

The news of the U.S. victory at the Battle of New Orleans was greeted with joy throughout the country. Even though it had taken place after the signing of the Treaty of Ghent, which ended the war (but before the official ratification of the treaty), many Americans linked the two in their minds, as if the battle had brought about the end of the war. Jackson instantly became a national hero. The fame and adulation Jackson won at New Orleans would help to propel him, less than fifteen years later, to the presidency.

Jackson stayed in New Orleans for several months, keeping the city under martial law even when most of its citizens felt they could and should return to civilian rule. He finally left to take command of the army of the Southern District. His next brush with fame—this one more controversial—came in 1817, when he was sent to stop the Creek and Seminole raids on white settlements. Jackson chased them south into Florida but, in an action that exceeded his orders and that was clearly more about taking territory out of Spanish hands than punishing Native American aggression, seized the towns of Saint Marks and Pensacola. He also put to death two British subjects who had been encouraging and aiding the Seminoles.

The British and Spanish governments were both incensed, causing an embarrassing situation for the administration of President James Monroe (1758–1831). But Secretary of State John Quincy Adams (1767–1848) convinced Monroe that Jackson's actions should be excused as being justified by the circumstances. And in 1819, Spain ceded (gave) Florida to the United States, resulting in Jackson becoming even more popular than before. In 1821 Jackson was appointed governor of Florida but, after employing his usual heavy-handed style, resigned after only four months and returned to private life in Tennessee.

Becomes president

In the 1828 election, Jackson ran against the incumbent Adams, this time as a candidate of the new Democratic Party. Presented as the candidate of change, reform, and democracy, Jackson won by a large margin. Thus was ushered in what would be called the era of Jacksonian democracy.

The satisfaction of winning was followed by a great personal loss for Jackson. His adored wife, Rachel, died of a heart attack soon after the election, and Jackson was convinced that the stresses of the campaign—during which the old talk of a scandal regarding the Jacksons' marriage had been brought up again—had helped to speed her death. When he arrived in Washington, D.C. for his inauguration, he was sixty-two years old, grief-stricken, and suffering from a persistent cough and chronic dysentery (a disease of the stomach and bowels).

A major issue of Jackson's first term involved the removal of Native Americans from their traditional lands into areas set aside for them, especially in the Oklahoma Territory. This movement of people, which severely disrupted their lives and cultures, was happening more and more as the nineteenth century progressed and white Americans moved in greater numbers into the western expanses of the United States. Jackson oversaw the signing of ninety treaties with Native Americans, including one that would force the Cherokee people out of Georgia, where they had lived for thousands of years.

Asserting that the treaty was unfair and illegal, the Cherokees appealed to the U.S. Supreme Court, which ruled in their favor. Jackson ignored the ruling, which had no impact if he was unprepared to enforce it. Thus the Georgia Cherokees were forced to make a journey of more than eight hundred miles along what they called the Trail of Tears, which led to Oklahoma. Many white Americans found this forced displacement of people shameful, but most westerners applauded it because it made more land available for settlement.

In foreign affairs, Jackson achieved some gains for the United States. During his first term the United States signed a treaty with Great Britain that opened up trade with the British West Indies, and another agreement arranged for France to repay Americans for damages suffered during the Napoleonic Wars (1803–15).

In the election of 1832, which was the first in which candidates were chosen at party conventions, Jackson ran against Henry Clay, who had been nominated by the new National Republican party. Jackson won the election easily. As his second term began, the nullification issue came to the forefront again, with South Carolina declaring that both the tariff of 1828 and the more recently passed 1832 tariff were null and void. The state also threatened to secede (separate) from the Union if the federal government tried to collect these taxes. Jackson pushed through Congress a bill that authorized the government to use force in the situation, if necessary; meanwhile, Speaker of the House Henry Clay (1777–1852; see biographical entry) came up with a compromise tariff that was acceptable to South Carolina. For now, the threat of a divided nation had been avoided.

By 1836, Jackson had been physically weakened by tuberculosis (a disease of the lungs), but he stayed in office until the end of his term and was happy to see his old friend Martin Van Buren elected as his predecessor. Jackson lived for eight more years at the Hermitage, plagued by financial worries but keeping a keen eye on national affairs until his death in 1845.

For More Information

Books

Brooks, Charles B. *The Siege of New Orleans.* Seattle: University of Washington Press, 1961.

Carter, Samuel. *Blaze of Glory: The Fight for New Orleans, 1814-1815.* London: Macmillan, 1971.

Heidler, David S., and Jeanne T. Heidler, eds. *Encyclopedia of the War of 1812.* Santa Barbara, Calif.: ABC-CLIO, Inc., 1997.

Heidler, David S., and Jeanne T. Heidler. *Old Hickory's War: Andrew Jackson and the Quest for Empire.* Mechanicsburg, Penn.: Stackpole Books, 1996.

Remini, Robert V. *Andrew Jackson and the Course of American Empire.* New York: Harper and Row, 1981.

Ward, John William. *Andrew Jackson: Symbol for an Age.* New York: Oxford University Press, 1955.

Web sites

"Andrew Jackson." *White House Biography.* [Online] http://www.whitehouse.gov/history/presidents/aj7.html (accessed on November 26, 2001).

Andrew Jackson—Seventh President. [Online] http://members.aol.com/icecold966/AJack.html (accessed on November 26, 2001).

War of 1812. [Online] http://www.galafilm.com/1812/e/index.html (accessed on November 26, 2001).

Francis Scott Key

Born August 1, 1779
Frederick County
(now Carroll County), Maryland

Died January 11, 1843
Baltimore, Maryland

Attorney

F rancis Scott Key was a successful attorney who served during the last year of the War of 1812 in the militia (small armies made up of troops residing in a particular state) of Washington, D.C. He only gained fame, however, after he wrote a poem that later became "The Star-Spangled Banner." Key was a witness to the British bombing of Fort McHenry. Inspired by the sight of the U.S. flag still flying after a bombardment that lasted twenty-four hours, Key wrote a poem on the back of a letter. It later gained popularity around the country, and in 1931 it became the national anthem of the United States.

Grows up to become a lawyer

Francis Scott Key's grandfather arrived in the United States from England about 1720, settling in Maryland's Frederick County (now known as Carroll County). Key was born on the family's twenty-eight-hundred-acre estate, Terra Rubra, located near the town of Frederick, Maryland (about forty miles north of Washington, D.C.). His father, John Ross Key, had

Portrait: Francis Scott Key.
Photograph reproduced by
permission of Archive Photos, Inc.

203

fought with distinction in the Revolutionary War (1775–83). Key grew to be a slender young man with dark blue eyes and a passionate nature who enjoyed horseback riding.

After graduating from St. John's College in Annapolis, Maryland, in 1796, Key studied law under Judge J. T. Chase. (In the early nineteenth century, those who wished to become lawyers underwent a period of training with an already established lawyer or judge rather than attending law school.) With his friend Roger B. Taney (1777–1864)—who would one day become chief justice of the U.S. Supreme Court, the nation's highest court—Key set up a law practice in Frederick in 1801. The next year he married Mary Tayloe Lloyd, the daughter of an army colonel, with whom he would have eleven children.

Key moves to Georgetown

In 1803 Key moved his law practice and his family to Georgetown, which is now a part of Washington, D.C. At that time, Georgetown had five thousand residents and was located only a few miles from the nation's capital. He had a successful law career and also was very active at St. John's Episcopal Church; he was a lay reader (a person who is not a minister but takes part in the service by reading from the Bible) and at one time even considered becoming a minister. Key also sang with the Georgetown Glee Club. An amateur poet, he wrote a hymn called "Lord, With Glowing Heart I'd Praise Thee" that was still being sung nearly two centuries later.

During the first decade of the nineteenth century, tensions mounted between Great Britain and the United States. The war in Europe between Great Britain and its allies and France, under the leadership of Emperor Napoleon Bonaparte (1769–1821), had led to trade restrictions that many in the United States felt were unfair. In addition, Great Britain had been impressing American sailors (forcing them into the British navy) it claimed were British citizens, and some Americans also thought that the British were involved in stirring up trouble with the Native Americans in the western territories. All of these factors led to the United States declaring war with Great Britain in June 1812.

The British burn Washington, D.C.

During the first two years of the war, Key sided with members of the Federalist political party, who opposed the Republican administration of President James Madison (1751–1836; see biographical entry) and did not support the war effort. But in 1814 the nature of the war shifted when the Napoleonic Wars (1800–1815) ended and Great Britain was able to devote more troops and resources to the conflict in North America. The British went on the offensive and seemed likely to invade several areas of the United States. Key now changed his own position on the war and enlisted in the militia of Washington, D.C., serving as an aide to General Walter Smith.

During the summer of 1814, Americans leaders believed that the British would attack Baltimore, an important East Coast shipping center with a large population. Therefore most of the U.S. forces in the region were sent to defend that city against attack. But in August 1814 Great Britain surprised the United States by marching toward Washington, D.C. After defeating a poorly prepared U.S. force at Bladensburg, Maryland (located just north of the capital), the British entered Washington, burning the U.S. Capitol, the White House, and other government buildings. Less than two days later, they left Washington and headed north toward Baltimore.

Key negotiates William Beanes's release

While the British army was marching north, some of its soldiers became disorderly and left their regiments to raid the towns and countryside that lay between Washington and Baltimore. In the town of Upper Marlboro, an elderly physician named William Beanes (1749–1828) led a group of residents who took it upon themselves to round up some of these misbehaving British soldiers. But when British officers heard of their actions, they arrested Beanes and imprisoned him on one of their warships.

Beanes's friends appealed to Key to help them win the doctor's release. Accompanied by Colonel John S. Skinner, a U.S. government agent in charge of prisoner exchanges, Key sailed out on a ship that was flying a flag of truce (announcing a temporary halting of hostilities) to meet the British fleet at the mouth of the Potomac River. He met with Commodore

Alexander Cochrane (1758–1832), the commander of the British naval forces in the Chesapeake Bay area, to discuss Beanes's release. At first the British refused to release Beanes, but after they read some letters from British prisoners attesting to their good treatment by the Americans, they let the doctor go.

At this moment, however, the British had already sent land forces to attack Baltimore and were about to begin a naval attack on nearby Fort McHenry. They told Key, Skinner, and Beanes that they would not be able to leave until after the battle. The Americans' ship was towed to Fort McHenry behind a British ship. As the British lined up their sixteen warships to begin bombing the fort, Key noticed that a huge American flag (it measure thirty feet by forty-two feet) was flying above it.

Key writes *The Star-Spangled Banner*

The bombardment began on September 13 and lasted for about twenty-four hours, with the British shooting both bombs and rockets (these were Congreve rockets, which made a bright red flare but tended to do little damage) at Fort McHenry. At the same time, U.S. land and naval forces fired on the British ships. Key and his friends waited through a tense night, wondering what the outcome would be. At dawn, Key saw that the huge U.S. flag was still flying. The British had been unable to penetrate the fort, and as their ground forces also had made no headway they retreated from the Baltimore area.

Intensely moved by the experience, Key was on his way back to shore when he began to write a poem based on his observations. He finished it after reaching his hotel in Baltimore. The next day, Key showed the poem to Joseph Hopper Nicholson (1770–1817), his wife's brother-in-law, who greatly admired it and took it to be printed. Originally titled "The Defence of Fort M'Henry," the poem was widely distributed and quickly gained popularity, even in areas of the country far from Baltimore. It was soon set to the tune of an old British drinking song, *To Anacreon in Heaven*. When actor Ferdinand Durang sang the song in public during an October 1814 performance, he called it *The Star-Spangled Banner*.

The Star Spangled Banner

Oh, say can you see, by the dawn's early light,
What so proudly we hailed at the twilight's last gleaming?
Whose broad stripes and bright stars, through the perilous fight,
O'er the ramparts we watched, were so gallantly streaming?
And the rockets' red glare, the bombs bursting in air,
Gave proof through the night that our flag was still there.
O say, does that star-spangled banner yet wave
O'er the land of the free and the home of the brave?

On the shore, dimly seen through the mists of the deep,
Where the foe's haughty host in dread silence reposes,
What is that which the breeze, o'er the towering steep,
As it fitfully blows, now conceals, now discloses?
Now it catches the gleam of the morning's first beam,
In full glory reflected now shines on the stream:
'Tis the star-spangled banner! O long may it wave
O'er the land of the free and the home of the brave.

And where is that band who so vauntingly swore
That the havoc of war and the battle's confusion
A home and a country should leave us no more?
Their blood has wiped out their foul footstep's pollution.
No refuge could save the hireling and slave
From the terror of flight, or the gloom of the grave:
And the star-spangled banner in triumph doth wave
O'er the land of the free and the home of the brave.

Oh! thus be it ever, when freemen shall stand
Between their loved homes and the war's desolation!
Blest with victory and peace, may the heaven-rescued land
Praise the Power that hath made and preserved us a nation.
Then conquer we must, for our cause it is just,
And this be our motto: "In God is our trust."
And the star-spangled banner forever shall wave
O'er the land of the free and the home of the brave!

After the war, Key's law practice continued to thrive. A highly intelligent man and an effective speaker, he served as District Attorney for the District of Columbia from 1833 to

1841 and also helped to negotiate some agreements between the United States government and various Native American groups (such as the Creeks in Alabama in 1833). He also became involved in the antislavery movement. During a trip to Baltimore in early 1843, Key became ill, and he died at the home of one of his daughters. After his death, a volume of Key's poetry was published, but none of its verses is as memorable as the one that became "The Star-Spangled Banner."

Key's famous song was sung by the Union Army during the Civil War (1861–65) and adopted as an anthem by the U.S. military during World War I (1914–18), but it did not become the nation's official anthem until it was recognized as such by Congress in 1931. Often criticized as a song that is very difficult for most people to sing, "The Star-Spangled Banner" has nevertheless not been seriously challenged as the national anthem. Monuments attesting to Key's contribution to American history have been erected at Mount Olivet Cemetery in Frederick, where he is buried, at Eutaw Place in Baltimore, and in Golden Gate Park in San Francisco, California.

For More Information

Books

Furlong, William R., and Byron McCandless. *So Proudly We Hail: The History of the United States Flag*. Washington, D.C.: Smithsonian Institution Press, 1981.

Kroll, Steven. *By the Dawn's Early Light: The Story of the Star-Spangled Banner*. New York: Scholastic, 1994.

Silkett, John T. *Francis Scott Key and the History of the Spar Spangled Banner*. Washington, D.C.: Vintage American Publishing, 1978.

Sonneck, Oscar George Theodore. *The Star Spangled Banner*. New York: De Capo, 1969.

Weybright, Victor. *Spangled Banner: The Story of Francis Scott Key*. New York: Farrar and Rinehart, 1935.

Web sites

War of 1812. [Online] http://www.galafilm.com/1812/e/index.html (accessed on November 26, 2001).

Worley, Stephen L. *Francis Scott Key*. [Online] http://www.theshop.net/slworley/fckey.html (accessed on November 26, 2001).

Thomas Macdonough

Born December 31, 1783
The Trap (now Macdonough), Delaware

Died November 10, 1825
At sea, aboard the ship *Edwin*

Naval officer

S everal of the relatively few battles in the War of 1812 that ended in victory for the United States were fought at sea or on inland lakes. In general, the U.S. Navy performed better than anyone could have expected, given its lack of preparation for fighting a war against Great Britain, which was known as the Mistress of the Seas because of the dominance of the British navy. Perhaps the brightest of the naval stars was thirty-year-old Thomas Macdonough, who led his men to an unexpected victory over a larger British fleet on Lake Champlain.

Thomas Macdonough was the sixth of ten children born to Major Thomas Macdonough, a physician and a veteran of the Revolutionary War (1775–83) who was active in Delaware politics, and his wife Mary Vance Macdonough. The major's father had emigrated from County Kildare, Ireland to the United States around 1730.

Gaining experience as a midshipman

Young Macdonough was orphaned at the age of eleven. Luckily, some of his father's powerful political friends were

Portrait: Thomas Macdonough. *Photograph reproduced by permission of The Granger Collection, Ltd.*

looking out for him, and managed to get him a commission (assignment) as a midshipman (the lowest-ranking officer) in the U.S. Navy. He was seventeen when he stepped aboard the ship *Ganges,* on which he traveled to the West Indies to take part in actions against the French, who were interfering with trade in the area. There Macdonough survived a bout with yellow fever, a serious disease common to tropical regions.

In 1801 the U.S. government ordered a reduction in the size of the navy, and Macdonough was almost pushed out. But his father's influential friends intervened again. Soon he was headed across the ocean to the Mediterranean region, where the U.S. Navy had gone to head off piracy by the Barbary States. These were countries along the northern coast of Africa (such as Algeria, Morocco, Tripoli, and Tunisia) who had broken treaties in which they had agreed not to interfere with American trade.

At the beginning of his tour of duty, Macdonough served on the USS *Constellation* under Captain Alexander Morris, who was very conscientious about training young seamen. Macdonough received a thorough education in all the skills a young naval officer would need, such as navigation and gunnery. He had been transferred to the *Philadelphia* when the ship succeeded in capturing an enemy ship, the *Mirboka*; Macdonough was made second officer on the captured vessel.

Moving up the ranks

In 1803 Macdonough joined the crew of the *Enterprise,* which was commanded by a dynamic young captain named Stephen Decatur Jr. (1779–1820), who also would become a naval star during the War of 1812. In this position Macdonough formed what would be a lifelong friendship with Decatur, and also took part in two important actions. In February 1804 he aided in the burning of his former ship, the *Philadelphia,* which had been captured by the enemy. Six months later Macdonough took part in the capturing of two Tripolitan gunboats. In recognition of his good performance, Macdonough was made an acting (not yet official) first lieutenant on the *Enterprise* (the promotion would become permanent in 1807).

Macdonough had recently returned to the United States when, in October 1806, he was ordered to Middletown, Connecticut, to join Captain Isaac Hull (1773–1825) in constructing new gunboats for the U.S. Navy. Macdonough spent three months in Middletown, during which he made some good friends, joined the Episcopal church, and met a young woman named Lucy Ann Shaler, whom he would marry six years later.

From 1807 to 1808 Macdonough served as first lieutenant aboard the *Wasp,* spending most of his time cruising along the Atlantic coast to enforce the Embargo Act. This law prohibiting trade between the U.S. and foreign countries was intended to punish France and Great Britain who, in the course of their own war with each other, had been harassing the U.S. shipping industry. The act was repealed in 1809.

The War of 1812 begins

The years 1807 and 1808 were not particularly active or interesting ones for members of the tiny U.S. Navy, so in 1810 Macdonough requested a leave of absence. He spent the next two years making profitable cruises aboard various merchant ships to ports in the East Indies, Great Britain, and India. But then, in June 1812, the United States declared war on Great Britain. The war was provoked by two major issues. The first was Britain's maritime policy of impressment in its war with France. This policy was where British officials boarded U.S. ships to capture deserters from their own navy, often wrongfully taking American citizens in the process. The other issues that led to the war was Great Britain's overly friendly relations with Native Americans. Americans believed that the British were encouraging Native Americans to attack white settlers who were moving west. The Native Americans believed that the settlers were encroaching (gradually taking over) on their land. It was at the beginning of the war that Macdonough returned to active duty. He was ordered to Washington, D.C., to join the *Constellation* as first lieutenant, but he arrived to find the ship not yet ready to go to sea.

The disappointed Macdonough was next given command of a division of gunboats stationed at Portland, Maine. Soon, however, he had a new assignment: to take charge of the U.S. fleet on Lake Champlain, a large body of water wedged between the borders of New York and Vermont. During the Revolutionary War there had been some major battles on the lake but it was now a sleepy, isolated place. The fleet there consisted only of two leaky gunboats and three transport sloops. The British also had maintained a presence on the lake, but it was not much more impressive than that of the United States.

Preparing the fleet at Lake Champlain

The energetic young officer immediately set out to build up the Lake Champlain fleet. Working under difficult conditions—weapons, supplies, equipment, and people (including craftsman to build ships as well as seamen to sail them) had to be moved inland to the lake from the Atlantic seacoast—Macdonough joined forces with Noah Brown (born c. 1770), a highly skilled shipbuilder from New York. They started by adding more guns to two of the existing sloops, the *Growler* and the *Eagle,* so that each were equipped with eleven guns. (Sloops were small warships with guns on only one deck.)

With the arrival of cold weather came a halt to the work, and in late 1812 Macdonough went into his winter quarters at Shelburne, Vermont. The spring thaw brought a renewed effort, but there was a setback during the summer of 1813. One of the officers serving under Macdonough made a strategic error when he sent the fleet's sloops too far down the Richelieu River (which branched off from Lake Champlain) and the *Growler* and *Eagle* were both captured by the British.

The two fleets are ready for battle

In July the Navy showed its confidence in Macdonough by making him a master-commandant. By September, Macdonough felt that his fleet of three sloops and two gunboats was ready for action, but the British had now retreated into Canadian waters. When 1814 began, both the United States and Great Britain stepped up their construction programs. By summer, the U.S. fleet consisted of thirteen ships, including Macdonough's flagship (the ship flying the American flag and on which Macdonough himself would sail during a battle) *Saratoga,* carrying twenty-six guns, and the *Ticonderoga* (seventeen guns) as well as three sloops and six gunboats.

Not yet satisfied, Macdonough asked the Navy to approve construction of another ship. Less than five weeks after construction had begun on this vessel, the 20-gun *Eagle* was launched on August 11.

U.S. lake patrols had detected signs that the British were ready to launch a major offensive. Indeed, the recently improved British fleet was ready, and fully expecting to destroy or capture the American ships. Captain George Downie (d. 1814) commanded the *Confiance* (thirty-seven guns), the *Linnet* (sixteen guns), the *Chubb* (eleven guns), and the *Finch* (eleven guns), along with twelve gunboats. (The brand-new *Confiance* would be under construction until just before the battle.)

Careful planning leads to victory

Macdonough thought long and carefully about how the United States should proceed, concluding that a cautious approach was best. He wanted to put off a confrontation until circumstances favored the U.S. side; in a June letter to a fellow naval officer, as quoted in David and Jeanne Heidler's *Encyclopedia of the War of 1812,* Macdonough had noted that "Tis better to save a force by retiring from a superior foe than to lose it even by hard fighting." Knowing that the British ships were equipped with many long-range guns, while the strength of the U.S. vessels lay in their short-range weapons, Macdonough decided to keep his ships inside Plattsburg Bay rather than sending them out onto the lake.

On the morning of September 11, the enemy appeared in Plattsburg Bay, and the battle began. The *Saratoga* and the *Confiance* were the first to engage, and the *Saratoga* immediately took a broadside (in which a ship fires all of the guns on one side at the same time) that killed forty men. The crews' drooping spirits were lifted when they heard the loud crowing of a rooster that had escaped from its cage and flown into the ship's sails. The men cheered and kept fighting.

In a battle that lasted only an hour and a half, dominance and luck kept shifting from one side to the other. Downie was killed in the first fifteen minutes of the battle, delivering a big blow to British morale. Macdonough fared better, although he was knocked down twice (once by the

Letters from Commodore Thomas Macdonough

The following letter comprises a part of Macdonough's report to Secretary of the Navy William Jones on the U.S. victory at Lake Champlain on September 10, 1814.

U.S. Ship Saratoga, Plattsburg Bay, September 13th, 1814.

SIR,

I have the honour to give you the particulars of the action which took place on the 11th instant, on this lake.

For several days the enemy were on their way to Plattsburg by land and water, and it being well understood that an attack would be made at the same time by their land and naval forces, I determined to await, at anchor, the approach of the latter.

At eight A.M. the look-out boat announced the approach of the enemy. At nine, he anchored in a line ahead, at about 300 yards distance from my line; his ship opposed the *Saratoga*, his brig to the *Eagle.*

In this situation, the whole force on both sides, became engaged, the *Saratoga* suffering much, from the heavy fire of the *Confiance.* I could perceive at the same time, however, that our fire was very destructive to her. The *Ticonderoga,* lieutenant commander Cassin, gallantly sustained her full share of the action. At half past 10 o'clock, the *Eagle* not being able to bring her guns to bear, cut her cable, and anchored in a more eligible position, between my ship and the *Ticonderoga,* where she very much annoyed the enemy, but unfortunately, leaving me exposed to a galling fire from the enemy's brig. Our guns on the starboard side being nearly all dismounted, or not manageable, a stern anchor was let go, the bower cut, and the ship winded with a fresh broadside on the enemy's ship, which soon after surrendered. Our broadside was then sprung to bear on the brig, which surrendered in about 15 minutes after.

The sloop that was opposed to the *Eagle,* had struck some time before, and drifted down the line; the sloop which was

severed head of a soldier). When the battle finally did come to an end, it was due to a brilliant move devised by Macdonough. Before the battle began, he had secured the *Saratoga* with a special anchor that allowed the ship to be maneuvered around without the aid of wind. Thus the Americans were able to surprise the British by pivoting the *Saratoga* around to deliver a fresh broadside to the *Confiance.* The British ship tried to respond with the same maneuver but it had been too heavily damaged, and the British fleet soon surrendered. British casualties (men killed, wounded, or captured) num-

with their gallies having struck also. Three of their gallies are said to be sunk, the others pulled off. Our gallies were about obeying with alacrity, the signal to follow them, when all the vessels were reported to me to be in a sinking state; then it became necessary to annul the signal to the gallies, and order their men to the pumps. I could only look at the enemy's gallies going off in a shattered condition, for there was not a mast in either squadron that could stand to make sail on; the lower rigging being nearly shot away, hung down as though it had been just placed over mastheads.

The *Saratoga* had 55 round shot in her hull, the *Confiance* 105. The enemy's shot passed principally over our heads, as there were not 20 whole hammocks in the nettings at the close of the action, which lasted, without intermission, two hours and twenty minutes.

...Acting lieutenant Vallette worked the 1st and 2nd division of guns with able effect. Sailing master Brum's attention to the springs, and in the order to wind the ship, and occasionally at the guns met my entire approbation; also captain Youngs, commanding the acting marines, who took his men to the guns, and in carrying my orders through the ship with midshipman Montgomery. Master's mate Joshua Justin had command of the third division; his conduct during the action was that of a brave officer. Midshipmen Monteath, Graham, Williamson, Platt, Thwing and acting-midshipman Baldwin, all behaved well and gave evidence of their making valuable officers. The *Saratoga* was twice set on fire, by hot shot from the enemy's ship.

I close, sir, this communication, with feelings of gratitude, for the able support I received from every officer and man attached to the squadron which I have the honour to command.

I have the honour to be etc.
T. MACDONOUGH

Source: "The War on Lake Champlain 2." Copies of Official Documents. [Online] http://www.cronab.demon.co.uk/lake2.htm (accessed on November 26, 2001).

bered more than one hundred, while the Americans lost only fifty-seven men. Most of the British ships were captured.

Hailed as a hero

The victory at the Battle of Lake Champlain (also called the Battle of Plattsburg) proved to be one of the finest moments in the entire history of the U.S. Navy. It crushed British hopes of gaining dominance and new ground in the north and put the United States in a stronger position for the peace negotiations, which had just begun at Ghent, Belgium. The victory also was a general morale booster for the American public, and particularly welcome after the late-August sacking of Washington, D.C., where the British burned many of the public buildings in the capital city.

Praised for the careful planning and foresight he had practiced before the battle as well as his coolness and bravery while it raged, Macdonough became a nationally known hero. He also received many material rewards, including a Congressional medal, $22,000 in prize money (naval crews were allowed to split the profits gained from captured ships), and even large plots of land donated by grateful citizens of New York and Vermont. On November 18, Macdonough was promoted to the rank of captain.

The war ended in early 1815. Macdonough went on to command the U.S. naval yard at Portsmouth, New Hampshire, for three years. In 1818 he was given command of the *Guerriere* and assigned to deliver U.S. diplomat G. W. Campbell to his post as minister (diplomatic representative) to Russia. Macdonough briefly joined the navy squadron stationed on the Mediterranean Sea, but a disagreement with the commanding officer there resulted in his return to the United States. In 1820 he assumed command of the seventy-four-gun *Ohio*, and four years later he returned to the Mediterranean, this time as commander of the squadron.

Macdonough had contracted tuberculosis (a serious disease of the lungs that was not then treatable) while serving on Lake Champlain, and he had never fully recovered. His health now took a turn for the worse, so he set out for the United States aboard the merchant ship *Edwin*. The forty-one-year-old Macdonough died at sea while he was still about six hundred miles from the U.S. coast. His body was taken to New York and given military honors and a memorial service there, then buried in Middletown, Connecticut.

For More Information

Books
Eckert, Edward K. "Thomas Macdonough: Architect of a Wilderness Navy." In ed., *Command under Sail: Makers of the American Naval Tra-*

dition, edited by James C. Bradford. Annapolis, M.D.: Naval Institute Press, 1985.

Heidler, David S., and Jeanne T. Heidler, eds. *Encyclopedia of the War of 1812.* Santa Barbara, Calif.: ABC-CLIO, Inc., 1997.

Hickey, Donald R. *The War of 1812: A Forgotten Conflict.* Urbana: University of Illinois Press, 1989.

Web sites

War of 1812. [Online] http://www.galafilm.com/1812/e/index.html (accessed on November 26, 2001).

"War of 1812." *KidInfo.* [Online] http://www.kidinfo.com/American_History/warof1812.html (accessed on November 26, 2001).

Dolley Madison

Born May 20, 1768
Guilford County, North Carolina

Died July 12, 1849
Washington, D.C.

First lady, wife of President James Madison

olley Madison gained fame not just because she was married to President James Madison (1751–1836; see biographical entry) but also as a vibrant, unforgettable individual in her own right. She was respected and admired for her lively, warm personality, her elegant but often unconventional sense of style, and her ability to make a wide variety of people feel comfortable. Valued by her husband both as a companion and for the grace and energy she brought to her role as first lady, she earned the nation's admiration during the War of 1812 when she kept official documents and other items—including a famous portrait of George Washington (1732–1799), the first president of the United States—out of British hands when Washington, D.C., was invaded and burned.

Raised as a Quaker

Madison's parents, John and Mary (Coles) Payne, were Virginia residents of English, Scottish, and Irish descent. Her parents were members of the Society of Quakers, a religion whose members believe that all people are equal, and

Portrait: Dolley Madison.
Photograph courtesy of the National Archives and Records Administration.

219

stress the values of hard work, cooperation, pacifism (a refusal to engage in violent conflict), and modest dress and manners. Dolley was born in North Carolina where her parents spent a year before returning to their Virginia plantation. She is sometimes referred to as Dorothy or Dorothea but was always called Dolley.

Growing up on the family's Virginia plantation, called Scotchtown, Dolley Madison was educated by private tutors and also attended the local Quaker school. At this time her grandmother became a major influence on her life because they shared a fondness for beautiful clothing and jewelry, which was discouraged by the Quaker religion. In 1783 when Madison was fifteen (and the same year in which the Revolutionary War [1775–83] ended), her father freed the slaves who worked on his plantation and moved his family to Philadelphia, Pennsylvania.

John Payne started a starch-making business that was not successful, and in 1789 his company went bankrupt. This failure plunged him into despair, and he died less than five years later. Meanwhile Dolley was witness to all the interesting political events taking place in Philadelphia during this period, especially the Constitutional Convention. At this meeting held between May and September of 1787, delegates from twelve of the thirteen colonies met to formulate a new government for the country. One of the delegates, and a major shaper of the Constitution, was future president James Madison.

Marriage and motherhood

Before Dolley met Madison, many young men were interested in the young woman with blue eyes and curly black hair. She resisted them all, however, until a Quaker lawyer named John Todd proposed. Dolley married him in 1790, and two years later she gave birth to a son named John Payne (called Payne). Another son, William Temple, was born the next year.

But in 1793 an epidemic of yellow fever swept through Philadelphia, killing both her husband and her youngest son. Madison also fell ill, but recovered to find herself a young widow with a son to support. Eventually she rejoined the social circle of which she had been a part before her husband's death, which included many politicians.

"The great little Madison"

Among her political acquaintances was Aaron Burr (1756–1836). One day he told her that his friend, a Virginia legislator named James Madison, wanted to meet her. Dolly had heard about Madison, who had already gained a reputation as a brilliant thinker and statesman. She called him "the great little Madison" in a letter she wrote to a friend, and indeed, Madison was only five feet four inches tall and weighed about a hundred pounds. He was a forty-three-year-old bachelor who always appeared very quiet and reserved in public, even though his friends found him charming and witty.

Despite the nineteen-year age difference, their personality differences, and Dolley's Quakerism, they were married on September 15, 1794. (Dolley was expelled from the Quaker church for marrying outside the Quaker community.) Their union lasted forty-two years and was, by all reports, full of love, friendship, and appreciation for each other's talents. Although they had no children, their household included Dolley's son Payne and her sister Anna and Madison's niece Nelly.

Soon the friendly, fashionable Dolley Madison was a popular Philadelphia hostess. Her shy husband seemed to blossom in her presence, becoming more talkative and even developing a love for dancing. In 1797 Madison retired from Congress and the family moved to his five-thousand-acre plantation, Montpelier, in Orange County, Virginia, where they lived the quiet life of a farming family.

Moving to Washington, D.C.

In 1801 President Thomas Jefferson (1743–1826) took office and appointed his trusted friend, colleague, and fellow member of the Republican Party James Madison as his secretary of state. The Madisons moved to Washington, D.C., the new capital of the United States.

Dolley Madison adapted as well to the Washington social world as she had to that of Philadelphia, but here she had an interesting new duty. Jefferson's wife had died many years earlier, and he asked Dolley to serve as hostess during White House functions—a role to which she was well suited.

James Madison was Jefferson's hand-picked successor as president. By the time he won the 1808 presidential election, his wife was already well known and much loved in Washington society. Dolley Madison always wore the latest fashions, and liked to make a stir by trying unusual styles (an example is her habit of wrapping a scarf around her head, which became known as the "Dolley turban.") Her dinner parties and banquets featured the delicious, rich food she loved (as her plump figure showed), including a new treat called ice cream.

A popular First Lady

Dolley brought a new style and several new traditions to the White House. Madison's election was followed by the first inaugural ball (a dance held when a new president takes office), and Dolley started the yearly tradition of the Easter Egg Roll on the White House lawn. Invitations to parties and other functions were extended not just to political figures but writers, artists, and other interesting people. A wide variety of people—from members of European royalty to Native American chiefs—were all treated in the same kind, relaxed manner. She also took a great interest in political matters, encouraging her husband to share his thoughts and ideas with her.

There were, of course, those who found fault with Dolley. She was criticized for her fondness for cards, racetrack gambling, snuff (a form of tobacco that is chewed), unconventional fashions, and fattening foods. Overall, Madison was extremely popular, however, and invitations to her functions were much sought-after. Every Wednesday evening she held special gatherings—which some called "Mrs. Madison's Crush" because they were often so crowded—where guests discussed the serious matters of the day, often with the president himself, in an informal setting.

The war comes closer to Washington

The War of 1812 between the United States and Great Britain was provoked by two major issues. The first was

Britain's maritime policy of impressment in its war with France. This policy was where British officials boarded U.S. ships to capture deserters from their own navy, often wrongfully taking American citizens in the process. The other issue that led to the war was Great Britain's overly friendly relations with Native Americans. Americans believed that the British were encouraging Native Americans to attack white settlers who were moving west. The Native Americans believed that the settlers were encroaching on (gradually taking over) their land.

During the War of 1812 Dolley toned down her entertaining somewhat but did not completely stop, for she thought that parties and gatherings would help to keep people's spirits high during a troubling time. For a while the war was fought at a considerable distance from the capital, Washington, D.C., but in the summer of 1814, the British landed in the Chesapeake Bay area (about fifty miles away). Few preparations had been made to defend the city.

On August 22 James Madison rode north to view the situation at Bladensburg, Maryland, where U.S. forces (comprising mainly militiamen, temporary members of state-sponsored armies that were generally inferior to regular army troops) were preparing to meet the British in battle. Dolley waited anxiously for news from her husband. His first message was reassuring, as recorded in Robert Rutland's *The Presidency of James Madison*: "The reports as to the enemy have varied every hour. The last and probably truest information is that they are not very strong ... and of course they are not in a condition to strike at Washington."

Two days later, the British defeated the outnumbered and less experienced American troops at Bladensburg and, in the evening, began to march toward Washington. Earlier that day, Dolley had received a second message from her husband, this one urgently instructing her to leave the city. She hurriedly packed official papers and documents in trunks, as well as much of the White House silver and other items.

Dolley had to leave behind most of her own personal belongings, but she made sure that a number of important documents and the famous portrait of George Washington by the celebrated American painter Gilbert Stuart (1755–1828) was saved. Due to a shortage of time and space it had to be cut out of its frame for removal. In her memoirs, Dolley remembered that she "lived a lifetime in those moments."

The British invade and burn the capital

As her carriage left Washington for the Virginia countryside, Dolley saw crowds of people who also were fleeing the city. Arriving at a roadside inn at Great Falls, Virginia, Dolley found the innkeeper reluctant to admit her. The tide of public opinion had turned against James Madison's apparent ineffectual handling of the war. Nevertheless the Madisons were reunited that night, but the president soon left her to rejoin the U.S. forces at Baltimore.

The British, meanwhile, had entered the nation's capital unopposed. Several officers went into the White House to find the table set for a banquet for forty people, and they proceeded to consume the food and wine that Dolley had intended for her own guests. Their meal finished, the British burned down the White House, destroying all of its contents; they also burned a number of other public buildings. Such destruction was unusual in countries that observed international standards of war, but the British were retaliating for the destruction of public buildings when the United States had sacked York, Canada, earlier in the war. The Madisons returned to Washington on August 27 to find much of the city destroyed. With the White House in ruins, the Madisons moved into a residence called the Octagon House, and Dolley Madison resumed her active social life.

More peaceful years

A treaty was signed with Great Britain on December 14, 1814, and American general Andrew Jackson (1767–1845; see biographical entry) dealt a final blow to the British with the Battle of New Orleans. In 1816 James Monroe (1758–1831; see biographical entry) was elected president, and the Madisons retired to Montpelier. Besides a beautifully decorated house, the plantation also comprised farm buildings and slave quarters (despite his opposition to slavery, James Madison never freed the slaves on his own plantation), pear orchards and grape arbors, and fields in which grains and tobacco were grown.

These years were not completely free from worry, however. Dolley's son Payne had grown up to be an irresponsible, restless young man prone to drinking and gambling. Eventually he was many thousands of dollars in debt, and James Madison had to repay these debts to keep his stepson out of jail.

Financial troubles

The Madisons' financial problems were made worse by a general depression in Virginia agriculture in the years

following the war. Determined not only to preserve important national records but to provide his wife with a source of
income after his death, James Madison began to organize the
papers he had produced during his long career in politics.
Dolley helped her husband to organize and edit the documents. She also nursed him throughout the illness that led to
his death in 1836.

In 1837 Dolley returned to Washington. Once again
she was an important figure on the Washington social scene,
offering advice to the first ladies of presidents Martin Van
Buren (1782–1862), John Tyler (1790–1862), and James Polk
(1795–1849). That same year, she was able to bolster her income by selling Madison's notes on the Constitutional Convention to Congress for thirty thousand dollars.

In 1844 Dolley was forced to sell Montpelier, which she
had left to the management of her son, a spendthrift and alco-
holic. Four years later, she sold Madison's correspondence to
Congress for twenty-five thousand dollars, but she did not receive the payment until just before her death. She made her last
public appearance at a White House reception in 1849, escorted
through the rooms of her former home by President Polk.

After a five-day illness, Dolley died in Washington on
July 17, 1849. She was eighty-one years old. Her funeral was attended by an impressive array of both officials (including the
president and his cabinet, diplomats, members of Congress,
Supreme Court justices, army and navy officers, and the mayor
of Washington, D.C.) and private citizens. Madison's body was
initially laid to rest in the Congressional Cemetery, but eventually her remains were removed to her beloved Montpelier.

For More Information

Books

Arnett, Ethel Stephens. *Mrs. James Madison: The Incomparable Dolley.*
Greensboro, N.C.: Piedmont Press, 1972.

Davidson, Mary R. *Dolly Madison: Famous First Lady.* New York: Chelsea
Juniors, 1992.

Flanagan, Alice K. *Dolley Payne Todd Madison, 1768–1849.* Danbury,
Conn.: Children's Press, 1997.

Gerson, Noel B. *The Velvet Glove, a Life of Dolly Madison.* New York: Penguin Putnam Books for Young Readers, 1975.

Madison, Dolley. *Memoirs and Letters of Dolley Madison, Wife of James Madison, President of the United States.* Boston and New York: Houghton Mifflin, 1888.

Moore, Virginia. *The Madisons: A Biography.* New York: The McGraw-Hill Companies, 1979.

Rutland, Robert Allen. *The Presidency of James Madison.* Lawrence, Kans.: University Press of Kansas, 1990.

Web sites

Dolley Payne Todd Madison: 1768–1849. [Online] http://www.whitehouse.gov/history/firstladies/dm4.html (accessed on November 26, 2001).

War of 1812. [Online] http://www.galafilm.com/1812/e/index.html (accessed on November 26, 2001).

James Madison

Born March 16, 1751
Port Conway, Virginia

Died June 28, 1836
Montpelier, Virginia

Politician, president of the United States

James Madison was a guiding light among the group of men who created and defended the United States Constitution, which established a government structure that continues to survive. A shy person of small stature—he stood only five feet, four inches tall and weighed about one hundred pounds—Madison achieved greatness as a political thinker. He was devoted to balancing the interests of the Union with individual liberties, and he was good at making compromises to achieve that balance. While serving as president during the unpopular and problematic War of 1812, Madison was criticized for weak leadership. Yet when the war was over, Americans were more optimistic than they had ever been, and Madison's popularity rose again. He is credited with leading the United States in a valiant struggle to retain its independence and national honor during the war.

A privileged childhood

James Madison was born into privilege. He was the oldest of twelve children of wealthy tobacco grower James

Portrait: James Madison. *Photograph courtesy of the National Archives and Records Administration.*

229

Madison Sr. and Nellie Conway Madison, who also came from a wealthy family. The future president was born at his maternal grandparents' home in Port Conway, Virginia and grew up at Montpelier, his family's five-thousand-acre plantation. Madison lived at Montpelier his whole life, except for those periods when his role as an elected official kept him away.

A period of doubt

After graduating from the College of New Jersey (now Princeton University), Madison considered a career as a minister but, unable to decide what path to take, he returned to Montpelier. There he entered one of the bouts of illness and depression that he was to experience throughout his adult life. An intellectual with a love of sophisticated culture, Madison felt isolated on the plantation, and was plagued by indecision about what to do with his life.

It wasn't long before Madison's gloom lifted, as he began to breathe the scent of rebellion that was in the air. At this time, the American colonies were starting to become annoyed with British rule. Leaders who spoke of independence and democracy were emerging, and Madison began to debate their ideas with a local group. In 1774 the soft-spoken but brilliant Madison was elected to Virginia's Committee of Safety, which would serve as the colony's government during the American Revolution (1775–83).

A young legislator gains experience

Two years later, Madison joined the Virginia Convention, where delegates would draft a new constitution and declaration of rights for their state. There Madison met another Virginia delegate named Thomas Jefferson (1743–1826), who had just returned from Philadelphia, Pennsylvania, where he had authored the Declaration of Independence. In 1778 he was appointed to serve on the Governor's Council under Governor Patrick Henry (1736–1799). When Jefferson succeeded Henry as governor of Virginia, Madison began to work closely with him, and the two began a lifelong collaboration and friendship.

The Revolutionary War was now in full swing. Madison served in the Continental Congress, the body established to serve as the colonies' central government, from 1780 to 1783. When he entered the Congress at age twenty-nine, he was the youngest representative. During these years he honed his skills as a debater and legislator, emerging from the experience as a seasoned politician.

The need for a new form of government

After serving as a delegate to the Annapolis Convention, a meeting called to resolve some trade issues between the states of Virginia and Maryland, Madison was appointed to the Virginia delegation to Constitutional Convention. Members of the convention fashioned a document called the Virginia Plan, their concept—authored primarily by Madison—of how the new government should be shaped.

The Constitution: Madison's brilliant plan

Most commentators agree that the formulation of the Constitution was Madison's greatest achievement. The government he proposed through the Virginia Plan included an elected executive (the president) with the power to veto legislation, a federal judiciary branch (the courts or justice system), and a two-body legislature (the law-making body, which in the United States is the Congress). Each branch would have certain responsibilities, but each would be controlled by a system of checks and balances. This meant that because the branches would be able to approve or disapprove each other's actions, none of them could become more powerful than the others.

In 1788 Madison was elected to the brand-new House of Representatives, and he soon became one of its most distinguished legislators. One of his first tasks was to assist in the passage of the Bill of Rights, a set of twelve amendments to the Constitution that were designed to safeguard such individual rights as the freedom to practice one's own religion, to express (and publish) one's beliefs, and to gather together to peacefully protest government policies.

Disagreeing with the Federalists

In 1789 George Washington (1732–1799) unanimously became the first president of the United States. However, by 1792, Madison and Jefferson had become increasingly opposed to the Federalist slant of Washington's administration. (The Federalist Party supported a strong central or federal government.) Gradually, those who agreed with Madison and Jefferson became known as anti-Federalists. When war broke out between Great Britain and France in 1793, differences between the two viewpoints became even more pronounced. Eager to maintain the commercial ties with Great Britain that had been re-established after the Revolutionary War, the Federalists sided with the British. The anti-Federalists sympathized with the French, who had assisted the United States so ably in its fight for independence and who had recently waged their own revolution.

A brief retreat to Montpelier

In 1796 Federalist John Adams (1735–1826) won the U.S. presidential election. Discouraged by what he saw as a decline in his own influence, Madison retired from Congress in 1797. Three years earlier, he had married Dolley Payne Todd (1768–1849; see biographical entry), a lively twenty-six-year-old widow he had met in Philadelphia. Probably concerned about his aging parents and perhaps longing for the tranquility of rural Virginia, Madison and his wife moved back to Montpelier. There he enjoyed a happy married life and ran his plantation while also keeping on eye on political developments.

Madison was soon pulled back into politics, however, by the passage of the Alien and Sedition Acts, which were designed, in part, to stifle criticism of the government. To Madison, this stirred memories of Great Britain's attempts to limit freedom in its former colonies. Convinced the laws were a direct threat to freedom of speech and freedom of the press and thus unconstitutional, he sponsored the Virginia Resolution in his state's legislature. This document, which says that states have the right to oppose federal laws they consider unconstitutional, was matched by a similar resolution sponsored by Jefferson in the Kentucky legislature.

A new political party is formed

Opposition to the Alien and Sedition Acts among the anti-Federalists was a leading factor in the formation of a new political party led by Madison and Jefferson. During the next several years, the Democratic-Republicans (eventually referred to as simply the Republicans) would gain dominance in national affairs as more and more citizens came to consider them the champions of ordinary people's interests.

In fact, by 1800 the political party had garnered so much popularity that Jefferson was elected as the nation's third president. He appointed Madison as secretary of state, which gave Madison responsibility for foreign policy issues. The two friends worked closely together through the major events of Jefferson's first term, especially the Louisiana Purchase, in which France sold a huge piece of territory west of the Mississippi to the United States for only fifteen million dollars. Both Jefferson and Madison were eager to acquire more territory into which U.S. settlers could move; in fact, this would be one of the motivations for the War of 1812, as the United States saw an opportunity to acquire land in both Canada and Spanish-held Florida.

Jefferson's second term was dominated by the growing problems connected to the ongoing war between England and France. Unable to dominate Great Britain militarily, Napoleon Bonaparte (1769–1821)—the emperor of France—had established the Continental System, which prevented neutral countries from trading with Great Britain. In response, Great Britain had put in place the Orders in Council, which similarly punished countries that continued to trade with France. The United States was caught in the middle, and its ships were being seized by both countries.

In addition, the British were carrying on a practice called impressment by which men they considered British citizens and deserters from their navy were taken from U.S. ships and forced back into military service. Many U.S. citizens (or former British citizens who had become Americans) had been illegally impressed. Americans were incensed by this practice, especially after the *Chesapeake-Leopard* incident, when the captain of the USS *Chesapeake* refused to allow British sailors from the HMS *Leopard* aboard to reclaim alleged deserters. As a result, the British attacked the *Chesapeake* and several were sailors killed.

Trying to avoid war

Convinced that the United States was not ready for another war with Great Britain, Madison urged Jefferson to try to resolve the problem through economic means. The resulting Embargo Act of 1807, which eliminated all U.S. trade with other nations, was intended to teach both France and Great Britain a lesson. The act, however, proved a disaster for the U.S. economy.

As Jefferson's second term came to an end, he wanted his friend Madison to succeed him. Despite growing dissatisfaction with the "Virginia dynasty"—the group of Virginia politicians, including Jefferson, Madison, and Monroe, that had dominated politics during the last two decades—Madison won the 1808 presidential election. With his victory he inherited the continuing problems of trade restrictions and impressment and the very real possibility of war. In his inaugural speech, Madison stated that the United States would not put up with interference from other nations, but this tough talk did nothing to change the situation.

"Mr. Madison's War"

Meanwhile, some young members of Congress felt passionately that war with Great Britain was a good idea. Nicknamed the War Hawks, these men (most of whom were from the western and southern states) resented British interference in U.S. trade and shipping and thought the United States should defend its national honor by striking back. They also claimed that the British were involved in arming Native Americans in the Northwest Territories (what would become the states of Ohio, Michigan, Indiana, Illinois, and parts of Minnesota) and even encouraging them to attack white American settlers in that region. The War Hawks believed that a war with Great Britain would give the United States a chance to expand its territory by annexing the British colony of Canada as well as Spanish-held Florida.

Toward the end of 1811, Congress began debating the prospect of war. The Federalists, many of them representing the northeastern states, argued that entering a war with Great Britain would only cause further damage to the American economy, and that an invasion of Canada was unnecessary and ill-advised. Seven months later, on June 1, 1812, Madison sent Congress a "War Message" in which he stated that Great Britain's actions had made war unavoidable.

Although Congress approved the declaration of war on June 18, the close votes in both the House of Representatives and the Senate showed that there was considerable opposition to the war. Not surprisingly, all of the Federalists in Congress had voted against the war, but a substantial number of Republicans also were against it. These divisions would grow deeper and more troublesome for Madison as the conflict, which his critics immediately began to call "Mr. Madison's War," continued.

Only a few days before the declaration of war was signed, Great Britain had cancelled its Orders in Council, but the slowness of communication (the news could only travel by ship across the Atlantic Ocean) meant that the news arrived too late; in addition, the British still did not agree to end the practice of impressment. The war would proceed, despite a startling lack of U.S. military and financial preparation for it. Neither the army nor the navy had adequate soldiers or sailors to effectively fight a war, and neither the secretary of war, William Eustis (1753–1825), nor the secretary of the navy, Paul Hamilton (1762–1816) had the experience to direct the effort.

A disappointing start

It's not at all surprising, then, that the first year of the war did not go smoothly. There were some unexpected victories at sea, such as the defeat of the HMS *Guerriere* by the USS *Constitution*, but the U.S. invasion of Canada failed due to poor planning and leadership and an over-reliance on state militias (armies made up not of professional soldiers but of private citizens who fight on an emergency, temporary basis), who often refused to fight. The surrender of U.S. troops at Detroit to a much smaller British force added to the mood of humiliation and anxiety that dominated the country as 1812 drew to a close.

Madison was just barely re-elected to the presidency in 1812. Widely faulted for weak leadership, he was especially criticized for failing to get rid of the incompetent people in his administration. The Federalists and a sizable number of Republicans who were dissatisfied with Madison backed New York statesmen DeWitt Clinton (1769–1828) in the election, and he almost beat Madison. The close election served as something of a wake-up call to Madison, who reshuffled his cabinet at the beginning of 1813. Eustis and Hamilton were replaced with John Armstrong (1758–1843) and William Jones (1760–1831), both men of solid military experience.

Both victories and defeats in 1813

During the course of the next year, the military began slowly improving as Congress authorized funds to build up its numbers and as younger, more skilled and dynamic officers were promoted to replace the Revolutionary War veterans who had been in charge at the beginning of the war. In 1813 the United States won a few significant victories, including those at York (now Toronto), on Lake Erie, and at the Battle of the Thames.

Madison had suffered from a long illness in the early summer of 1813 from which he nearly died. His recovery was about all he had to celebrate, though, especially after some ominous news arrived from Europe in the fall. Great Britain and its allies had defeated Napoleon's troops at the Battle of Leipzig, and the tide in the Napoleonic Wars seemed to be turning. The French emperor was on the run now, and his defeat would free up thousands of British troops for service in the war with the United States.

Meanwhile, addressing Congress at the end of 1813, Madison tried to sound optimistic about the prospects for a U.S. victory, but there was no overcoming the bleak mood that prevailed in Congress and around the country. On December 30, however, a glimmer of hope arrived in the form of an offer from Great Britain to begin peace negotiations. Madison quickly approved the offer. Another year of war remained, though, before peace would be reached.

The British burn Washington, D.C.

In July 1814 Madison and a few other leaders began to worry that the British were planning to attack Washington,

D.C. Armstrong, however, strongly believed that Great Britain's target would be Baltimore, Maryland, a major shipping center and a more strategic target than the nation's capital. Therefore, Armstrong devoted most of the available military resources (especially troops) to Baltimore. As August approached, however, it became clear that an attack on Washington was probable, and defensive preparations were quickly begun.

The British landed in the Chesapeake Bay on August 18 and began their march toward Washington, which they had decided to attack from the north. On August 24 a force of inexperienced, hastily assembled U.S. troops—most of them militiamen—were thoroughly defeated by the British force at Bladensburg, Maryland. The British then marched south and entered Washington, which most residents had already left. After visiting Bladensburg just before the battle began, Madison had retreated into the Virginia countryside outside of Washington, D.C. He was joined at a roadside inn by his wife Dolley, who had left the capital with a load of official documents and other treasures, including a famous portrait of George Washington.

In retaliation for the burning of public buildings when U.S. troops occupied York in Canada, the British ransacked and destroyed the Capitol, the president's home, and other government buildings. Then they marched north to attack Baltimore, but they found that city much better defended. Unable to defeat Baltimore's U.S. defenders with either their land or naval forces, the British retreated.

In Ghent, Belgium, peace negotiations between the United States and Great Britain began in August. Madison sent a set of able statesmen representing a variety of backgrounds and viewpoints: diplomat John Quincy Adams (1767–1848); James Bayard (1767–1815), a Federalist senator known for his moderate views; Speaker of the House Henry Clay (1777–1852; see biographical entry), the leader of the War Hawks; and Madison's longtime, trusted ally Albert Gallatin (1761–1849), the former secretary of the treasury.

In October, Madison heard the first, discouraging news about what was happening in Ghent. The British were asking for too much, especially in their demand that most of the Northwest Territory be made into a Native American homeland. It appeared that the United States would continue fighting the war as 1815 approached. As the year drew to a close, a mood of discontent prevailed over much of the United States. The newspapers expressed impatience with Congress and with Madison's administration. In New England, delegates to a special meeting called the Hartford Convention expressed heir complaints against the way they felt the Madison administration had treated their region.

End of the war

With the new year, however, came a change of fortune—or at least of attitude—for the United States. On January 8, after a series of preliminary skirmishes (small gunfights or battles), the British attacked New Orleans with a large force of seasoned soldiers who had recently fought Napoleon's troops in Europe. Under Major General Andrew Jackson's (1767–1845; see biographical entry) strong leadership, a diverse assortment of regular soldiers, militiamen, Native American allies, and even pirates won a lopsided victory for the United States. The British lost about two thousand men (including three hundred dead and five hundred captured) and the Americans only seventy (including only about a dozen killed).

The news of the signing of the Treaty of Ghent ending the war arrived in the United States in February 1815. As it turned out, the British had given up their previous demands, and both sides had agreed to return to the *status quo antebellum,* the situation that had existed before the war. None of the issues over which the war had supposedly been fought were mentioned in the treaty, for the Orders in Council had been cancelled in June 1812, and impressment was no longer an issue (since the end of the Napoleonic Wars, Great Britain's need for more soldiers had dropped off). In military and political terms, the War of 1812 had ended in a draw.

A new spirit of pride and optimism

Against all expectations, the United States had fought off a much bigger, more experienced force, and now peace was at hand. The Treaty of Ghent had gained nothing for the United States, but that hardly mattered to Americans. After the months and even years of gloom as the war continued with no victory in sight, they were basking in the light of triumph. In the wink of an eye, Madison was transformed from the much-criticized head of a nation at war to the leader of a victorious people who considered themselves capable of almost anything now that they had (or felt that they had) brought Great Britain to its knees. Madison was popular again, and his remaining two years as president were pleasant.

An active retirement

In the presidential election of 1816, Madison was succeeded by his fellow Republican (and member of the Virginia dynasty) James Monroe (1758–1831). Madison retired to Montpelier, where he took up farming again and experimented with new, scientific approaches to agriculture. He offered advice to Monroe when called upon, and helped Jefferson establish the University of Virginia, also serving as the university's rector (president) after Jefferson's death in 1826.

Eighty-six years old when he died at Montpelier, Madison was buried in the family cemetery. In a document titled *Advice to My Country*, which Madison specified was to be opened only after his death, he expressed his wish for the nation he had helped to found: "The advice nearest to my heart and deepest in my convictions is, that the union of the states be cherished and perpetuated."

For More Information

Books

Ketcham, Ralph. *James Madison: A Biography.* Charlottesville: University Press of Virginia, 1971; reprinted., 1992.

Leavell, J. Perry, Jr. *James Madison.* New York: Chelsea House, 1988.

Madison, James. *Letters and Other Writings of James Madison, Published by Order of Congress.* Edited by Philip Fendall. Philadelphia, Penn.: Lippincott, 1865.

Malone, Mary. *James Madison.* Springfield, N.J.: Enslow, 1997.

McCoy, Drew R. *The Last of the Fathers: James Madison and the Republican Legacy.* Cambridge and New York: Cambridge University Press, 1991.

Polikoff, Barbara. *James Madison: 4th President of the United States.* Ada, Okla.: Garrett Educational Corp., 1989.

Rakove, Jack. *James Madison and the Creation of the American Republic.* New York: HarperCollins, 1990.

Rutland, Robert A. *James Madison: The Founding Father.* New York: Macmillan, 1987; reprint, Columbia: University of Missouri Press, 1997.

Web sites

"James Madison." *White House History.* [Online] http://www.whitehouse.gov/history/presidents/jm4.html (accessed on November 26, 2001).

"James Madison: His Legacy." *James Madison Center.* James Madison University. [Online] http://www (accessed on November 26, 2001).

"Madison, James." *American Presidents, Life Portraits.* [Online] http://www.americanpresidents.org/presidents/president.asp?/PresidentNumber=4 (accessed on November 26, 2001).

President James Madison, 4th President of the United States. [Online] http://www.library.advanced.org/12587/contents/personalities/madison/jm.html (accessed on November 26, 2001).

James Monroe

Born April 8, 1758
Westmoreland Country, Virginia

July 4, 1831
New York, New York

Secretary of state,
secretary of war, president of the United
States

M onroe played a key role in the War of 1812, serving as secretary of state during the conflict and also taking over the job of secretary of war in its last few months. He was one of several figures whose wartime accomplishments helped to propel them into political office. In Monroe's case, that office was the presidency. A tall, plain-looking, warm-hearted man who wore the old-fashioned clothes of the Revolutionary War period (1775–83), Monroe was admired for his honesty, his good judgment, and his ability to gauge the mood of his country's citizens.

Caught up in the revolutionary spirit

James Monroe was the eldest of four children born to Spence and Elizabeth Jones Monroe on the family's six-hundred-acre (fairly small, by the standards of the time) plantation in Westmoreland Country, Virginia. When Monroe was sixteen years old his father died, and his much wealthier uncle Joseph Jones, who lived in nearby King George Country, became his guardian. Jones had no children of his own and took a special interest in his young nephew.

Portrait: James Monroe.
Photograph courtesy of The Library of Congress.

241

In 1774 Monroe entered William and Mary College in Williamsburg, Virginia. He was proud of being the first person his family to attend college, but his time at William and Mary would be short. Monroe soon got caught up in the revolutionary spirit that had overtaken the thirteen colonies of America as they declared their independence from Great Britain and began the war that would establish the United States of America, and he enlisted in the Third Virginia Regiment in the spring of 1775.

A strong sense of public service

In 1779 Monroe came back to Virginia in the hope of raising a regiment so that he could serve as a field commander rather than a staff assistant. He felt discouraged when he could not find enough recruits to make up a regiment. It was at this bleak moment in his life that Monroe met Thomas Jefferson (1743–1826), who was then serving as governor of Virginia. Monroe began a friendship with Jefferson, who was fifteen years older, that would last until Jefferson's death in 1826.

In 1786 Monroe married Elizabeth Kortright, the daughter of a New York merchant, who was admired for her beauty as well as her polished, formal manners. The couple moved to Fredericksburg, Virginia, where Monroe set up a law office. After three years Monroe bought a plantation in Albemarle Country, only a few miles from Jefferson's home, Monticello, and within twenty miles of the plantation of future president James Madison (1751–1836; see biographical entry), whom Monroe also had befriended. Monroe ran his farm while also practicing law and serving in the state legislature.

An active role in the new government

Elected to the U.S. Senate in 1790, Monroe worked closely with both Madison—who was then serving in the House of Representatives—and Jefferson, who was serving as vice president under George Washington (1732–1799). The three Virginians were united in their disapproval of the financial policies put forth by Treasury Secretary Alexander Hamilton (c. 1775–1804). They also felt that Washington's administration and followers, who were called Federalists because they advocated a strong central or federal government, favored merchants and city dwellers over farmers and plantation owners and that they were too friendly with Great Britain. With Jefferson and Madison, Monroe took part in the formation of a new political party, whose members came to be known first as Democratic Republicans and later simply as Republicans.

Washington appointed Monroe as minister to France from 1794 to 1796. He then was elected governor of Virginia in 1799. While serving three one-year terms in that office, Monroe demonstrated his strong leadership ability through his calls for legislative actions and his skillful handling of Gabriel's Rebellion, a slave uprising that took place in 1800.

Negotiating the Louisiana Purchase

In January 1803 Monroe was appointed by now president Jefferson to serve as a special envoy (representative) to France to negotiate a site at the mouth of the Mississippi River that Americans could use as a port. Arriving in Paris in April, Monroe met with Robert Livingston (1746–1813), the U.S. minister to France, who had just learned that French emperor Napoleon Bonaparte (1769–1821) was willing to sell all of Louisiana to the United States for fifteen million dollars.

Even though their orders did not authorize such a move, the two Americans immediately signed an agreement with the French. The Louisiana Purchase (an area of more than eight hundred thousand square miles that included the present-day states of Arkansas, Missouri, Iowa, North Dakota, South Dakota, Nebraska, Oklahoma, most of Kansas, and parts of Minnesota, Montana, Wyoming, Colorado, and Louisiana) nearly doubled the size of the United States and opened up a huge new area for settlement.

After four months in France, Monroe moved on to London, where he would serve as the U.S. minister to Great Britain until 1807. During these years he worked hard to get the British to recognize the rights of the United States as a neutral nation, but he could make little headway. A particularly thorny issue was the British practice of impressment, by which sailors (many of them recognized as American citizens by the United States but not by Great Britain) were forcibly removed from U.S. ships and made to serve in the British navy.

Near the end of 1806, Monroe and special envoy William Pinkney (1764–1822) reached an agreement with Great Britain regarding trade issues, but because it did not resolve the impressment issue, Jefferson and Madison (who was serving as secretary of state) rejected it. Monroe returned home in a resentful mood about the treaty, and for the next several years his relationships with Jefferson and Madison were strained. He even allowed some Republican friends to present him as a presidential candidate, running against Madison in the election of 1808, but Madison easily won the election. For the next few years, Monroe kept busy as a Virginia state legislator and also served another term as the state's governor.

Appointed secretary of state

Monroe's rift with the president was healed in 1811, when Madison asked his old friend to become secretary of state. Monroe's diplomatic experience made him a good candidate for the job, and Madison also hoped the move would repair the damaging splits that had occurred in the Republican Party. Monroe quickly became one of Madison's closest advisors. He also built a loyal following in Congress, especially among the group of young leaders called the War Hawks, who favored war with Great Britain as the only way to resolve the continuing issues of neutral trade rights and impressment.

In July 1811 Madison met with Augustus J. Foster, Great Britain's minister to the United States, to try to reach a peaceful solution, but neither country wanted to budge on its demands or practices. Congress met in November and began to seriously discuss the possibility of war. Monroe did his part to support the president, even writing prowar editorials for the *National Intelligencer,* the newspaper that was the administration's main mouthpiece.

When war with Great Britain was declared in June 1812, Monroe remained optimistic that it would end quickly, since he believed that Great Britain was too busy with the war in Europe to carry on a long conflict in North America. Meanwhile, he longed to command soldiers in the field. Madison, however, did not want to offend more experienced officers by assigning Monroe a rank higher than theirs, so Monroe stayed in Washington, D.C., to help plan the war effort.

The war continues

By the end of 1812, disastrous army campaigns in the northwest and along the Niagara River had reflected poorly on Secretary of War William Eustis (1753–1825), who resigned his position as a result. Madison made Monroe the temporary head of the war department, and during the two months he held this job he managed to push a military expansion program through Congress and plan an invasion of Canada for the coming spring. In February, John Armstrong (1758–1843) took over as secretary of war and Monroe returned to his State Department duties. From now on, Armstrong and Monroe would see each other as rivals (because both had set their sights on the presidency), and Armstrong would make sure that Monroe never got the military command he wanted.

In February 1813 the Russian government offered to mediate a peace agreement between the United States and Great Britain. Monroe and Madison immediately accepted, and they sent Treasury Secretary Albert Gallatin (1761–1849) and Senator James Bayard (1767–1815) to St. Petersburg, Russia, to represent the United States. Great Britain, however, rejected the offer, stating that they preferred to negotiate directly with the United States. Toward the end of the year, the British sent their own offer to begin peace talks. Now Speaker of the House Henry Clay (1777–1852; see biographical entry) joined Gallatin and Bayard, as well as diplomat John Quincy Adams (1767–1848) and U.S. chargé d'affaires in Russia (in charge of the diplomatic mission or embassy when no ambassador is in place) Jonathan Russell (1771–1832).

Great Britain launches a counteroffensive

Although there had been a few significant American victories in 1813, in general the war was not going well. The war between Great Britain and France ended with Napoleon's defeat in the spring of 1814. As a result of Great Britain's victory, they mounted a major offensive against the United States, and many more British troops began to arrive in North America. The British had targeted the Chesapeake Bay as one of three areas of concentration (the others were Lake Champlain in the northeastern United States and the Gulf Coast region, including Florida, Mississippi, Alabama, and Louisiana). Some U.S. leaders, including Monroe, feared that the British would attack Washington, D.C., but Armstrong insisted that the larger city—and important shipping center—of Baltimore would be their target, not the nation's capital.

In July 1814 Monroe was finally able to convince Madison to provide for Washington's defense by establishing a new military district that included Washington and the Potomac River. Still, the city remained very poorly defended, mostly by militia troops that had been gathered in haste and had not received much training. In August, the British landed at the Chesapeake Bay and began to march toward the capital.

The British reached the town of Bladensburg, located just north of Washington, D.C., on August 24. Met by a ragtag, inexperienced U.S. force, the British won an easy victory, even though they were outnumbered. The British could now proceed to Washington, where they arrived that same evening. They spent about twenty-four hours in the city, burning many public buildings, and then departed.

Returning to the capital

Monroe was one of the first leaders to return to Washington, D.C., arriving on August 27, and immediately setting to work at the State Department. Meanwhile, Armstrong had been blamed for allowing the attack on Washington, and he resigned on September 5. Madison made Monroe acting secretary of war, and he would be in charge of both the state and war departments for the next nine months.

At the same time, the peace negotiations between the United States and Great Britain had been going on in Ghent, Belgium. During the summer of 1814, Madison and Monroe had removed impressment as an issue to be included in the talks (since the end of the war against France had eliminated Great Britain's need for more seamen, impressment was no longer practiced). Nevertheless, the negotiations had stalled over the British demands for adjustments of the Canadian border and for a Native American homeland in the Northwest Territory (an area of land that would become the states of Ohio, Michigan, Indiana, Illinois, and parts of Minnesota).

Discouraged, U.S. leaders braced themselves for a new campaign in 1815. Toward the end of 1814, however, the deadlock was broken when Great Britain, unwilling to begin another season of fighting in North America, gave in on its demands.

The war comes to an end

In the months before and even the weeks after the signing of the Treaty of Ghent, more battles took place (the slowness of communications, which had to travel on ships across the Atlantic Ocean, meant that it took almost two months for news of the peace to arrive in the United States). Major General Andrew Jackson (1767–1845; see biographical entry) was in charge of U.S. forces in the area of the Gulf Coast, and Monroe worked closely with him to prepare for a British invasion. His quick responses to Jackson's requests for troops and supplies helped Jackson's men defeat a much larger British force at the Battle of New Orleans on January 8, 1815.

Monroe resigned from the War Department on February 15, two days after the news of the Treaty of Ghent arrived in Washington. Exhausted and ill, he took the next six months off, retreating to his plantation to rest. When Monroe returned to work at the State Department, he negotiated the Rush-Bagot agreement, by which the United States and Great Britain agreed to restrict the number of warships on the Great Lakes.

As the presidential election of 1816 approached, it was generally assumed that Monroe would be the Republican nominee, thus continuing the "Virginia dynasty," which is how some referred to the dominance of Virginia leaders (especially Jefferson, Madison, and Monroe) in national politics. The Federalist Party had fallen more and more out of favor due to its opposition to the war, and the end of the conflict in what many considered a victory for the United States seemed to be the final blow. The Federalists did put forth a candidate, New York Senator Rufus King (1755–1827), but Monroe beat him easily.

"The Era of Good Feelings"

Monroe's victory signaled a temporary end to the two-party system (in which those with similar views and goals banded together in factions or political parties). This was seen as a positive change by Monroe and other Republicans, who believed that political parties created harmful divisions in the nation and that candidates should win or lose by their own personal merits.

In the same spirit of harmony, Monroe chose a cabinet with representatives from different parts of the country. Thus his team of advisors included southerner William Crawford (1772–1834) as treasury secretary, New Englander Benjamin Crowninshield (1772–1851) as secretary of the navy, and westerner John C. Calhoun (1782–1814) as secretary of war. The important job of secretary of state went to the very experienced diplomat, John Quincy Adams, who would later follow in the footsteps of his father, John Adams (1735–1826), to become president of the United States.

Also in keeping with the new mood of harmony and conciliation, Monroe went on two goodwill tours of the nation, visiting New England and the middle Atlantic states in 1817 and parts of the west and south in 1819. He was warmly received wherever he went, and particularly in Boston, Massachusetts, where a crowd of forty thousand turned out to cheer him. This represented a remarkable change of heart in a region that had been strongly opposed to the War of 1812 and to Madison's administration. A writer for a Federalist newspaper remarked that an "Era of Good Feelings" seemed to be dawning, and from then on that phrase would be associated with Monroe's first term as president.

A new president begins his job

Monroe's first term as president was marked by two significant domestic (affecting the internal United States, rather than its relations with foreign countries) crises. One was the Panic of 1819, a period of economic hardship when unemployment rose while farm prices fell and businesses failed. The other domestic issue that arose was that of Missouri's admission as a state.

The Missouri Compromise

During the early part of the nineteenth century, tension was mounting over the issue of slavery, which was still practiced in the southern United States. In 1818 when Missouri applied to join the union as a slaveholding state, the number of states on each side of the issue was equal. Admitting Missouri as a slave state would upset the balance.

Monroe's view of the president's limited role in legislative matters required him to stay out of the debate over Missouri, but he gave his approval to a compromise proposed by Henry Clay. Missouri would be admitted as a slave state, but at the same time Maine would be admitted as a free state, and slavery would be permanently banned beyond the northern and western borders of Missouri. Although the compromise settled this specific problem, slavery would continue to be a troubling issue and a major factor in the outbreak of the American Civil War (1861–65).

The Monroe Doctrine

Monroe ran unopposed in the 1820 presidential election and won all but one electoral college vote. His second term was marked by an important development in the foreign policy of the United States. At this time, many Latin American nations were declaring their independence from Spain, which had colonized South and Central America during the previous two centuries. Like many Americans, Monroe was deeply sympathetic to these nations' struggle for freedom. He wanted to lend them the moral support of the United States. Monroe was opposed, however, to offering them military support, because he did not want to provoke the European nations into intervening.

In March 1822 he announced that the United States was establishing diplomatic relations with La Plata (which later became Argentina), Chile, Peru, Colombia, and Mexico. The next year, Great Britain proposed a joint British-U.S. declaration of opposition to European intervention in American affairs. After considering the proposal, Monroe and Adams rejected it, fearing that it would make the United States appear to be in Great Britain's shadow. Instead, Monroe wanted to establish the United States as the leading power in the Americas.

That is why he decided to use his annual message to Congress, delivered on December 2, 1823, to state that the

A cartoon illustrating the Monroe Doctrine, which stated that the United States would consider any interference in American affairs an aggressive act. *Photograph reproduced by permission of Corbis Corporation (Bellevue).*

United States would consider any interference in American affairs an aggressive act. For its part, the United States would not intervene in any other nation's affairs. Monroe emphasized that the United States now considered the Americas closed to any further European colonization. This policy—known in Monroe's day as the American System but later called the Monroe Doctrine—would gain even greater significance in the twentieth century, when it would be used to justify U.S. intervention in Latin American affairs (a use that was not intended by its author).

Leaving the presidency

Monroe left the White House in March 1825 and kept busy by helping Jefferson run the recently established University of Virginia. His friendships with Jefferson and Madison continued, and he grew even closer to Madison after Jefferson's death in 1826. Monroe attended Virginia's Constitutional Convention in 1829 and was chosen to serve as its president, but he was now too feeble to take a very active role, although he did deliver several speeches.

Monroe died on July 4, 1831, the fifth anniversary of the deaths of Jefferson and John Adams. His New York City funeral was attended by a host of officials, and huge crowds assembled to watch the funeral procession. In newspapers across the nation, journalists paid tribute to the tall, dignified man who had lent his sound judgment and so many years of service to the country he loved. Monroe was buried in New York, but was eventually re-interred in Richmond, Virginia.

For More Information

Books

Ammon, Harry. *James Monroe: The Quest for National Identity.* New York: McGraw-Hill, 1971.

Dangerfield, George. *The Era of Good Feelings.* New York: Harcourt, Brace & World, 1963.

Heidler, David S., and Jeanne T. Heidler, eds. *Encyclopedia of the War of 1812.* Santa Barbara, Calif.: ABC-CLIO, Inc., 1997.

May, Ernest R. *The Making of the Monroe Doctrine.* Cambridge: Belknap Press, 1975.

Web sites

Ammon, Harry. "James Monroe." *Grolier Online Biography.* [Online] http://www.grolier.com/presidents/ea/bios/05pmonr.html (accessed on November 26, 2001).

"James Monroe." *The American President.* [Online] http://www.american-president.org/theseries.htm (accessed on November 26, 2001).

"James Monroe." *Presidential Explorations.* http://library.thinkquest.org/11492/cgi-bin/pres.cgi/monroejames (accessed on November 26, 2001).

"James Monroe: Fifth President 1817–1825." *White House Biography.* [Online] http://www.whitehouse.gov/history/presidents/jm5.html (accessed on November 26, 2001).

Oliver Hazard Perry

Born August 20, 1785
South Kingstown, Rhode Island

Died August 23, 1819
At sea near Venezuela

Naval officer

The War of 1812 was a relatively short conflict with few clear battle victories for either side, yet the United States emerged from it with a new feeling of pride and confidence. Naval officer Oliver Hazard Perry helped to create that feeling through his bold leadership and personal courage, especially during the Battle of Lake Erie. In his book titled *Amateurs to Arms!: A Military History of the War of 1812*, historian John R. Elting writes about this battle: "It had been a small clash on the edge of nowhere between two improvised fleets with mostly greenhorn [inexperienced] crews.... [yet no] major sea battle was ever more valiantly and sternly fought." Perry's starring role in this small but important clash was the highlight of his brief career.

An early love for the sea

Born in 1785 in South Kingstown, Rhode Island, Oliver Hazard Perry was the son of naval officer Christopher Raymond Perry. Perry's mother, Sarah Wallace Alexander Perry, instilled an early love of books and learning in her son, but his greatest passion, even when he was still a young boy, was for the sea.

Portrait: Oliver Hazard Perry. *Photography courtesy of The Library of Congress.*

In 1798 during what was later called the Quasi War, France began attacking U.S. merchant ships in the Caribbean Sea (the body of water that lies between the southern coast of the United States and the northern coast of South America). The United States responded by sending its own navy to the region. Perry's father was given command of the warship *General Greene* and assigned to defend U.S. shipping in the Caribbean. A year later, fourteen-year-old Perry wrote to his father to request permission to join the navy. The elder Perry appointed his son a midshipman (a junior sailor who is still in training) on the *General Greene*. The ship cruised around Cuba and Haiti, and Perry began to gather the seagoing experience that would help him build his naval career.

The Quasi War ended in 1800, but the next year the United States became involved in another conflict in the Mediterranean Sea (the body of water that lies south of Europe and north of Africa). For years, pirates from the North African countries known as the Barbary States (Tripoli [now Libya], Algeria, and Tunisia) had forced European countries to pay tribute (a cash payment) or face having their ships captured. The United States sent its navy to the region to put an end to this practice.

Serving in the Mediterranean

In 1802 Perry—just seventeen but already a lieutenant—sailed for the Mediterranean aboard the *John Adams*. He spent the next eighteen months assisting in such duties such as escorting convoys (merchant ships that sailed in groups for protection), enforcing the blockade, and general patrolling of the area. After returning to the United States, Perry lived in Newport, Rhode Island. Perry continued his studies, pursuing mathematics and astronomy with the same enthusiasm he brought to his fencing, marksmanship (shooting guns), and horseback riding. He was tall, handsome, and very polite, and he became a popular figure in the Newport social scene.

Commander of a gunboat squadron

In 1807 twenty-two-year-old Perry was given the job of supervising the building of seventeen gunboats for the U.S.

Navy. Gunboats were small, armed ships used mostly for patrolling rivers and harbors. When construction was completed, Perry became the commander of the gunboat squadron (a group of ships assigned to a special duty) based at New York City. He was soon dissatisfied with this coastal duty, however, and in 1809 he was thrilled to be given command of the schooner (a type of ship with two or more masts at its front and back ends) *Revenge*.

At sea on the *Revenge*

At this time Great Britain and France were at war with each other and carrying on the practices that would soon bring about the War of 1812, including the harassment of U.S. shipping and the impressment or forcing of soldiers into military service. The British had seized the U.S. merchant ship *Diana,* and in July 1810 Perry led a mission to the coastal waters off southern Georgia, near the border with Spanish-held Florida, to recover her. While making off with the *Diana,* the *Revenge* was approached by a British warship called the *Goree.* In a show of boldness that he would exhibit throughout his career, Perry prepared to fight. The *Goree* backed off, and Perry won the admiration of those who heard about the encounter.

Perry now received orders to return for coastal duties in the north. Assigned to conduct a survey of some Rhode Island harbors, Perry was, on February 2, 1811, cruising in a thick fog when the *Revenge* ran aground (got into water that was too shallow and hit the bottom of the ocean), causing damage to the ship. The *Revenge* eventually sank, but Perry managed to save the crew and some of the property aboard the ship. Since a valuable ship had been lost, the Navy investigated the incident, but Perry was found to be blameless and was even praised for his actions.

Since he was now without a ship, Perry requested a leave of absence from naval duty. He took this opportunity to get married, wedding Elizabeth Champlin Mason on May 5, 1811 (the couple would go on to have a daughter and three sons). Perry's domestic tranquility was soon interrupted, however, by the coming of war between the United States and Great Britain.

At war with Great Britain again

For several years the United States had tried to avoid war, countering the practices it condemned through economic rather than military means. But measures like the Embargo Act of 1807, which prevented ships from entering or leaving American ports and thus put an end to shipping, had only hurt the United States more. Americans were especially angry about U.S. citizens being impressed into the British navy. In addition, many U.S. citizens believed that Great Britain was arming and encouraging Native Americans to attack whites, and some thought that war with Great Britain would offer a chance to expand U.S. territory into Canada and Florida. All of these factors led to the June 18, 1812, declaration of war against Great Britain.

Convinced that war would be declared, Perry had requested sea duty in May 1812. Instead, he was given command of the same squadron of gunboats whose construction he had previously supervised. Perry's job was to defend the city of Newport and, despite his disappointment at serving so close to shore, he devoted himself to his task. In August he was promoted to the rank of Master Commandant.

A special task on Lake Erie

Still unwilling to give up his dream of more active service, Perry wrote to Commander Isaac Chauncey (1772–1840), who was in charge of U.S. naval actions on the Great Lakes (including lakes Ontario, Erie, Huron, Michigan, and Superior). These bodies of water held great strategic importance, for whoever controlled the lakes—especially Ontario and Erie—controlled the only efficient supply and transport routes in the northwest. Chauncey wrote back that he had a special job in mind for Perry, who was soon ordered to report to Chauncey's headquarters at Sacket's Harbor, New York, on Lake Ontario.

Perry arrived at Sacket's Harbor on February 17, 1813, and a little less than a month later he left to begin the special job that Chauncey had assigned him. He was to go to the new U.S. naval base at Presque Isle (now Erie, Pennsylvania) to supervise the construction of a fleet of ships for duty on Lake Erie (working with a talented shipbuilder named Noah Brown) and also collect the smaller boats that were already there. He also was to lead the United States in taking control of Lake Erie. Chauncey, meanwhile, would concentrate his own efforts on Lake Ontario.

Overcoming obstacles to ready the fleet

Perry tackled the assignment with his usual determination, but he faced many problems, including bitterly cold weather and the difficulty of gathering the wood needed to build ships. Another major obstacle to overcome was the lack of able seamen to serve on the ships. As the spring and early summer progressed, Perry found that he had only about 120 sailors who were fit for service, since many of the men were suffering from an illness called lake fever. Chauncey had agreed that Perry would need about 750 men to carry out his mission. However, Perry maintained that Chauncey was unwilling to send enough to attain that level and also kept the most experienced and capable soldiers for his own fleet. The bad feelings between the two men almost resulted in Perry's resignation, but Chauncey and other officers convinced him to stay. Eventually, with the arrival of some volunteers from the Pennsylvania militia (small armies made up of troops residing in a particular state) and from the army of Major General William Henry Harrison (1773–1841; see biographical entry), Perry was able to put together an adequate force.

Another big problem still remained though. There was a sand bar at the mouth of the Presque Isle harbor that lay only about seven feet beneath the surface of the water. That was too shallow to allow passage of Perry's two largest ships, the *Lawrence* and the *Niagara*. Also, Perry needed to move five other ships a distance of eighty miles upstream from the town of Black Rock (located down the Niagara River, which connects lakes Ontario and Erie) in order to reach Presque Isle. En route the ships would have to pass by British-held Fort Erie. The British also had a squadron of ships stationed on Fort Erie, under the command of Robert Barclay (1785–1837), a one-armed veteran of Great Britain's war with France. This fleet was waiting outside the Presque Isle harbor to prevent the Perry's ships from entering.

The task might have been impossible without the help of what came to be known as "Perry's luck." During the late spring and early summer of 1813, the U.S. Army had made progress against the British along the Niagara River, and the British were forced to evacuate Fort Erie. Thus the ships were able to proceed up towards Presque Isle, and when they reached the harbor, Barclay's fleet was gone. Although it was rumored that Barclay had left to attend a dinner banquet, it is more likely that he had gone for provisions. In any case, the U.S. ships arrived safely at Presque Isle.

Perry would need more luck to get the *Lawrence* and *Niagara* across the sand bar and into the open lake. Their heavy guns were removed, and a device called a camel—large boxes or barges filled with water which were positioned partly under the ship, then emptied to become buoyant—was used to lift the ships enough to allow them to pass over the sand bar. The *Lawrence* got clear, but the *Niagara* became stuck in the sand.

Just at this moment, with the *Niagara* disabled and the *Lawrence* completely unarmed, Barclay's squadron appeared about a mile offshore. Perry called on his famous luck again and made an incredibly bold move: he sent two of his smaller ships toward the British, firing their guns. Barclay had no idea that the U.S. squadron was not really battle-ready and, assuming that he was outgunned, turned his ships around and left the area for his base at Amherstburg in what is now Ontario, Canada.

Plans and preparations for a battle

In mid-August, Master Commandant Jesse Duncan Elliott (1782–1845) arrived with 100 men. The Americans now had 530 crew on their ships, while the British had 440 (only 10 per British ship were trained seamen; all in all the U.S. had more experienced sailors). Perry's flagship (the ship that carries the battle's top commander) would be the *Lawrence,* and Elliott would command the *Niagara.* Each of these ships was equipped with twenty guns.

Also participating in the battle were the *Caledonia* (three guns); the *Somers* (two guns); the *Trippe* (one gun); and the gunboats *Tigress, Porcupine, Scorpion,* and *Ariel,* each with one to four guns. Barclay's six-ship opposing squadron included the HMS *Detroit* (eleven guns), the HMS *Queen Charlotte* (seventeen guns), the *Lady Prevost* (thirteen guns), the *General Hunter* (ten guns), the *Little Belt* (three guns), and the *Chippeway* (one gun).

His squadron complete—and with the *Lawrence* flying a blue flag with white lettering that read, "Don't Give Up the Ship," the last words uttered by Captain James Lawrence (1781–1813), who had died in an earlier sea battle—Perry sailed west, ready to disrupt the British supply lines and engage them in battle if possible. The U.S. fleet set up their base at Put-in-Bay on Bass Island. Perry ordered that sand be spread on the decks of the ships, so that in the event of a brutal battle the sailors would not slip on the blood that was bound to be spilled.

Meanwhile, Barclay was under pressure to engage the U.S. fleet in battle. His supplies were running dangerously low, his men had not been paid, and he also had to support a huge group of Native American allies, who were camped with their families at Amherstburg. A victory on Lake Erie would secure his supply lines. In addition, Sir George Prevost (1767–1816), the overall commander of the British troops in Canada, was urging Barclay to confront the Americans.

The Battle of Lake Erie

On September 10 the British squadron was sighted about nine miles west of Put-in-Bay and the U.S. fleet sailed out to meet it, the *Lawrence* in the lead. The battle began just before noon. The plan had been for the *Lawrence* to close in quickly on the British, because it did not have the long-range guns needed to attack from a distance. The *Niagara* was to follow closely and engage the *Queen Charlotte,* while the smaller vessels took on the enemy's smaller ships. For reasons unknown, Elliott failed to bring the *Niagara* close and instead hung back, ignoring signals to proceed.

The British concentrated most of their guns on the *Lawrence,* which suffered heavy damage. During the first two hours or so of the battle, eighty per cent of the *Lawrence*'s crew was killed or wounded, although Perry remained essentially unhurt. In the middle of all the chaos, Perry's pet dog

George Prevost: Competent but too cautious

Sir George Prevost served competently as Canada's governor and as overall commander of British military forces in Canada during the War of 1812, but his career ended in shame after he was blamed for the British defeat at Lake Champlain.

The son of a Swiss-born officer in the British army, George Prevost was born in 1767 in New Jersey, where his father was then stationed. He was educated mostly in England, and always groomed for a military career. Prevost entered the army in 1779 and rose steadily through the ranks, becoming a brigadier general in 1798. He served for several years in the British colonies of Barbados, St. Lucia (where he also was the lieutenant governor), and Dominica in the Caribbean region, where he was much respected for his leadership.

Prevost returned to England in 1805 and stayed until 1808, when he returned to Canada to serve as both lieutenant governor and lieutenant general in Nova Scotia. In this position Prevost achieved both political and military success, building a reputation as a skilled and decisive leader. Thus he seemed well qualified to take command of all the British forces in North America, an assignment he assumed on July 4, 1811. In October, he also was sworn in as Canada's head colonial administrator. Prevost's ability to speak French fluently allowed him to gain the confidence and support of Canada's influential French-Canadian leaders.

When the War of 1812 began, the British had only about nine thousand regular troops stationed in Canada, which comprised many thousands of square miles of territory to defend from a possible U.S. invasion. At this time the Canadian population was only about three hundred thousand, compared to a U.S. population of about eight million. In addition, Great Britain was too busy fighting Napoleon (the leader of France, with whom Great Britain had been at war since the 1790s) in Europe to devote many resources to the new conflict in North America.

In view of these factors, Prevost adopted a defensive strategy for Canada that involved waiting for the enemy to attack, delaying confrontations, and avoiding mistakes. Gradually Prevost became known as a leader who was nonaggressive to the point of timidity, and who did not like to

stuck its head out of a hole that had been shot in his cabin and yelped in terror. Eventually Perry had to order wounded men who were not too severely disabled to return to their battle positions because there were not enough uninjured men to continue the fight.

take any risks. Almost immediately after the start of the war, Prevost began negotiating a truce (a halt in the war) with Major General Henry Dearborn (1751–1829), the overall commander of the U.S. troops. But this proved to be only a short ceasefire.

Prevost's cautious approach worked fairly well during the first two years of the war. But in early 1814, Great Britain defeated France and was able to send many more troops to North America. British leaders felt that a more aggressive approach was now possible, but Prevost had trouble adjusting to this change. His over-cautiousness would soon prove disastrous.

In September 1814 Prevost was ordered to take control of Plattsburg, New York, a town strategically located on Lake Champlain (which formed a border, on the north, with Canada). Prevost headed there with ten thousand troops but halted before he reached the town and settled down to wait for the arrival of the British fleet on Lake Champlain. When the fleet did arrive, Prevost pushed its commander, Captain George Downie, to attack the U.S. fleet. Meanwhile, the U.S. commander, Captain Thomas Macdonough, had wisely anchored his ships inside Plattsburg Bay, where their short-range guns would be most effective. Downie's hastily prepared ships were at a disadvantage, and the battle ended in the complete destruction of the British fleet, as well as the death of its commander.

Prevost was supposed to launch a simultaneous land attack, but he waited until the battle was almost over to order it. As soon as he heard the news of the naval defeat, he ordered his troops to retreat, even though his top officers felt the army could easily take Plattsburg.

As a result of his cautiousness, Prevost's career ended under a cloud of shame. He was recalled to England, where a naval court of inquiry that investigated charges brought against him by James Yeo, the commander of British naval forces on the Great Lakes, blamed Prevost for the defeat on Lake Champlain. Prevost requested a second hearing to clear his name, but he died on January 5, 1816, before the hearing could be held.

Sources: Heidler, David S., and Jeanne T. Heidler, eds. Encyclopedia of the War of 1812. *Santa Barbara, Calif.: ABC-CLIO, Inc., 1997;* War of 1812. *[Online] http://www.galafilm.com/1812/e/index.html (accessed on November 26, 2001).*

A daring transfer

Finally all of the guns on the *Lawrence* had been put out of commission. This is the point at which most commanders would have given up the battle, but Perry was no ordinary commander. Instructing his crew to surrender the

Lawrence to the British as soon as he was clear of the ship, Perry climbed into a rowboat with five seamen and headed through a steady rain of bullets and fire toward the *Niagara,* which had finally moved closer and was about a quarter mile away. At first Perry stood in the rowboat, hoping that by doing so he would encourage his men to keep fighting, but finally his crew convinced him to sit down.

Perry boarded the Niagara and immediately took over the ship's command, sending Elliott to rally the smaller vessels. Perry brought the *Niagara* right through the middle of the formation of British ships, raking them with broadsides (all guns on one side of a ship firing at more or less the same time) from both sides of the Niagara. The British were surprised by this move and in the confusion of trying to get into a better position, the *Detroit* and the *Queen Charlotte* collided.

Within fifteen minutes the battle ended. All of the British ships had been captured or sunk, and all of the British commanders and deputies (second-in-command officers) had been killed or wounded, so the British had no choice but to surrender. In a battle that lasted about three hours, the British had lost 140 men (46 killed and 94 wounded) while the Americans lost 123 (27 killed and 96 wounded), two-thirds of them from the crew of the *Lawrence.*

Following the battle, Perry sent two messages informing his superiors of the U.S. victory, and both soon became famous. His message to Secretary of the Navy William Jones (1760–1831) read, "It has pleased the almighty to give to the arms of the United States a signal victory over their enemies on this lake." To Harrison, he wrote "We have met the enemy and they are ours: two ships, two brigs, one schooner and a sloop."

Showered with praise and rewards

The Battle of Lake Erie represented the biggest U.S. victory of the war to that date, and the first time the U.S. Navy had defeated an entire British squadron rather than just one ship. It also changed the course of the war, for it left Canada vulnerable to invasion from the west. In fact, Perry was soon occupied with ferrying Harrison's army of thirty-five hundred men across Lake Erie to recapture Detroit, which had been surrendered to the British during the first year of the war. From there, the U.S. troops chased the retreating British to Moraviantown on the Thames River. There also the Americans were victorious, even managing to kill Tecumseh (c. 1768–1813; see biographical entry), the great Shawnee leader whose attempt to form a Native American alliance had threatened white settlement.

Within a few weeks, Perry gave up his command and headed for the East Coast. Along the way, he found that people had already heard about the Battle of Lake Erie and that they were eager to praise and reward him. In addition to earning a promotion to captain and an extra $5,000 in prize money, Perry was recognized by Congress and received awards from various state legislatures and city governments. The officers and other men who had served with him also received awards: three months' pay for officers and swords for ordinary sailors.

Perry was assigned command of the *Java*, which was still under construction. The finished *Java* soon proved to have structural problems and had to be refitted, which was a major disappointment to Perry. Meanwhile, he led the effort to harass the British as they retreated down the Potomac River following their invasion of Alexandria, Virginia (which occurred a few days after their August 24, 1814 sacking of Washington, D.C.). He also participated in the Battle of Baltimore on September 12 through 14, at which the U.S. forces turned back an attempted British invasion.

Conflicts with his fellow officers

After the war, Perry went back to sea in command of the *Java*, but this would prove an ill-fated cruise. Tension arose between Perry and another officer, John Heath, and Perry hit Heath, which violated naval rules condemning striking a fellow officer. A court-martial (military court) ruling found both parties guilty, but they were punished only with private scoldings. This outcome did not satisfy Heath, who felt that the injury to his honor called for a duel with Perry. Although he agreed to the duel, Perry refused to fire a weapon and simply stood with his hands by his sides when Heath fired. Fortunately, the shot missed Perry, and Heath did not push the matter further.

Perry also was involved in a battle of words with Jesse Elliott, who had been widely faulted for failing to bring the *Niagara* into action properly at the Battle of Lake Erie. Some said Elliott had deliberately backed away from the fight. In his official report on the battle, Perry had avoided criticizing Elliott and had even praised him, but Elliott felt that Perry should do or say more to restore Elliott's reputation. He even implied that it was he, and not Perry, who had saved the day at the Battle of Lake Erie. Convinced that he had been more than generous to Elliott, Perry refused to defend him further. Elliott challenged Perry to a duel but Perry refused to participate, instead making official charges of his own against Elliott (nothing was to come of these charges).

In 1819 Perry was put in command of the *John Adams* and the *Nonesuch* and sent on a diplomatic mission to the South American country of Venezuela, which had recently gained its independence from Spain. After he had completed his mission, Perry contracted yellow fever—a tropical disease then common in the region—and died aboard the *Nonesuch* a few days after his thirty-fourth birthday. Perry was buried at Port of Spain, Trinidad, but in 1826 his body was moved to Newport, Rhode Island. His home state erected a handsome granite marker to commemorate his deeds in service of the United States.

For More Information

Books

Dillon, Richard. *We Have Met the Enemy: Oliver Hazard Perry, Wilderness Commodore*. New York: McGraw-Hill, 1978.

Elting, John R. *Amateurs to Arms!: A Military History of the War of 1812*. Da Capo Press, 1995. Reprint. Originally published by Algonquin Press, Chapel Hill, N.C., 1991.

Heidler, David S., and Jeanne T. Heidler, eds. *Encyclopedia of the War of 1812*. Santa Barbara, Calif.: ABC-CLIO, Inc., 1997.

Hickey, Donald R. *The War of 1812: A Forgotten Conflict*. Urbana: University of Illinois Press, 1989.

Web sites

"Oliver Hazard Perry." *Ohio History Central*. [Online] http://www.ohiohkids.org/ohc/history/h_indian/people/ohperry.html (accessed on November 26, 2001).

"Oliver Hazard Perry." *U.S. Brig Niagara, Erie, Pennsylvania.* [Online] http://www.brigniagara.org/perry.htm (accessed on November 26, 2001).

War of 1812. [Online] http://www.galafilm.com/1812/e/index.html (accessed on November 26, 2001).

Zebulon Montgomery Pike

Born January 5, 1779
Lamberton, New Jersey

Died April 27, 1813
York, Canada

Explorer, army officer

A career army officer who gained fame for his expeditions through Minnesota, Colorado, New Mexico and other areas in the years before the War of 1812, Zebulon Montgomery Pike later distinguished himself as a wartime general. He led the U.S. forces that attacked York, Canada, in April 1813 and was killed toward the end of that battle. Pike gave his name not only to a U.S. warship, the *General Pike*, that saw action later in the war, but to Pike's Peak mountain, located near Pueblo, Colorado.

An ambitious young soldier

The son of Major Zebulon Pike and Isabella Brown, Zebulon Montgomery Pike was born in Lamberton, New Jersey (now part of Trenton). His family had emigrated (came from another country) to the United States in 1635 and went on to establish a long military tradition. His ancestor Captain John Pike had fought in the early colonial wars against the Native Americans, and his father served in the American Revolution (1775–83) and was a career army officer.

Portrait: Zebulon Montgomery Pike.
Photograph courtesy of the National Archives and Records Administration.

267

The Lewis and Clark Expedition

With the Louisiana Purchase the United States acquired an area covering more than eight hundred thousand square miles (including the present-day states of Arkansas, Missouri, Iowa, the part of Minnesota that is west of the Mississippi River, North Dakota, South Dakota, Nebraska, Oklahoma, most of Kansas, the parts of Montana, Wyoming, and Colorado that are east of the Rocky Mountains, and Louisiana west of the Mississippi but including the city of New Orleans) for only fifteen million dollars. With the purchase came a whole new set of problems but also, as President Thomas Jefferson saw it, opportunities.

And opportunities were definitely what he had in mind when he decided to send off his private secretary, Meriweather Lewis and Lewis's friend and fellow army officer William Clark to explore the new territory. The Lewis and Clark expedition was the nation's first overland exploration of the American west and northwest. From May, 1804 to September 1806, Lewis and Clark covered eight thousand miles of land between St. Louis, Missouri, and the coast of what is now Washington state. Jefferson wanted them to find the fabled "Northwest Passage," an inland water route that would make it much easier to travel between the Atlantic and Pacific Oceans. Although they did not find such a passage, their journey was a success and their experiences and observations proved invaluable.

For most of his childhood Pike's family lived in New Jersey and western Pennsylvania. When he was fourteen, his father was assigned to Fort Washington on the Ohio frontier. The elder Pike's commander was General James Wilkinson (1757–1825), who would later gain notoriety as a spy for the Spanish and as an unpopular commander during the War of 1812. Eager to play the role of a dashing soldier like his father, young Pike joined the army at fifteen. He served briefly under his father, then under Revolutionary War hero General "Mad Anthony" Wayne (1745–1796), who had earned his nickname for his bravery and quick temper.

Under Wayne's command, Pike helped to ferry supplies to forts along the Miami River. From 1795 to 1799 he did the same kind of work on the Ohio and Mississippi Rivers, gaining some valuable experience in supervision and serving as an agent for the private contractors who supplied the army with food, clothing, and other provisions. He was commissioned as

The so-called "Corps of Discovery" set out with forty-eight men, including hunters, soldiers, and boatmen as well as Lewis's African American slave, York. Following the Mississippi River north, they crossed the Rocky Mountains and the present-day states of Montana and Idaho. Then they traveled into what is now Oregon via the Snake and Columbia rivers. They reached the Pacific Ocean in November 1805 and built Fort Clapsop, where they spent the winter. On the return voyage, the corps split into two groups, with Lewis leading a party along the Yellowstone River and Clark venturing into north-central Montana. The two groups reunited before returning to St. Louis.

The Lewis and Clark expedition gathered extensive and carefully documented information on the geography, plants, and animals of the American west. They also learned much about the Native Americans who lived in the areas they covered, and their encounters with these people were remarkably positive. While wintering in North Dakota they had encountered a Shoshone woman named Sacajawea who served as an interpreter and whose presence helped to establish the group's peaceful intentions.

Source: Heidler, David S., and Jeanne T. Heidler, eds. Encyclopedia of the War of 1812. Santa Barbara, Calif.: ABC-CLIO, Inc., 1997.

an ensign (the lowest-ranking officer) in the army's Second Infantry in 1799 and was made a first lieutenant a year later, when he was twenty. Pike served a few uneventful years with the frontier army, waiting for a chance to make his name.

During this period, Pike was trying to augment his patchy education by studying French, Latin, Spanish, mathematics, and science on his own. In March 1801 he eloped with his cousin Clarissa Brown, despite her father's disapproval. The couple would have five children, but only one daughter, Clarissa, would survive longer than her father (Clarissa would marry the son of William Henry Harrison [1773–1841; see biographical entry], another major figure in the War of 1812).

Seeking the source of the Mississippi River

In 1803 the United States acquired a huge expanse of territory from France (the acquisition was called the

Louisiana Purchase; see chapter 2), nearly doubling the size of the nation. Americans were eager to know what lay in this vast wilderness, and in 1804 President Thomas Jefferson (1743–1826) sent an expedition headed by Meriweather Lewis (1774–1809) and William Clark (1770–1838) to survey the new territory. Meanwhile, General Wilkinson—whom Jefferson had appointed governor of Louisiana—was also interested in sponsoring an expedition. Pike was assigned the task of locating the source of the Mississippi River thought to be somewhere in the newly acquired territory.

Pike left St. Louis (in what is now Missouri) on August 9, 1805, accompanied by twenty men and carrying enough provisions to last four months. Traveling along the Mississippi in a seventy-foot keelboat (a large, shallow boat often used to transport goods up and down rivers) they proceeded north into what is now the state of Minnesota. By this time, the bitterly cold weather of the northern winter had set in, so the expedition halted near the Falls of Saint Anthony (close to the present-day cities of Saint Paul and Minneapolis).

They built a rough stockade, and then Pike and some of his men continued moving north, dragging their supplies through the snow on a sled. In early February they found Leech Lake in northern Minnesota, and Pike decided that this was the source of the Mississippi River (he was wrong; actually the source is located a little west, at Lake Itasca). Pike visited several British fur trading posts and informed the traders that they were trespassing on U.S property; he also met with various Native American tribes in the area. Then he returned to St. Louis, arriving on April 30, 1806.

Another expedition

Less than three months later, Pike embarked on another journey. This time, Wilkinson instructed him to look for the sources of the Arkansas and Red Rivers. He also was to gather information about the Spanish settlements in New Mexico. At this time Spain was still in control of a major portion of what would eventually become part of the United States, including Florida, Texas, New Mexico, and California. Relations between Spain and the United States were somewhat uneasy, and Pike was told not to offend or alarm the Spanish.

Leaving St. Louis on July 16 with a crew of twenty-three men (including Wilkinson's son), Pike headed west, following a route up the Missouri and Osage rivers in central Missouri to the Arkansas River. On November 15 the expedition sighted the Rocky Mountains, and a week later they reached the site of what would become Pueblo, Colorado. They paused briefly and attempted to climb to the top of the tallest mountain in the Rocky Mountain range. They were not successful, and Pike claimed that no one would be able to scale this mountain. Fourteen years later Major Stephen Long's expedition would reach the top of the mountain eventually called Pike's Peak.

Pike explored the headwaters (source) of the Arkansas River and then turned south in search of the Red River's source. The expedition crossed the Sangre de Cristo Mountains in southern Colorado, crossing into the Spanish territory of New Mexico. On the banks of the Conejos River (a tributary of the much larger Rio Grande) they built a fort.

Spanish authorities became concerned about Pike's presence, although he assured them he was only there to protect the area from Native Americans. He was taken to Sante Fe and then to Chihuahua, where he was questioned by the chief commander of the region. Pike's papers (including his records of the expedition) were taken from him, so that he later had to reconstruct them from memory as well as from some notes he managed to hide in gun barrels (Pike's papers were returned to the U.S. government about one hundred years later). Pike was to return to Natchitoches, Louisiana, about a year later.

Returning to a controversy

While Pike was in New Mexico, a scandal had erupted over the alleged treasonous (assisting the enemy during war) misdeeds of Aaron Burr (1756–1836), a former vice president of the United States, who was accused of having bought land in the West with the intention of setting up a separate empire there. Wilkinson, Burr's partner in these schemes, had exposed him to Jefferson. Pike's connection to Wilkinson and the timing of his expedition made it look like he might himself be a collaborator.

Pike claimed that he knew nothing about what Burr and Wilkinson had been plotting. He had assumed that the information he had gathered in New Mexico would be used by the U.S. government in the event (which many thought likely) of war with Spain. Secretary of War Henry Dearborn (1751–1829) believed Pike and cleared him of any wrongdoing; nothing could be proven against Wilkinson, either.

The publication of Pike's rather poorly written report on his expedition was overshadowed by that of Lewis and Clark. Nevertheless, Pike's report provided a great deal of useful information about the West. Pike speculated that the Great Plains would never be inhabited by white Americans (the settlers of the late nineteenth century would prove him wrong on that point) and that New Mexico held many opportunities for trade.

A wartime commander

Pike had been promoted to the rank of captain in August 1806; he was made a major in 1809 and a lieutenant colonel in 1810. He served as a battery commander of the army's Sixth Regiment, then as a deputy quartermaster general at New Orleans, again serving under Wilkinson. In April 1811 Pike was given command of the U.S. troops stationed at Baton Rouge. He put them through a rigorous training program, and they performed well at the Battle of Tippecanoe (when U.S. forces fought against an allied Native American force in northern Indiana in November 1811).

The United States declared war against Great Britain in June 1812. The war was provoked by two major issues. The first was Britain's maritime policy of impressment in its war with France. This policy was where British officials boarded U.S. ships to capture deserters from their own navy, often wrongfully taking American citizens in the process. The other issue that led to the war was Great Britain's overly friendly relations with Native Americans. Americans believed that the British were encouraging Native Americans to attack white settlers who were moving west. The Native Americans believed that the settlers were encroaching on (gradually taking over) their land.

At the time the war began, Pike was promoted to the rank of colonel and assigned to lead the Fifteenth Regiment on the Lake Champlain (located between the border of New York and Vermont) frontier. By October, Dearborn and other strategists had decided that the United States would invade Montreal, one of Canada's most important and well defended cities. Pike's six hundred men were ready and waiting at Plattsburg, New York (on the shore of Lake Champlain) when the plan was abandoned.

Pike, however, received permission to lead an advance into Canada on November 21. They met and scattered a small group of Canadian soldiers and Native American warriors, burned the enemy camp, and headed back toward the U.S. border. On the way, Pike's troops had a skirmish with what turned out to be another U.S. force, and there were five casualties (two killed, three wounded).

The Battle of York

In spring 1813 U.S. leaders planned to invade Canada through the cities of Kingston and York (present-day Toronto), both of which were major shipbuilding centers; York also was the capital of upper Canada. Too sick to command the attack on York himself, Dearborn assigned the task to Pike. In preparing his men for the coming battle, Pike gave strict orders that in the event of a victory they were to respect the enemy's personal property; no looting would be tolerated. Loading seventeen hundred troops onto the ships of Commander Isaac Chauncey's (1772–1840) fleet, Pike himself boarded the *Madison*. From aboard the ship he directed the landing of the troops on the morning of April 27. A company of riflemen was the first to attack. Then Pike jumped into a boat and, after reaching shore, led the charge inland to reach the town's fort. Meanwhile, Chauncey's naval forces backed up the army with covering fire from their ships.

Soon the British commander, General Roger Hale Sheaffe (1763–1851), could see that his troops would not win the battle. He drew his regular soldiers back into the fort and prepared to retreat to Kingston, destroying military equipment in order to keep it out of enemy hands. Foreseeing a victory, Pike halted his troops six hundred feet away from the fort. He was sitting on a tree stump interrogating some prisoners when suddenly there was a terrible explosion. The fort's magazine (ammunition storehouse) had been ignited, and several hundred pounds of gunpowder as well as a huge quantity of ammunition had blown up with great force and deafening noise.

"Honor and glory await my name"

Rocks and other debris were scattered for three hundred yards around the site of the explosion, which killed or severely wounded more than one hundred Americans as well as about forty of the British and Canadian soldiers. Pike was among the victims, when a huge rock fell on him crushing his ribs and breaking his back. He passed his command to Colonel Cromwell Pearce (1772–1852), telling his men "Push on my brave fellows and avenge your general." Pike was carried back to the *Madison* in great agony. Having heard the victorious cheers of his men as they entered the fort, and having requested that the captured British flag be placed beneath his head, Pike died. His body was taken to Sacket's Harbor and buried at Fort Tompkins.

In the disorder and lack of strong leadership that followed the battle, the American troops forgot Pike's orders and went on a rampage through the town of York, looting and burning public buildings. They were angered over the rumored discovery of a scalp in one of the government offices (it was said that the British paid Native Americans for the scalps of U.S. citizens) and also distraught over the magazine explosion and the death of their beloved general.

In a letter Pike wrote to his father before the battle, he seemed to anticipate the possibility that he might not survive it, as well as the honorable reputation that he would earn for himself, as stated in John K. Mahon's *The War of 1812*: "If success attends my steps, honor and glory await my name—if defeat, still should it be said we died like brave men and conferred honor, even in death, on the American Name."

Where to Learn More

Books

Elting, John R. *Amateurs to Arms!: A Military History of the War of 1812.* Algonquin Press, Chapel Hill, N.C., 1991. Reprint, New York: Da Capo Press, 1995.

Heidler, David S., and Jeanne T. Heidler, eds. *Encyclopedia of the War of 1812*. Santa Barbara, Calif.: ABC-CLIO, 1997.

Hickey, Donald R. *The War of 1812: A Forgotten Conflict*. Urbana: University of Illinois Press, 1989.

Hollon, W. Eugene. *The Lost Pathfinder: Zebulon Montgomery Pike*. Norman: University of Oklahoma Press, 1949.

Jackson, Donald, ed. *The Journals of Zebulon M. Pike, with Letters and Related Documents*. 2 vols. Norman: University of Oklahoma Press, 1966.

Mahon, John K. *The War of 1812*. Da Capo Press, 1991. Reprint. Originally published by University of Florida Press, Gainesville, Fla., 1972.

Terrell, John Upton. *Zebulon Pike: The Life and Times of an Adventurer*. New York: Weybright and Talley, 1968.

Web sites

War of 1812. [Online] http://www.galafilm.com/1812/e/index.html (accessed on November 26, 2001).

Zebulon Pike—Explorers and Travelers. [Online] http://www.kcmuseum.com/explor05.html (accessed on November 26, 2001).

Josiah Quincy

Born February 4, 1772
Braintree, Massachusetts

Died July 1, 1864
Washington, District of Columbia

Politician, reformer

When the War of 1812 began, Massachusetts native Josiah Quincy was serving in the House of Representatives. A strong Federalist—the party that was against the war and often criticized the Republican administration of President James Madison (1751–1836)—Quincy's was the loudest of the voices of opposition as Congress debated the prospect of war. He resigned from the House soon after the declaration of war was signed, but continued to express his disapproval after he was later elected to the Massachusetts state legislature. Quincy later became mayor of Boston and president of Harvard University.

A well-established, respected family

Josiah Quincy was born in Boston on February 4, 1772, to a well-respected Massachusetts family. His ancestor Edmund Quincy had arrived from England in 1633, settling in the town of Mount Wollaston (which became Braintree, then Quincy) and gradually acquired great influence in the community. Quincy's father (also name Josiah), a prominent lawyer and ardent supporter of the American Revolution

Portrait: Josiah Quincy.
Photograph reproduced by permission of Hulton/Archive.

277

(1775–83), died of tuberculosis (a disease of the lungs) when Quincy was three. Quincy's mother, Abigail Phillips Quincy, was the daughter of a Boston merchant and the sister of Massachusetts lieutenant-governor William Phillips. After his father's death, Quincy's family became dependent on Abigail's father, a stern, religious man who decided to send his six-year-old grandson to boarding school.

Quincy entered Phillips Academy, which his mother's cousin had recently established at Andover, Massachusetts, becoming its youngest student. As discussed in a biography of Quincy titled *Josiah Quincy, 1772–1864: The Last Federalist* by Robert A. McCaughey, the school's goal was to "promote True Piety [religious obedience] and Virtue" through strict discipline and unrelenting academic work. Quincy was later to recall his days at Phillips with little fondness, and he never developed the strict, rigid attitudes toward religion that the school (and his grandfather) tried to teach him.

Attending Harvard College

Although he was not the best student, Quincy graduated Phillips Academy and was encouraged to further his education. As a wealthy young man of New England, he was expected to attend Harvard College, located close to Boston in Cambridge, Massachusetts. Besides being one of the most prominent colleges in the United States, twenty-one of Quincy's relatives on both sides of his family had gone to Harvard, so Harvard it was.

At this period in its history, Harvard featured a loose academic structure and a fairly liberal approach to religion, which suited Quincy well. There was little emphasis on competition; grades and examinations were not considered very important. Nevertheless, Quincy worked hard at his studies and benefited from them, taking courses in such subjects as Greek, Latin, Mathematics, and Metaphysics (philosophy). He also was given many opportunities to learn and practice public speaking, and developed skill in this area that would serve him well in later life, when he would come to be considered a great orator (speechmaker). Quincy graduated first in the class of 1790.

A young lawyer

Now eighteen years old, Quincy felt that becoming a lawyer was his most likely career option, even though the idea did not excite him much. At this time the path to becoming an attorney involved not academic study but an apprenticeship (when a young person would work for an established professional for little or no money, and thereby learn and acquire a trade). Thus Quincy spent three years working in the Boston office of attorney William Tudor. He passed the bar (the examination attorneys must pass to qualify to practice) in 1793 but never took many cases, for his family's wealth meant that he did not have to make much money.

Though he lacked enthusiasm for being a lawyer, Quincy wanted very much to serve the public by getting involved in politics. While waiting for a good opportunity to do so, he kept busy by participating in many organizations, including the Massachusetts Historical Society and the American Academy of Arts and Sciences. He also started investing in real estate, which helped to increase his wealth.

Tall, handsome, and sociable, Quincy also was known for his impetuous (doing things suddenly, without much thought) nature. Thus it must have hardly surprised his friends when they learned that, during the summer of 1795, he had become secretly engaged to Eliza Susan Morton—the twenty-two-year-old daughter of a New York merchant—a week after meeting her. Wedded on June 6, 1797 in New York City, the Quincys had a happy marriage of fifty-three years and raised seven children.

A taste for politics

Quincy entered politics in 1796, when he began to participate in Boston's city government. His speeches were widely admired, and he was appointed Town Orator in 1798. As part of Boston's wealthy elite, it was natural for Quincy to identify himself as a Federalist. This conservative political party tended to appeal to those who believed in a strong federal (national) government and whose interests lay in business and city life, while the Democratic Republicans (who later became known simply as Republicans), many of whom were farmers and plantation owners, did not want the federal government to violate the rights of the individual states.

The twenty-eight-year-old Quincy hoped to be elected to the U.S. Congress in 1800 but lost to William Eustis (1753–1825), a Revolutionary War veteran who was twice his age and who would, at the beginning of the War of 1812, serve as secretary of war. Two years later, John Quincy Adams (1767–1848; a future president of the United States) won the Federalist nomination over Quincy, but Adams subsequently lost to Eustis. Although he served briefly in the Massachusetts state legislature, Quincy had to wait until 1804 for another chance to run for the U.S. Congress. This time, he beat Eustis. For the next forty-five years, Quincy would hold some kind of public or semipublic (e.g., college presidency) office.

A committed Federalist

Quincy was a committed Federalist at a time when the Federalist Party was beginning a rapid decline. As the nineteenth century began, the Democratic Republican Party was gaining strength as more and more Americans stressed the values of individualism, democracy, and expansion (the movement of people into the western reaches of the North American continent). They agreed with prominent statesman Thomas Jefferson (1743–1826) that the United States was essentially an agrarian (rural, farming) nation. Federalists, by contrast, tended to focus on urban concerns and viewed the United States as comprising the east coast and the original thirteen states. They believed in a strong central government that was run by well-educated people from the top rungs of society, and they preferred to maintain the status quo (things as they are) in all things, including the issue of expansion.

In 1800 Thomas Jefferson had been elected president, and he was re-elected in 1804, when Quincy came to Washington, D.C. for the first time. The U.S. Congress also was dominated by Republicans, but Quincy did not despair. Like other Federalists, he assumed that the Republicans would soon demonstrate their inability to govern the nation and the Federalist Party would regain its earlier dominance. Meanwhile, he intended to raise his voice on issues that he—and the citizens of Massachusetts who had elected him—cared about.

One such issue involved the Louisiana Purchase, the 1803 deal by which the United States bought from France a huge parcel of western land for a very low price. The Federalists opposed the purchase because they feared the federal government could not control an area of such size, and because they did not want the southern and western states to become more powerful than those in the northeast (where most Federalists were concentrated). But there would prove to be no way for the Federalist to stem the tide of westward expansion that they so disliked and feared.

An unhappy member of Congress

Quincy moved his family south from Boston to Washington, D.C. in the fall of 1805. At that time, the capital was a small town located in a swampy area that many people found downright unhealthy. Its population increased when Congress was in session, but most of these temporary residents from all parts of the country were strangers to each other, and there were few cultural events to divert them. Quincy did not enjoy his time in Washington, particularly after the first two winters, when his wife and growing family no longer came with him. He did, however, make one solid if unlikely friendship. John Randolph (1773–1833), a Republican member of Congress from Virginia, was the chairman of the Ways and Means Committee who, like Quincy, came from a wealthy, cultured background. The two also shared a distaste for Thomas Jefferson's egalitarian (belief in human equality) style of politics.

Quincy was re-elected to Congress in 1806 and 1808; he would have preferred not to run in 1810 but Federalist Party leaders pressured him to do so, and he was again elected. Quincy was depressed and exasperated during his first two terms, due to the Republican dominance of national politics. In addition, he had been told to follow the Federalist strategy of keeping quiet and making no waves until it was time for the party to come again to the foreground. But Quincy finally decided, on his own, that he wanted to take a more active role in Congress and register the Federalist viewpoint, even if few people wanted to listen.

A leading voice of opposition

Beginning with the Tenth Congress in 1807, Quincy began to make very dramatic speeches of opposition to Republican measures. Instead of trying to find some middle ground with those with whom he disagreed, he intentionally took the most extreme positions possible. His speeches were very provocative and forceful, and sometimes contained personal attacks on people whose ideas he opposed. Other members of Congress frequently rose to interrupt and object to his statements. Quincy was soon considered the leading minority voice in Congress, even though other Federalists were often alarmed by his extremism.

An example of this extremism occurred when Congress was debating whether the territory of Louisiana (originally part of the Louisiana Purchase, which Quincy had opposed) should be admitted as a state. Quincy declared that if Louisiana was allowed to join the Union without the consent of the original thirteen states, those states would be justified in seceding (separating) from the United States. At this early stage in the nation's development, talk of secession stirred up fears of war and disorder, and Quincy was criticized for suggesting such a thing, even if he had done it mostly as a symbolic gesture.

Meanwhile, the Napoleonic Wars (1803–15; a long conflict between France and Great Britain and its allies) were raging in Europe. Both France and Great Britain had tried to inflict damage on each other by forbidding trade between their enemy and neutral countries. These restrictions had harmed the United States, as many ships were seized on the high seas. In addition, the British navy was attempting to bolster its numbers by impressment, which meant that sailors Great Britain considered British citizens were taken from American ships and forced to serve in the British navy. This practice caused much outrage in the United States, particularly because many of the sailors forced into the British navy were American citizens.

The prospect of war

Anxious to avoid war, Jefferson responded in December 1807 with the Embargo Act, which ended U.S. trade with other countries. But this act did not punish Great Britain and France, as intended, as much as it did the merchants, ship owners, and sailors of the northeastern United States. Southern planters who had previously sold vast quantities of tobacco, rice and cotton to Great Britain also were hurt.

Being a Federalist, Quincy had loudly opposed the Embargo Act in Congress. In fact, the law proved so unpopular that the Federalists enjoyed a brief surge in popularity: twice as many of them were elected to the Eleventh Congress as had been elected to the Tenth. For his part, Quincy maintained that the embargo was actually part of a Jefferson administration conspiracy to bankrupt the northeastern states and destroy the Federalist Party. He refused to believe that the act was part of a strategy to avoid war through the use of economic measures; in fact, Quincy steadfastly declared that war was not a possibility.

Subsequent measures (including the Non-Intercourse Act and Macon's Bill Number 2) also failed to improve matters, and the United States seemed to be moving steadily toward war. Helping to push things along in this direction was a group of young congressmen, most of them from the western and southern states, who felt that a war with Great Britain was necessary to regain the honor of the United States and also, perhaps, gain some new territory. The War Hawks, as they were called, pressured reluctant President James Madison (1751–1836), who had been elected in 1808, to make a declaration of war.

War becomes a reality

When the Twelfth Congress convened in November 1811, the looming war was the main topic of debate, with the War Hawks pushing for measures to help prepare the United States for a conflict. Quincy chose the unusual strategy of joining the War Hawks in calling for military preparedness. He declared that he was tired of hearing talk of war and thought that the best way to silence it was to call Madison's bluff (to make him either declare war or stop discussing it).

Quincy still did not really believe that the United States would go to war with Great Britain. Like other Federalists, he thought that the issues of neutral countries' trading rights and impressment could be easily resolved by other means, and that such a conflict would cause far more economic hardship than any benefit that might be gained. In addition, he found the idea of invading Canada—as promoted by War Hawks like Kentucky's Henry Clay (1777–1852; see biographical entry)— ridiculous and unnecessary. Quincy also noted the irony of protecting maritime (seagoing) rights with a war that would be fought on land.

At the same time as the nation was moving toward war, the Federalist Party was losing more and more ground. In fact, in Quincy's state of Massachusetts—formerly a Federalist stronghold—voters had elected a Republican governor in 1811. In addition, the majority of representatives in the state's legislature were Republicans.

For the moment, though, Quincy was still the leading Federalist in Congress, and in the early months of 1812, when it had become obvious even to him that war was a distinct possibility, he tried to work against it. But in June 1812, Madison delivered a war message to Congress, and the House and Senate both voted in favor of war. However, the vote revealed a sizable opposition, of which Quincy's voice was the loudest. Quincy had joined forty-eight other members of Congress—including some Republicans—in voting against the war, and it was he who wrote the statement of dissention (disagreement), which was signed by thirty-four Federalists. As quoted in Donald R. Hickey's *The War of 1812*, the statement warned that the United States was "rushing into difficulties, with little calculation about the means, and little concern about the consequences."

Leaving the U.S. Congress

The Twelfth Congress met for the last time in the fall of 1812, after the war had gotten off to an unpromising start. Although Quincy's career as a national legislator ended when he resigned at the end of the congressional session, he continued to make speeches about the folly of the conflict. In January 1813 Quincy suggested that the war was being used a way to make sure that Secretary of State James Monroe (1758–1831)—Madison's fellow Virginian, fellow Republican, and close friend—would become the next president.

Returning to Boston, Quincy focused on his ties with the Massachusetts Historical Society, the American Academy of Arts and Sciences, and Phillips Academy. He also went to work to make his estate in Braintree a model farm, introducing new and experimental farming methods as well as lecturing and publishing articles on farming-related topics (such as the various uses for manure). Quincy was active in the Washington Benevolent Society, a charitable organization sponsored by the Federalist Party, and in the Boston Hussars, a militia unit made up of wealthy Federalists who conducted showy exercises and parades but never actually fought in the war.

Before 1813 was over, Quincy was elected to the Massachusetts state senate, and in that position he continued to speak out against the war. But Quincy's fellow Federalists were increasingly embarrassed by his outspokenness, and he was not chosen as a delegate to the Hartford Convention (a meeting at which representatives from several New England states expressed their grievances against the Madison administration). Quincy's influence continued to decline, and in 1820 the Federalists dropped him as a senatorial candidate.

Quincy was, however, able to run for the legislature's lower house (the state equivalent of the House of Representatives), and he was elected. In 1821 his fellow legislators chose him to serve as Speaker (a top leadership post), but he soon resigned his office to become a judge in Boston's Municipal Court. In this role he spoke out against jail conditions and the city's treatment of its poor residents.

The Mayor of Boston, and the President of Harvard College

That same year Quincy ran for mayor of Boston but was not elected; he was, however, elected in 1823. He immediately began a series of rigorous reforms: the city's streets were thoroughly cleaned for the first time in its two-hundred-year history; municipal (city) water and sewer systems were introduced; as a public health measure, burials were prevented in certain crowded areas; and a professional fire department was established. Quincy also cracked down on gambling and prostitution, added six new, wide streets, and oversaw the building of the Faneuil Hall Market (also called Quincy Market), a large building with space for markets that is still in use today. Quincy was re-elected five times, but was finally voted out of office in December 1828.

It did not take Quincy long to find another job, however. In January 1829, he became president of Harvard College. When Quincy took over this position, the college was dominated by a very disorderly atmosphere, both academically and socially, and he set about reforming it. Theorizing that if students were treated like gentlemen, their behavior would improve, Quincy improved the food and service provided by the school and made a rule that students be addressed as "Mister." He also instituted a standardized grading system to replace the haphazard grading methods that had previously existed, and helped to build up the college's law school.

Quincy's sixteen years at Harvard included a short period of student rebellion—during which he was burned in effigy (a model presenting him was burned)—that eventually died down. When Quincy resigned in 1845, the college had grown considerably. After his retirement, Quincy commented that he had gotten so accustomed to the noisy college campus that the quiet of the city streets actually kept him awake at night!

Quincy lived for almost twenty more years, keeping busy with literary works (including a history of Boston and a memoir about John Quincy Adams) but generally avoiding politics. When the Civil War began in 1861, Quincy supported President Abraham Lincoln (1809–1865) in the struggle to preserve the Union. In his last public address, given when he was ninety two, he urged the public to stand behind their president. Quincy died on July 1, 1864, after the Union victory had been assured.

For More Information

Books

Heidler, David S., and Jeanne T. Heidler, eds. *Encyclopedia of the War of 1812*. Santa Barbara, Calif.: ABC-CLIO, Inc., 1997.

Hickey, Donald R. *The War of 1812: A Forgotten Conflict*. Urbana: University of Illinois Press, 1989.

McCaughey, Robert A. *Josiah Quincy, 1772–1864: The Last Federalist*. Cambridge, Mass.: Harvard University Press, 1974.

Web sites

War of 1812. [Online] http://www.galafilm.com/1812/e/index.html (accessed on November 26, 2001).

Winfield Scott

Born June 13, 1786
Petersburg, Virginia

Died May 29, 1866
West Point, New York

Military officer

During the War of 1812, Winfield Scott was at the beginning of what would turn out to be a brilliant military career. He was one of several young officers whose talents were recognized after the first two disastrous years of the war. Promoted to the rank of brigadier general, he led his troops to an inspiring victory at the Battle of Chippewa. A strong leader who believed in discipline and whose personal bravery sometimes verged on recklessness, Scott went on to play a major role in the war between the United States and Mexico (1846–48). He also successfully negotiated solutions to other conflicts, and he worked to make the United States Army a more professional and efficient operation.

A military tradition

Winfield Scott was born on June 13, 1786, on his family's estate, Laurel Branch, which was located about fourteen miles from Petersburg, Virginia. His paternal grandfather had emigrated (come to live from another country) to the United States from Scotland in 1746, and members of his family had

Portrait: Winfield Scott.
Photograph reproduced by permission of Hulton/Archive.

been politically active during the colonial period. Scott's father, William, who died when he was six years old, had been a captain during the Revolutionary War (1775–83). His mother, Ann Mason Scott, raised her four children alone after her husband's death, and died herself when Scott was seventeen. He would later write in his autobiography that his beloved mother had been the inspiration for all his success.

Scott was educated at home until he was twelve years old, then sent to several boarding schools. Because of a legal technicality, he did not inherit his family's estate and all of the wealth that went with it. That meant that he had to borrow money to enroll in William and Mary College in Williamsburg, Virginia. Though a popular choice for many young men like himself, William and Mary did not suit Scott's personality. He thought the students were not religious enough.

Scott left college after only one year, having decided to become a lawyer. In the early nineteenth century, lawyers trained for their profession by becoming apprentices (low-paid assistants) to established attorneys, then taking the bar examination (a test that lawyers must pass before beginning their careers). Thus Scott went to work in the Petersburg office of David Robinson. He passed the bar in 1807. However, he only had practiced law for one year when he decided to join the army. Tensions were building between Great Britain and the United States over trade issues and sailors' rights, especially during and after the *Chesapeake* and *Leopard* affair, when the British removed some U.S. sailors by force and made them serve in the British navy. This practice of removing soldiers was called impressment.

"...the bugle and the drum"

Convinced it was his duty to defend his country, Scott signed up with the Virginia militia (a state-sponsored army that is available for federal government service on a temporary basis). As he later stated in his autobiography, this is where he first "heard the bugle and the drum. It was the music that awoke the ambition." This taste of soldiering inspired Scott to seek a commission (an assignment as an officer) in the United States Army. He went to Washington, D.C., and managed to speak personally with President Thomas Jefferson (1743–1826), who promised Scott that he would receive a commission as soon as possible.

In early 1809 Scott was made a captain in an artillery unit. It is said that after hearing the news he immediately bought himself a full dress uniform and spent several hours in front of two mirrors, admiring himself from every angle. That same year, Scott was assigned to join the army at New Orleans, where he arrived on April 1. He soon displayed not only an eagerness and ability to learn that would continue to mark his behavior, but the sharp tongue that would continue to get him into trouble.

Punished for misconduct

In 1807 Scott had been present at the Richmond, Virginia, trial of Aaron Burr (1756–1836), a former vice president who was accused of treason (he was eventually found innocent). Also involved in the scandal was an army general named James Wilkinson (1757–1825), although no charges were brought against him. Learning that Wilkinson was his commanding officer, Scott spoke openly against him, calling him a "liar and a scoundrel" who was as treasonous as Burr. Even though almost everybody agreed with Scott, such open criticism of a fellow officer went against the army's code of conduct.

Scott was court-martialed (brought before a military court) and found guilty of conduct unbecoming an officer and a gentleman in 1810. His punishment was having to leave military service for one year. Scott used the year to study military history and British military manuals, so that by the end of this period he was probably better prepared for war than any other U.S. officer.

A promising young army officer

When Scott's one-year punishment was finished, he joined the staff of Wade Hampton (1751–1835), who had taken over for Wilkinson at New Orleans. In the meantime, the tensions between the United States and Great Britain had been mounting. The United States was upset with Britain because of its maritime policy of impressment, and because of its overly friendly relations with Native Americans. (Americans believed that the British were encouraging the Native Americans to attack white settlers who were moving west.) These issues led to the June 1812 declaration of war. Although the United States had declared the war, the country was unprepared militarily. The fact that high-ranking officers were in short supply worked to Scott's benefit: normally his court martial would have been a great strike against him, but now the army overlooked this blemish and promoted him to lieutenant colonel. He was made second-in-command of an artillery regiment stationed in Philadelphia, Pennsylvania.

During the first year of the war, the United States had a three-pronged plan for invading British-controlled Canada. Troops were to cross the border in the Northwest Territory, at Detroit (in what is now the state of Michigan); at the Niagara River, which connects lakes Ontario and Erie in the northeastern United States; and at Lake Champlain, about 250 miles northeast of the Niagara, between New York and Vermont. Assigned to the Niagara front, Scott took his regiment to Buffalo, New York, reporting to the joint commanders, Brigadier General Alexander Smyth (1765–1830) and Stephen Van Rensselaer (1764–1839), on October 12, 1812. He saw his first major action the next day, at the Battle of Queenston.

The Battle of Queenston

U.S. troops crossed the Niagara into Canada from Lewiston, New York, attacking the British position on the riverbank and nearby cliffs of Queenston, in what is now Ontario, Canada. Scott did not arrive with the first attachment of troops, entering the battle after the commanding officer, Colonel Solomon Van Rensselaer (1774–1852; a relative of Stephen Van Rensselaer) was wounded. Although the American troops held their own at first, the arrival of British reinforcements, as well as the refusal of U.S. militia to join the fight, doomed their effort. Scott was taken prisoner and barely escaped being killed by Native American warriors (taking part in the battle as allies of the British) who did not know, or did not want to admit, that the fight was over.

Released in November in exchange for a captured British officer, Scott returned to duty in January 1813. In March, he was made a full colonel and a regimental commander. This would prove to be a bad year for the American side, and especially for Scott, who was continually frustrated by what he saw as the inefficiency and incompetence of the military's high command. On May 28, Scott had a chance to exhibit his own leadership skills when he planned and led a successful attack on British-held Fort George (located on the Canadian side of the Niagara River, downstream from Lake Ontario). Scott was the first to enter the fort, and he personally halted a trail of burning gunpowder that led to a magazine (ammunitions storehouse) and seized the British flag.

Preparing for a new campaign

Scott was put in command of the captured fort, and worked on building up its defenses. In October, he joined the U.S. troops fighting along the St. Lawrence River, annoyed by the repeated defeats suffered by the U.S. side and increasingly convinced that American soldiers needed better training. After the battle on the St. Lawrence, Scott was sent to Albany, New York to take part in preparations for the spring campaign of 1814.

As the war continued, U.S. leaders finally responded to the military's generally poor performance by getting rid of some of the older, less competent officers and promoting younger ones who had proven themselves on the battlefield. One of the latter was Scott, who became the army's youngest brigadier general in the spring of 1814. He was put in charge of his own brigade in the army headed by Jacob Brown (1778–1828), which was assembling at Buffalo, New York.

In Buffalo, Scott put into place a rigorous training program. His soldiers drilled for up to ten hours per day, six days per week. In addition, Scott made sure that his men kept up the highest standards of sanitation (cleanliness, or the lack thereof, was a huge problem in the military and contributed to a high incidence of illness), dress, discipline, and courtesy. By the time the summer arrived, Scott's troops were more than ready for battle. Major changes had taken place not only in their physical condition and military skills but in how they felt about themselves: they now had self-respect, and also deep respect for the commander who had brought them to this point.

Troops perform well at Chippewa

In 1814 the United States continued to pursue the plan, which still called for an invasion of Canada launched across the Niagara River. Scott and his men would carry out their part of this plan on July 4 and 5, when they met the British at the Battle of Chippewa (which took place on the Chippewa River, a tributary of the Niagara). Dressed in new gray jackets because the usual blue wool used for uniforms had been unavailable, Scott's troops led the advance. British general Phineas Riall (1775–1850) had assumed they were militiamen when he saw the unusual color of their uniforms, but after witnessing the coolness and skill with which the men marched, maneuvered, and shot, Riall exclaimed, "Those are regulars, by God!" (meaning, regular soldiers).

The United States won the Battle of Chippewa, marking the first time American regular soldiers had beaten British regulars in an evenly matched clash. The U.S. public rejoiced in the victory, and Scott was given much of the credit, even though some said that his aggressiveness put soldiers' lives in danger unnecessarily.

Despite the loss at the Chippewa River, the British army kept moving north along the Niagara, looking for chances to catch the Americans unprepared. On July 25 another heated battle took place, this one at Lundy's Lane, just west of Niagara Falls. The two armies fought through the day, and the U.S. troops finally forced the British to retreat, but with the arrival of reinforcements around nightfall the British surged back. Scott had two horses shot from under him before he was finally badly wounded, shot in the shoulder and hit in the ribs with a cannonball. The American troops were forced to retreat to Fort Erie, and the battle ended in a draw.

Acclaimed as a war hero

Although Scott's wounds kept him out of the rest of the war, his fame as a military hero had spread throughout the nation and he received many honors, including a gold

Remembering Lundy's Lane

The following reminiscence was written by William Dunlop, a surgeon present after the Battle of Lundy's Lane, which took place near Niagara Falls in New York on July 25, 1814.

"... the misery their quarrels lead to...."

It would be a useful lesson to cold-blooded politicians, who calculate on a war costing so many lives and so many limbs as they would calculate on a horse costing so many pounds [British money] ... to witness such a scene, if only for one hour.

This simple and obvious truth was suggested to my mind by the exclamation of poor woman. I had two hundred and twenty wounded turned in upon me that morning, and among others an American farmer, who had been on the field either as a militia man or a camp follower. He was nearly sixty years of age, but of a most Herculean frame. One ball [cannon ball] had shattered his thigh bone, and another lodged in his body, the last obviously mortal. His wife, a respectable elderly looking woman, came over under a flag of truce, and immediately repaired to the hospital, where she found her husband lying on a truss of straw, writhing in agony, for his sufferings were dreadful.

Such an accumulation of misery seemed to have stunned her, for she ceased wailing, sat down on the ground, and taking her husband's head on her lap, continued long, moaning and sobbing, while the tears flowed fast down her face; she seemed for a considerable time in a state of stupor, till awakened by a groan from her unfortunate husband, she clasped her hands, and looking wildly around, exclaimed, "O that the King and the President were both here this moment to see the misery their quarrels lead to—they surely would never go to war without a cause that they could give as a reason to God at the last day, for thus destroying the creatures that He hath made in his own image."

In half an hour the poor fellow ceased to suffer.

Source: War of 1812. *[Online]* http://www.galafilm. com/1812/e/index.html (accessed on November 26, 2001).

medal and proclamation of thanks from the U.S. Congress. Scott was not content to settle for wartime glory, however, and immediately set out in pursuit of new goals and accomplishments. Scott was named by President James Madison (1751–1836) as one of only six generals to remain on active duty in the peacetime army. In 1815, following a trip to Europe to study French military methods, Scott published *Rules and Regulations for the Field Exercise and Maneuvers of Infantry*, a manual to aid the army in the training of soldiers.

In March 1817 Scott married Maria Mayo of Richmond, Virginia, and went to New York City to take up his position as head of the army's Eastern Division. During the next two decades, he would play an important role as a peacekeeper and negotiator rather than as a warrior. In the late 1820s and 1830s, Scott was called upon to help settle several conflicts that arose from the resistance of Native Americans to being resettled on land that the government had put aside for them. In June 1932, for instance, President Andrew Jackson (1767–1845; see biographical entry) assigned Scott to help negotiate an end to an uprising of Sac and Fox tribes in Illinois and Wisconsin territories.

The Mexican-American War

Scott reached what may be considered the peak of his career during the 1840s. In 1841 President John Tyler (1790–1862) named him commander in chief of the U.S. Army, a title he would hold for the next twenty years. By now Scott had earned the nickname "Old Fuss and Feathers" due to his fondness for ceremony and insistence on a strict dress code and tight discipline. He was strongly opposed to the use of alcohol, and reportedly once ordered that any soldier found drunk would be forced to dig a grave his own size, so that he could see where he would end up if he kept drinking. Scott labored to make the army more professional by constantly trying to improve training methods and enforce discipline. However, his job was made more difficult by limited funds and general lack of interest on the part of the federal government.

Scott had an opportunity to prove his brilliance as a battle strategist and commander when, in May 1846, the United States went to war with Mexico over disputed territory in Texas. At the beginning of the war, Scott had to stay in headquarters to plan and coordinate strategy, even though he would have preferred to be in the field with the soldiers. A fundamental disagreement with President James K. Polk (1795–1849), who wanted a quick end to the war and urged a more aggressive approach than Scott thought it wise to make, led to Scott being replaced by General Zachary Taylor (1784–1850). Taylor could not achieve a victory any more rapidly, so in the end command of the war effort shifted back to Scott. This time, he would go to Mexico to lead the campaign himself.

On March 9 Scott led a ten-thousand-man invasion force in a historic amphibious (involving both land and sea forces) landing at the Mexican coastal city of Vera Cruz. At the end of March, the Mexicans surrendered the city to the United States. Scott now pointed his army inland toward Mexico City, the capital of Mexico, which is located more than two hundred miles from the coast. During the spring and summer, Scott's forces won impressive victories at Cerro Gordo, Contreras, and Churabusco, leading to an unsuccessful armistice (peace agreement) and the resumption of conflict in early September.

Again honored as military hero

After more battles at Molino del Rey and Chapultepec, the United States forces entered Mexico City on September 13, and the war was soon over. Scott took command of a temporary military government, a job he did so well that he was asked by a group of Mexican leaders to take over as Mexico's dictator (absolute ruler). Scott declined the offer and returned home in February 1848 to a hero's welcome similar to that he had received for his role in the War of 1812. Despite continuing tensions between Scott and Polk (and Polk's attempts to discredit him), Scott was again honored with a gold medal from Congress.

Scott had long harbored a wish to hold an elected office, and in 1852 the Whigs (one of two political parties now dominant in American politics) nominated him as their presidential candidate. However, Scott's tendency to switch sides on slavery, which was a major issue in the election, caused him to alienate members of his own party, and he lost the election to Democrat Franklin Pierce (1804–1869).

In 1855 Scott was promoted to lieutenant general, a title that only George Washington (1732–1799) had previously held. Despite his advancing age, he continued to take part in attempts to negotiate disputes, such as the conflict with Great Britain over who controlled the San Juan Islands in the Pacific northwest. Scott was seventy-five years old when, in 1861, the

Civil War began. He planned the defense of Washington, D.C., should the Confederacy (the Southern states) attack, and also developed a special strategy for winning the war. Known as the Anaconda Plan, it called for dividing and economically strangling the South. The plan would eventually be implemented and was credited with helping the North win the war.

Scott retired from the army in November 1861. He spent the remaining five years of his life traveling to Europe and writing his memoirs, and with the ending of the Civil War he witnessed the preservation of the Union he had served for fifty-three years.

For More Information

Books

Elliott, Charles W. *Winfield Scott: The Soldier and the Man.* New York: Macmillan, 1937.

Heidler, David S., and Jeanne T. Heidler, eds. *Encyclopedia of the War of 1812.* Santa Barbara, Calif.: ABC-CLIO, Inc., 1997.

Scott, Winfield. *Memoirs of Lieutenant General Scott.* 2 vols. New York: Sheldon and Company, 1864.

Smith, Arthur D. Howden. *Old Fuss and Feathers: The Life and Exploits of Winfield Scott.* New York: Greystone Press, 1937.

Web sites

General Winfield Scott. [Online] http://msnhomepages.talkcity.com/ResortRd/ballykissangel2/WinfieldScott.html (accessed on November 26, 2001).

Winfield Scott. [Online] http:///www.tulane.edu/~latner/Scott.html (accessed on November 26, 2001).

Winfield Scott: General. [Online] http://library.thinkquest.org/12587/contents/personalities/wscott/ws.html (accessed on November 26, 2001).

Tecumseh

Born c. 1768
Old Piqua
(near present-day Springfield, Ohio)

Died October 5, 1813
Moraviantown, Canada
(near present-day Chatham, Ontario)

Warrior, tribal chief

Tecumseh was a Shawnee war chief and one of the most influential of all Native American leaders. Respected by both friends and enemies as a powerful public speaker and a dynamic, humane person, he tried to convince Native Americans from many different tribes to join together to keep white settlers from taking over traditional Native American lands. Tecumseh had won many recruits and become a serious threat to white American settlement in the Northwest Territory when, during the War of 1812, he decided to ally himself and his people with the British side. His death during the Battle of the Thames spelled the end of his dream of a Native American confederacy.

Grows up during conflict

The son of a veteran Shawnee warrior named Puckesinwa and Methoataske, a woman who may have been of Creek or Cherokee origin, Tecumseh was born in the Shawnee village of Old Piqua, which was located on the Mad River in what is now western Ohio. His name means "flying or springing across." Tecumseh's people had lived in the Ohio River

Portrait: Tecumseh.
Photograph reproduced by permission of Corbis Corporation (Bellevue).

Valley for thousands of years—farming, fishing, hunting the plentiful game in the area, and sometimes warring with other Native American tribes. But the last quarter of the eighteenth century brought a major change to the lives of the Shawnees and other Native Americans as white American settlers began to enter the area called the Northwest Territory (including the present-day states of Ohio, Indiana, Illinois, Michigan, and parts of Minnesota) by the U.S. government.

The lifestyles of the Native Americans and whites of European descent were very different, and conflicts soon arose. One of the major conflicts involved the concept of property, for most Native Americans believed that land could not be owned by any one person but must be shared by all. Although Americans made treaties to obtain land from various representatives of Native American tribes, other Native Americans did not recognize such agreements. At the same time, some Americans also failed to live up to the terms of treaties. As a result, violent attacks by each side upon the other became increasingly common.

Tecumseh grew up in the midst of this time of great chance and conflict, and in 1774 the violence touched his life directly when his father was killed by Long Knives (the Native American term for whites) in the Battle of Point Pleasant. Three years later, the Shawnee chief Cornstalk (called Cornplanter in some sources), whom Tecumseh greatly admired, also was killed by whites. Enraged and alarmed by the prospect of losing both their land and their lives, Shawnees stepped up their attacks on white settlements.

The U.S. government was not long in responding to this threat to its citizens. In May 1779 an army force led by Colonel John Bowman attacked the Shawnee settlement of Old Chilicothe (in Ohio). Even though there were more American than Native American losses, the attack sent ripples of terror through the entire Shawnee tribe. Soon about one-third of them (one thousand people) decided to leave the area and settle in what is now southeastern Missouri. Tecumseh's mother was one of these. She left her ten-year-old son in the care of his sister Tecumpease. Tecumseh's brother Chicksika (whose intense hatred for white people dated to their father's murder) also took responsibility for him, teaching him the skills of hunting and war that he would need as a Shawnee man.

Emerges as a leader

Tecumseh's courage and leadership ability were evident early in his life, when he would organize and lead hunting parties with other young boys. When he was about fifteen years old, he took part in his first battle, fighting against white settlers on the Mad River. After witnessing Chicksika being slightly wounded, Tecumseh fled the battle. Although he soon returned and was forgiven by the other warriors for running away, Tecumseh remembered the incident with shame and was determined never to repeat it.

In the years that followed, Tecumseh took part in many fights as the Shawnee attempted to protect their territory. At seventeen, he participated in an attack on a white settlement near present-day Maysville in which all of the settlers but one were killed. The warriors brought the one survivor back to their camp and spent the next day torturing him to death. Tecumseh was horrified by this act and spoke out against it, claiming that torturing prisoners was not an honorable way for a warrior to behave. His speech was so convincing that those involved promised to stop this practice. The incident was an early hint of Tecumseh's considerable powers as an orator (speechmaker) as well as his compassion for other human beings.

Recruits tribes to resist whites

Now a young man—and passionately opposed to white encroachment (gradually taking over) on Native American lands—Tecumseh traveled around with his brother, visiting their mother's village in Missouri as well as both Shawnee and Miami settlements in southern Illinois. In 1788 Tecumseh witnessed Chicksika's death by whites in a clash near Nashville, Tennessee. Two years later, he headed north again. He became a follower of a Miami chief named Little Turtle (c. 1752–1812), who was calling for Native Americans to join together to oppose whites.

Again, the U.S. government response to Native American resistance took the form of military action. Troops under General Josiah Harmar (1753–1813) clashed with warriors in 1790, and the next year Tecumseh took part (as the leader of a scouting party) in a battle against forces under General Arthur St. Clair (1736–1818), who was then the governor of the

Northwest Territory. The same year, Tecumseh again traveled south, rallying the Shawnee as well as Creeks and Cherokees to resist whites and building a reputation as a dynamic leader.

Meanwhile, the U.S. Army improved its efforts to stem Native American aggression through better planning and increased supplies. On August 20, 1794, U.S troops under General "Mad" Anthony Wayne (1745–1796) defeated a Native American force in the Battle of Fallen Timbers on the Maumee River in Ohio. The Americans lost 38 soldiers, while several hundred warriors—including another of Tecumseh's brothers, Sauwauseekau—were killed.

The battle was followed by a two-month conference attended by about a thousand Native Americans from twelve tribes. On August 3, representatives of the tribe signed the Greenville Treaty, in which they agreed to give a large area of land that included most of what is now Ohio to the U.S. government in exchange for a $10,000 annuity (yearly payment). Tecumseh did not sign the treaty and, furious that those who had would give away so much land, he refused to acknowledge the agreement. Since Little Turtle was among the treaty's signers, Tecumseh now became the leading chief of those Native Americans who opposed white settlement. He began to express the idea that treaties signed by individuals were not valid, since the land belonged to all Native Americans.

Tenskwatawa, the Prophet

Meanwhile, another member of Tecumseh's family was making a name for himself. Tecumseh's brother Laulewasika (1775–1836) was an unpopular figure who—like many Native Americans who had adopted, to varying degrees, white ways—was addicted to alcohol. But in 1805 Laulewasika claimed to have had a vision in which the Great Spirit (the Native American version of a supreme being or god) showed him the path that Native Americans must take to survive.

Changing his name to Tenskwatawa (which means "the open door"), he began to preach that Shawnees must return to their own traditions, abandoning the use of the tools, clothing, weapons, and especially alcohol of white people. Instead, they should develop their traditional farming skills and refuse to accept anything from whites on credit. Tenskwatawa established a settlement at Greenville, Ohio, where a steadily increasing number of followers joined him.

Tenskwatawa's movement was essentially a religious one, while Tecumseh's goals were more political. Still, he recognized that by teaming up with his brother he could recruit more warriors for his own cause. Thus Tecumseh and Tenskwatawa joined forces, together promoting the goals of land shared in common by all Native Americans, and an alliance or confederacy that erased the boundaries (and, hopefully, the sometimes deep-seated animosities) between tribes.

Their numbers grew, and eventually the area around Greenville had been so depleted of game and fish (along with increasing numbers of white settlers moving into the area) that the two leaders began to look for a new location. With permission from the Potawotami and Kickapoo tribes, they settled on a spot on the west bank of the Tippecanoe River (in present-day Indiana), where it meets the Wabash River. The settlement became known as Prophet's Town.

Tecumseh began traveling southward to try to gain more recruits, even venturing as far as Florida. He also went north to Canada, establishing links with the British and acquiring weapons, ammunition, and clothing from them. As he spoke to various tribes, Tecumseh often received a cool reception from older leaders, who felt threatened by the Shawnee chief and who warned their people about the dangers of making alliances with old enemies. Many younger warriors, however, embraced Tecumseh's ideas with enthusiasm. By 1810 Tecumseh had gained the support of members of the Sauk, Winnebago, Creek, Cherokee, and Seminole tribes and about one thousand of them had gathered at Prophet's Town.

Tecumseh meets with Harrison

During the same period that Tecumseh was winning recruits to his cause, William Henry Harrison (1773–1841; see biographical entry), the governor of the Northwest Territory, was doing everything he could to make his region safe for white settlement. In 1809 he persuaded chiefs of the Delaware, Miami, and Potawatomi tribes to sign the Treaty of

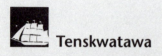

Tenskwatawa

During the War of 1812 the United States was testing and proving the depth of its independence from Great Britain. At the same time the Native Americans were involved in a desperate struggle to hold on to the lands and lives they had known for thousands of years. White settlers were moving west in large numbers, and many Native Americans were responding with violent resistance. During this period, two leaders emerged to direct the effort to bring Native American peoples together to resist white encroachment. They were Shawnee war chief Tecumseh, who led the political and military aspects of the resistance movement, and his brother Tenskwatawa, who provided the spiritual dimension that reinforced Tecumseh's ideas.

The brothers were born in a Shawnee village in what is now Ohio. Born in 1775 and seven years younger than Tecumseh, Tenskwatawa was originally named Lalawethika (which means "Noisemaker"). While he was growing up, the Native Americans who lived in the Northwest Territory were beginning to experience many difficulties as white people moved onto their lands. Their lives were being disrupted by poverty and violence. Tecumseh and Lalawethika's father, for instance, died soon after the younger child's birth, killed in a confrontation with whites.

Some Native Americans were finding an escape in alcohol, which was often offered to traded to them by whites who hoped it would make them easier to manipulate. Lalawethika became addicted to alcohol at a very young age. Short and physically unattractive, with a badly scarred face, he made himself unpopular with his frequent boasting and unwillingness to participate in the hunting and fishing expeditions in which other young men took part. He seemed a hopeless case until, in 1805, a change occurred in him.

It was at this stage in his life that Lalawethika claimed to have a vision (possibly after drinking himself into a stupor) in which he spoke with the Master of Life (also called the Great Spirit, the highest god to Native Americans). Stating that he had been shown the best way for Native Americans to avoid the torment for which they seemed headed, he changed his name to Tenskwatawa (meaning "the Open Door;" translated by whites as the "Prophet") and quit drinking. He began preaching that Native Americans must give up the evil white ways they had adopted, especially the

Fort Wayne, by which they gave away three million acres of land for $7,000 and an annuity of $1,750. When he heard about the treaty, Tecumseh was enraged, insisting that the chiefs involved—whom he threatened to kill—had had no right to make such a deal. By this time Harrison had heard ru-

drinking of alcohol, but also the use of white clothing, farming methods, and even guns. They must return to their traditional customs and regard each other as brothers.

Like Tecumseh, Tenskwatawa was a persuasive speaker, and he soon had a growing following among the Shawnee. Within two years, members of other Native American nations also had joined his movement. In 1808, having searched for a site that was sufficiently isolated, Tenskwatawa established a settlement for his followers at a place in Indiana Territory where the Wabash and Tippecanoe Rivers meet. Called Prophet's Town by whites, the village was known as Tippecanoe by the Native Americans.

In the summer of 1811, after a meeting with the governor of the Indiana Territory, William Henry Harrison, Tecumseh traveled south to gain more followers for his movement. Believing that Tecumseh's absence would allow a more effective strike against Prophet's Town, Harrison led a force of U.S. soldiers there. While they were camped close to the village, Tenskwatawa worked his warriors into a frenzy as he urged them to attack the American camp. He assured them that his magical powers would protect them from the whites' weapons.

Although Harrison's troops were initially overwhelmed by the attack, which came in the early morning hours of November 7, 1811, they were able to drive back the warriors. The next day, they destroyed Prophet's Town. Tenskwatawa's followers were so angry with him that for some time his life was in danger; they tied him up and threatened to kill him. When Tecumseh returned to find the settlement in ruins and his followers scattered, he banished Tenskwatawa to keep him from doing more harm.

The damage, however, was already done and Tenskwatawa would never regain the popularity he once knew. After the War of 1812, Tenskwatawa fled into Canada where he was supported by the British government, who Tecumseh had sided with during the war. In 1826, Tenskwatawa returned to the United States just in time for the forced removal of the Native Americans to land set aside for them in Kansas. He died in 1836.

Sources: Heidler, David S., and Jeanne T. Heidler, eds. Encyclopedia of the War of 1812. Santa Barbara, Calif.: ABC-CLIO, Inc., 1997; "Tenskwatawa," in Encyclopedia of World Biography Supplement, Vol. 20. Gale Group, 2000.

mors of the two charismatic Shawnee leaders who had attracted such a following, and the rumors made him nervous. Wrongly assuming that Tenskwatawa was in charge, Harrison invited him to a meeting at Vincennes, the territorial capital, in August 1810.

Tecumseh attended Harrison's meeting in place of Tenskwatawa. In Benjamin Drake's book, *Life of Tecumseh,* a witness at the meeting described the Native American leader as "about six feet high, straight, with large, fine features, and altogether a daring, bold-looking fellow," who brought with him four hundred warriors in full war paint. The meeting grew tense and almost came to blows, but Tecumseh and his followers eventually retreated. In 1811 there was another meeting between Tecumseh and Harrison, which was more peaceful (thanks to the presence of U.S. soldiers) but no more productive. According to Tecumseh's biographer R. David Edmunds, Harrison may have been Tecumseh's sworn enemy but he also admired him, writing that "the implicit obedience and respect which the followers of Tecumseh pay to him is really astonishing and … bespeaks him one of those uncommon geniuses, which spring up occasionally to produce revolutions and overturn the established order of things."

The Battle of Tippencanoe

Soon after his 1811 meeting with Harrison, Tecumseh set off for the south to attempt to win converts from tribes in Mississippi, Georgia, the Carolinas, Alabama, Arkansas, and Florida. Harrison took advantage of Tecumseh's absence, marching a thousand soldiers toward Prophet's Town with the intention of teaching those gathered there a lesson. Harrison's army camped a few miles from the settlement waiting for an opportunity to attack. Meanwhile, Tecumseh had instructed Tenskwatawa to strictly avoid any kind of conflict with the whites. Tenskwatawa, however, disobeyed Tecumseh's instructions by ordering an attack on Harrison's men during the early morning hours of November 7, 1811.

The U.S. troops were taken by surprise and suffered many casualties, but they managed to chase away their Native American attackers. The next day, the Americans burned Prophet's Town. Tecumseh returned in early 1812 to find the settlement in ruins, and his brother disgraced by the defeat. Tecumseh exiled his brother and vowed to seek revenge for what would become known as the Battle of Tippecanoe. Still, his dream of a powerful Native American alliance had suffered a major blow.

Despite the Native Americans' defeat, attacks on white settlers increased. Instead of seeing the Native Americans' loss of their traditional lands as the motivation for these attacks, many Americans (including Harrison) blamed the British, accusing them of encouraging and aiding the Native Americans in their violent resistance. Some even claimed that British officials paid warriors for white scalps (it was a Native American custom to remove and retain the scalp of fallen enemies).

Tecumseh allies with the British

The War of 1812 between the United States and Great Britain began in June 1812. It was provoked by two major issues. The first was Britain's maritime policy of impressment in its war with France. This policy was where British officials boarded U.S. ships to capture deserters from their own navy, often wrongfully taking American citizens in the process. The other issue that led to the war was Americans' belief that Great Britain was encouraging Native Americans to attack white settlers who were moving west. When the war began both the United States and Great Britain knew that it would be a great advantage to have as many Native Americans as possible on their side. The British gained the upper hand when Tecumseh—convinced that the a British victory would mean the establishment of a Native American homeland within U.S. territory—decided to join the British the same month that the war began.

When Tecumseh aligned himself with the British, he brought with him thousands of warriors. In fact, the U.S. agent in charge of Native American matters, William Jones, estimated that about ten thousand Native Americans had aligned themselves with Great Britain. (Of course, not all of these were warriors, for the men brought their families with them to the British camps, and feeding them all would become a major burden for the British.) During the next year and a half, Tecumseh and his men would fight in several important battles (such as those at the Raisin River, Fort Meigs, and Fort Stephenson), and some commentators have asserted that the Native American presence was a major factor in the inability of the United States to successfully invade Canada.

In the summer of 1812, Tecumseh was given command of all Native American forces and made a brigadier general in the British army, a rare honor for a Native American. He was introduced to General Isaac Brock (1769–1812; see biographical entry), commander of the British forces in the northwest region, and the two immediately liked and respected each other. Tecumseh's warriors were beside Brock's soldiers on August 15, when U.S. troops under General William Hull (1753–1825) surrendered at Detroit. Even though he had more men than Brock, Hull had been spooked by the prospect of an attack that included Native Americans, who were known among whites for their brutality. Tecumseh, however, was known for taking mercy on prisoners and for preventing needless slaughter and torture, and everyone knew that his word could be trusted.

Tecumseh was deeply saddened when Brock was killed in October at the Battle of Queenston. His replacement was the overweight Colonel Henry Procter (1763–1822), who failed to gain the Shawnee chief's respect. On September 10, 1813, the Americans won a major battle on Lake Erie and thus gained dominance on that important body of water. With his supply lines now cut off, Proctor ordered his troops to retreat from the Detroit area—of which they had had control for more than a year—and move toward eastern Canada. Adamant that the British should turn and face the Americans instead of fleeing, Tecumseh was incensed. As a local newspaper (the *Weekly Register*) reported several weeks later, Tecumseh told Procter, "We must compare our father's conduct to a fat animal, that carries its tail upon its back, but when affrighted, he drops it between his legs and runs off...." He continued, "Our lives are in the hands of the Great Spirit. We are determined to defend our lands, and if it be his will, we wish to leave our bones upon them." These words would prove prophetic.

On October 2 U.S. troops under Harrison set out in pursuit of Procter's fleeing force, which was moving along the Thames River in what is now southeastern Ontario. Three days later, the two armies met near Moraviantown (near the present-day city of Chatham). Procter had 430 regular soldiers and Tecumseh's 600 Native American warriors, while Harrison had 3000 troops. The ensuing battle did not last very long, for the British were soon surrounded and caught in a crossfire. The Native American warriors were less willing to give up, until the news that Tecumseh had been killed began to spread.

The news was true, for Tecumseh had been shot in the chest. His body was never found, although many stories were told about what had happened to the famous Shawnee. Some American soldiers later claimed to have cut strips of skin from Tecumseh's body as souvenirs, while other reports claimed that his corpse was carried away by his warriors and buried in a nearby swamp. Admired by so many—whether British, Native American, or U.S. citizen—Tecumseh would become a North American folk hero famous for his speaking skills, his bold leadership, and his personal integrity. Yet the confederacy of Native American tribes that he envisioned would never materialize. With his death, the dream was crushed, and white settlement would continue its relentless push across the northwestern, then western, U.S. territories.

For More Information

Books

Drake, Benjamin. *Life of Tecumseh*. Manchester, N.H.: Ayer Company, 1988.

Eckert, Allan W. *A Sorrow in Our Heart*. New York: Bantam, 1992.

Edmunds, R. David. *Tecumseh and the Quest for Indian Leadership*. Boston: Little, Brown, 1984.

Gilbert, Bill. *God Gave Us This Country: Tekamthi and the First American Civil War*. New York: Anchor/Doubleday, 1989.

Sugden, John. *Tecumseh's Last Stand*. Norman: University of Oklahoma Press, 1985.

Niles Register, November 6, 1813, p. 175.

Web sites

Edmunds, R. David. *Tecumseh*. [Online] http://www.historychannel.com/cgi-bin/frameit.cgi?p (accessed on November 26, 2001).

"The War of 1812 and Tecumseh." *Bkejwanong: Walpole Island First Nation*. [Online] http://www-personal.umich.ed/~ksands/War.html (accessed on November 26, 2001).

Tecumseh: Warrior-Statesman of the Shawnees. [Online] http://members.tripod.com/~RFester/tecum.html (accessed on November 26, 2001).

William Weatherford

Born c. 1781
Coosauda Village (in present-day Alabama)

Died March 9, 1824
Monroe County, Alabama

Native American warrior

William Weatherford was one of several leaders of mixed Native American and European heritage who became prominent during the Creek War, which took place at the same period as—and was closely related to—the War of 1812. A Native American people who lived in what are now Alabama and western Georgia, the Creeks were divided in their response to white Americans settling on their lands; the violent resistance chosen by one faction, the Red Sticks, caused the U.S. government to take action. A man of eloquence, courage, and leadership ability, Weatherford was drawn into the conflict somewhat reluctantly. But he did choose to lead his people against the United States, with disastrous results.

Choosing to live as a Creek

In the early nineteenth century, it was not at all uncommon in Creek communities to see people who were the offspring of Creek women and men of European heritage, usually traders of British or Scottish origin. Because these mixed-race children often faced discrimination from whites but none in Creek society, which was matrilineal (kinship is determined through the mother, not the father), they often chose to live within the Creek world. Weatherford's family had European ties that went back several generations: his French great-grandfather had been the commander of a French fort located near the junction of the Coosa and Tallapoosa rivers in central Alabama.

Weatherford's mother was named Sehoy III, and his father was a red-haired Scot named Charles Weatherford, who ran a trading post near the village of Coosauda, where his son was born. Young William grew to be a handsome boy with black eyes, light-colored hair, and pale skin. Although he could have passed as white, he chose to live among his mother's people and spent his early years absorbing their values. These included loyalty to one's clan (a smaller group within the tribe), respect for one's elders, and a general concern for others. In addition to his mother, Weatherford was strongly influenced by his uncle, Alexander McGillivray, a mixed-race Creek chief who taught him to speak English (he chose not to learn to read and write, however).

Creek boys practiced the skills needed to hunt and fish early in their lives, but they also spent a fair amount of their time playing sports and games. Weatherford became known for his horseback riding skills when he was still very young, and he also enjoyed playing a lacrosse-like game that was popular among the Creeks. At fifteen, he went through an initiation ritual that ushered him into adulthood, at which time he received the name he would use as a warrior: Red Eagle. Like other young Native American men, Weatherford dreamed of proving himself in battle and bringing home the scalp of an enemy (Native Americans customarily cut off the scalps of their dead enemies).

Tensions caused by white settlement

Weatherford came to manhood at a troubled time in Creek history. The tribe had split into the Lower Creeks, who favored peaceful adaptation to the presence of whites in their territory, and the Upper Creeks, who tended to resist such encroachment (gradually taking over land). In the years following the American Revolution (1775–83), the state of Georgia had entered into several treaties by which the Creeks agreed to give up pieces of their land. But not all of the Creeks approved of or honored these treaties. As a young man, Weatherford would have been aware of the growing tension not only between his people and whites, but within the Creek nation.

Weatherford's father Charles became involved in this tension by serving as a source of information for the U.S. government, informing them about what the Creeks were doing or planning to do. Another white man who took a strong interest in the Creeks was Benjamin Hawkins (1754–1816), who in 1796 was appointed by the U.S. government to serve as its agent to the Creek nation. Determined to bring what he and other Americans defined as "civilization" to the Creeks, Hawkins worked hard to persuade them to adopt white ways of government, agriculture, and lifestyle.

Tecumseh seeks Creek followers

In 1897 the U.S. government fueled resentment by building a road from Athens, Georgia to Fort Stoddert, Alabama, directly through Upper Creek territory. Meanwhile, the Lower Creeks had been cooperating with Hawkins and becoming increasingly adapted to white society. By 1811 the Upper Creeks were still angry about the road and also hostile to the Lower Creeks' acceptance of white encroachment. The stage was now set for the arrival of Tecumseh (c. 1768–1813; see biographical entry), a war chief of the Shawnee people (who lived in the Northwest Territory, or what is now Michigan, Ohio, Indiana, Illinois, and parts of Minnesota)—and the son of a Creek mother—who traveled south that fall to gain followers for his cause.

A charismatic person and a very effective speaker, Tecumseh dreamed of an alliance of many different Native American peoples, all of whom would put aside their differences to present a united front to resist white settlement of their lands. By now the War of 1812 was about to start, and Tecumseh hoped to use this conflict between Great Britain and the United States to Native American advantage. He hoped to convince the Creeks to join him in helping the British—whom Tecumseh believed would treat Native Americans fairly—beat the Americans.

Before leaving his home in what is now Indiana, Tecumseh had met with Indiana's governor, William Henry Harrison (1773–1841; see biographical entry), informing him that his people would not accept the presence of whites on their lands. On his way to the Creek territory, Tecumseh stopped to visit the Chickasaw people in what is now Mississippi, but they wanted to keep the peace with the United States. He also was unable to convince the Choctaws. On September 20 Tecumseh arrived at the village of Tuckabatchee, where the Creeks were holding a major meeting called the Grand Council.

Violent incidents increase

Tecumseh made a very powerful speech to the assembled Creek leaders, urging them to come together with other tribes to resist the whites. Weatherford was present at the meeting and rose to speak against Tecumseh's proposal. He said that violently resisting the United States could only end in disaster for the Creeks. The Americans, he pointed out, had already beaten the British once during the American Revolution and would surely do so again. Weatherford asserted that all whites were the enemies of Native Americans, and that the Creeks should remain neutral in the coming war or, if forced to take sides, align themselves with the United States.

Although he had not convinced Weatherford or the Lower Creek leaders, Tecumseh did find followers among the Upper Creeks, especially among their younger warriors. A full-fledged resistance or reform movement sprang up, with several individuals following the lead of Tecumseh's brother Tenskwatawa by claiming to be "prophets" whose magic would provide warriors protection from harm during battle.

Beginning in the spring of 1812, a series of violent incidents occurred that would eventually bring tensions to a head. Two white men were murdered and, on Hawkins' urging, their Upper Creek killers were ordered executed by some Lower Creek chiefs. In early 1813 a group of Creeks who were returning from a visit to the Northwest Territory murdered seven white families who were living in a settlement at the mouth of the Ohio River. Hawkins demanded that the killers be turned in to the U.S. government for prosecution, but instead the Lower Creek chiefs began having the band of murderers killed themselves. The Upper Creeks retaliated by killing several would-be executioners and destroying villages of Creeks who associated with Hawkins.

Agreeing to lead the Red Sticks

The hostile Upper Creeks now began to be known as Red Sticks, a name that refers to the Creek custom of displaying a red war club to indicate war. During the summer of 1813 Weatherford agreed to lead the Red Sticks; however, he may have been forced into this through threats against his family's safety. By this time, Weatherford was thirty years old and a prosperous plantation owner and breeder of fine race horses who frequently hosted guests—both Native American and white—at his home. He had married, but had lost two wives, Mary Moniac and Sapoth Thlaine, and was the father of four children. He had much to lose, and he neither approved of the Red Sticks' cause nor expected it to have a good outcome. Nevertheless, he declared that he would share his people's fate, whatever it might be.

In July another prominent mixed-race Creek named Peter McQueen (c. 1780–1820) led a Red Stick party to Pensacola in Spanish-held Florida. The Spanish authorities, who hoped to use the Creek War to strengthen their own position in the region, had offered to furnish the Red Sticks with guns and ammunition. Meanwhile, a U.S. militia officer named Colonel James Caller had learned of the expedition and led a force of about 180 soldiers to attack it. On July 27 they met McQueen's party, which was returning from Pensacola, at Burnt Corn Creek. The U.S. force had the upper hand at first but then the Red Sticks rallied, and Caller's troops had to retreat.

Even though the Americans got away with most of the supplies the Red Sticks had just received from the Spanish, the Red Sticks considered this a victory for their side. The Battle of Burnt Corn bolstered their confidence, while at the same time sounding a warning bell for the United States. The governors of Tennessee and Georgia quickly authorized fifteen hundred militia from each state to put down the Creeks, who they believed were being urged into violent confrontation by the British and aided by the Spanish. In addition, they knew that a victory against the Creeks could open even more land to white settlement.

The attack on Fort Mims

The Red Sticks now decided that they would attack two U.S. forts in the area, Fort Mims and Fort Pierce, to avenge the attack against them at Burnt Corn Creek. Weatherford was asked to formulate a plan of attack and he did, though still convinced that this war was pointless. More than seven hundred warriors gathered at Flat Creek and began the fifty-mile journey to Fort Mims. As they approached the fort, Weatherford urged them to spare the women and children he knew were inside, but this request would not be honored.

Fort Mims had really only existed for about a month, for it had been hastily constructed after the Battle of Burnt Corn as a refuge for panicky settlers in the region who were worried about Native American attack. Inside were about 300 people, including 120 militiamen and 16 regular soldiers. Fort Mims was not very well protected, and some recommended improvements had not been made. The officer in charge, Major Daniel Beasley, kept the fort's gate open at all times and asked his troops to do no more than play cards all day.

On Sunday, August 29, several reports of Native Americans gathering nearby had reached the fort, but since no evidence could be found, they were ignored. The fort's noon bell had been designated as the Red Sticks' signal to start their attack, and as soon as it sounded their war whoops could be heard by those within the fort. Beasley ran to shut the gate and was killed on the spot, and the Red Stick warriors leapt over his body to enter the fort. Soon a terrible massacre was underway within the fort, with women and children killed alongside the male settlers and soldiers. It was later reported that Weatherford deeply regretted this slaughter of innocent people but could do nothing to stop it.

It was estimated that about 250 to 275 of the occupants of Fort Mims were killed or taken prisoner during the attack, while somewhere between 20 and 40 escaped. Between 200 and 300 Red Sticks also were killed during the attack. News of the massacre at Fort Mims (in which the total number killed was often exaggerated) spread across the Unit-

ed States, and white settlers who lived in Creek territory were, of course, particularly terrified. In Tennessee, militia general Andrew Jackson (1767–1845; see biographical entry) was put in command of one of several militia forces to be sent to fight the Creeks. Meanwhile, Weatherford set up his headquarters at Holy Ground, a place where the Creeks performed religious rituals. He also sent out a message that any Native Americans who did not help the Red Sticks would be punished.

Creek warriors attacking the inhabitants at Fort Mims. About 250 people, including women and children, were killed by the Creek during the massacre. *Photograph reproduced by permission of Hulton/Archive.*

A campaign to stop the Red Sticks

On October 12 Jackson's force met up with troops commanded by Brigadier General John Coffee (1772–1833) near Huntsville, Alabama. Despite a severe shortage of food and supplies, Jackson formulated a bold plan that involved attacking Red Stick villages in succession and finally reaching and taking Pensacola, thereby halting Spanish aid to the Red

Sticks. On November 2, Jackson sent Coffee and with 900 soldiers to the village of Tallushatchee. The troops formed a loop around the village, catching the Red Sticks in a deadly crossfire in which 186 were killed (including some women and children); 84 women and children were taken prisoner. On the American side, only 5 were killed, and 41 wounded.

When Weatherford heard that the village of Talledega had decided to side with Jackson, he immediately sent his warriors to surround the village. Hearing of this, Jackson moved to defend the village with two thousand troops. Arriving on November 9, he sent his army into the same loop or crescent formation that had been so effective at Tallushatchee. In the battle that followed, seven hundred Red Sticks escaped due to a break in the U.S. line, but about three hundred were killed, while Jackson lost less than twenty soldiers.

Though disheartened by these defeats, the Creeks were consoled by the knowledge that their policy of burning crops and supplies before the Americans could take them had caused further suffering for the U.S. troops. However, another crushing blow came in December when a force under General Ferdinand L. Claiborne (1773–1815) won a victory at Holy Ground that disgraced the Red Stick prophets, who had claimed that the enemy could not harm that sacred place. Weatherford was present at this battle, and reportedly made a daring leap—mounted on his horse, Arrow—from a high bluff into the Alabama River while fleeing from pursuing U.S. troops.

The Battle of Horseshoe Bend
Battles fought in January at the villages of Emuckfau and Enotachopco also ended in defeat for the Red Sticks, paving the way for the final blow. The strongest concentration of Red Sticks was at Horseshoe Bend (called Tohopeka by the Creeks), a place where the Tallapoosa River bends into a loop, forming a peninsula of land surrounded on three sides by the river. There the Red Sticks had about one thousand warriors, plus almost three hundred women and children. They put up a breastwork (a protective barrier) at the opening of the settlement.

During the opening months of 1814, Jackson's assault on the Creeks were put on hold due to problems with supplies and dwindling troop numbers (the terms of service of many of the militiamen who had accompanied him to Creek territory had ended). However, in March, bolstered by reinforcements, he was ready to proceed again. On March 26 he arrived at Horseshoe Bend with almost three thousand soldiers, who immediately began firing at the Red Sticks' breastworks. Meanwhile, some of the Native Americans allied with Jackson swam across the river at the back side of the village and stole a number of Red Stick canoes. The canoes were used to ferry U.S. troops back to attack the Red Sticks from behind.

Despite having many more men than the U.S. side, the Red Sticks had fewer guns and could not fight as effectively. Seeing how badly things were going for the Red Sticks, Jackson offered them a chance to surrender, but they refused. They had a reputation for fighting to the death, and in this circumstance most of them would live up to that reputation. Finally the battle ended in a victory for the United States. More than eight hundred Red Sticks had been killed, and more than three hundred were taken prisoner.

A dramatic surrender scene

The Battle of Horseshoe Bend was a crushing defeat for the Creeks, effectively destroying their will to continue the fight. Though elated over the victory (and rewarded with a promotion to major general), Jackson was disappointed that Weatherford had not been captured. In fact, Weatherford was not present at the battle, having left the village a few days earlier (apparently he was convinced the Americans would not attack there).

Jackson now quickly constructed Fort Jackson on the site of the same French fort that Weatherford's grandfather had once commanded. When Creek chiefs began arriving at the fort to work out truce agreements, Jackson demanded that they turn in Weatherford. Hearing of Jackson's order, Weatherford decided to turn himself in and spare the chiefs the trouble. He rode to Fort Jackson on Arrow, shooting a deer on the way. Arriving at Jackson's tent, Weatherford introduced himself, catching the U.S. general very much by surprise.

Weatherford reportedly told Jackson that he would like to keep fighting but that his people were now scattered, forcing him to surrender. He asked no mercy for himself, but requested that Jackson aid the Creek women and children who had fled into the woods after the battle and were struggling to live. Pleased with Weatherford's courage, Jackson offered him a drink, and Weatherford gave Jackson the deer he had shot. They had a long conversation, but when it became apparent that the soldiers and Native American allies in the fort were growing increasingly hostile to Weatherford's presence, Jackson sent him on his way.

The Creek war was now over and, as Weatherford had predicted, it had ended in disaster for the Creeks. With the Treaty of Fort Jackson, the entire Creek nation (including those who had fought alongside the Americans) were forced into signing away twenty million acres of their land. Weatherford settled on a farm in lower Monroe County, Alabama, raising horses and respected by his neighbors. He married Mary Stiggins in 1817 and went on to have five children with her, making a total of nine by his three wives.

In late February 1824 Weatherford was on a hunting expedition when someone killed an albino deer. Declaring that this was an omen of death, Weatherford immediately returned to his home. Three days later, he died. Weatherford was buried near the village of Little River, close to his family's plantation on the Alabama River.

For more information

Books

Griffith, Benjamin W., Jr. *McIntosh and Weatherford: Creek Indian Leaders*. Tuscaloosa: The University of Alabama Press, 1988.

Martin, Joel W. *Sacred Revolt: The Muskogees' Struggle for a New World*. Boston: Beacon Press, 1991.

Keefe, John M. "William Weatherford." *Encyclopedia of the War of 1812*, edited by David S. Heidler, and Jeanne T. Heidler. Santa Barbara, Calif.: ABC-CLIO, Inc., 1997.

Where to Learn More

Books

Altoff, Gerald. *Amongst My Best Men: African-Americans and the War of 1812*. Put-in-Bay, Ohio: The Perry Group, 1996.

Arthur, Stanley Clisby. *Jean Lafitte, Gentleman Rover*. New Orleans, La.: Harmanson, 1952.

Berton, Pierre. *Flames Across the Border: The Canadian-American Tragedy, 1813-1814*. Boston: Little, Brown, 1981.

Brant, Irving. *James Madison*. Vols. 4 and 5. Indianapolis: Bobbs-Merrill, 1941, 1961.

Brooks, Charles B. *The Siege of New Orleans*. Seattle: University of Washington Press, 1961.

Carter, Samuel. *Blaze of Glory: The Fight for New Orleans, 1814-1815*. London: Macmillan, 1971.

Cleaves, Freeman. *Old Tippecanoe: William Henry Harrison and His Time*. New York: Charles Scribner's Sons, 1939.

Coit, Margaret L. *John C. Calhoun: American Portrait*. New York: Houghton Mifflin, 1950.

Coles, Harry L. *The War of 1812*. Chicago: University of Chicago Press, 1965.

Crane, Jay David, and Elaine Crane, eds. *The Black Soldier: From the American Revolution to Vietnam*. New York: William Morrow, 1971.

Dillon, Richard. *We Have Met the Enemy: Oliver Hazard Perry, Wilderness Commodore*. New York: McGraw-Hill, 1978.

Dowd, Gregory Evans. *A Spirited Resistance: The North American Indian Struggle for Unity, 1745-1815*. Baltimore: Johns Hopkins University Press, 1992.

Dudley, William S., and Michael S. Crawford, eds. *The Naval War of 1812: A Documentary History*. Washington, D.C.: Naval Historical Center, vol 1, 1985; vol. 2, 1992.

Edmunds, R. David. *The Shawnee Prophet*. Lincoln: University of Nebraska Press, 1983.

Edmunds, R. David. *Tecumseh and the Quest for Indian Leadership*. Boston: Little, Brown, 1984.

Elting, John R. *Amateurs to Arms!: A Military History of the War of 1812*. Da Capo Press, 1995. Reprint. Originally published by Algonquin Press, Chapel Hill, N.C., 1991.

Fredrikson, John C. *Officers of the War of 1812*. Lewiston, New York: Edwin Mellan Press, 1989.

Furlong, William R., and Byron McCandless. *So Proudly We Hail: The History of the United States Flag*. Washington, D.C.: Smithsonian Institution Press, 1981.

Griffith, Benjamin W., Jr. *McIntosh and Weatherford: Creek Indian Leaders*. Tuscaloosa: University of Alabama Press, 1988.

Heidler, David S., and Jeanne T. Heidler, eds. *Encyclopedia of the War of 1812*. Santa Barbara, Calif.: ABC-CLIO, Inc., 1997.

Heidler, David S., and Jeanne T. Heidler, eds. *Old Hickory's War: Andrew Jackson and the Quest for Empire*. Mechanicsburg, Penn.: Stackpole Books, 1996.

Hickey, Donald R. *The War of 1812: A Forgotten Conflict*. Urbana: University of Illinois Press, 1989.

Hitsman, Jay McKay. *The Incredible War of 1812: A Military History*. Toronto: University of Toronto Press, 1972.

Hollon, W. Eugene. *The Lost Pathfinder: Zebulon Montgomery Pike*. Norman: University of Oklahoma Press, 1949.

Ketcham, Ralph. *James Madison*. New York: Macmillan, 1970.

Kroll, Steven. *By the Dawn's Early Light: The Story of the Star-Spangled Banner*. New York: Scholastic, 1994.

Lloyd, Alan. *The Scorching of Washington: The War of 1812*. Washington, D.C.: Robert B. Luce, 1974.

Mahon, John K. *The War of 1812*. Da Capo Press, 1991. Reprint. Originally published by University of Florida Press, Gainesville, Fla., 1972.

Maloney, Linda M. *The Captain from Connecticut: The Life and Naval Times of Isaac Hull*. Boston: Northeastern University Press, 1986.

Mayo, Bernard. *Henry Clay: Spokesman for the West*. Boston: Houghton Mifflin, 1936.

McCaughey, Robert A. *Josiah Quincy, 1772–1864: The Last Federalist.* Cambridge, Mass.: Harvard University Press, 1974.

Moir, John. "An Early Record of Laura Secord's Walk." *Ontario History* 51 (1959): 105–08.

Remini, Robert V. *Andrew Jackson and the Course of American Empire.* New York: Harper and Row, 1981.

Remini, Robert V. *Henry Clay: Statesman for the Union.* New York: W.W. Norton, 1992.

Rutland, Robert, ed. *James Madison and the American Nation, 1751-1836.* New York: Simon and Schuster, 1994.

Rutland, Robert, ed. *The Presidency of James Madison.* Lawrence: University of Press of Kansas, 1990.

Roosevelt, Theodore. *The Naval War of 1812.* 2 vols. 3rd ed. New York: Putnam's Sons, 1900.

Schroeder, John H. "Stephen Decatur: Heroic Ideal of the Young Navy." In *Command Under Sail: Makers of the American Naval Tradition*, ed. James C. Bradford. Annapolis, Md.: Naval Institute Press, 1985.

Skeen, C. Edward. *John Armstrong, Jr., 1758-1843; A Biography.* Syracuse, N.Y.: Syracuse University Press, 1981.

Smith, Arthur D. Howden. *Old Fuss and Feathers: The Life and Exploits of Winfield Scott.* New York: Greystone Press, 1937.

Sonneck, Oscar George Theodore. *The Star Spangled Banner.* New York: Da Capo, 1969.

Sugden, John. *Tecumseh's Last Stand.* Norman: University of Oklahoma Press, 1985.

Terrell, John Upton. *Zebulon Pike: The Life and Times of an Adventurer.* New York: Weybright and Talley, 1968.

Vogel, Robert C. "Jean Lafitte, the Baratarians, and the Historical Geography of Piracy in the Gulf of Mexico." *Gulf Coast Historical Review* 5 (1990): 63-77.

Web Sites

Documents on the War of 1812. [Online] http://www.hillsdale.edu/dept/History/Documents/War/FR1812.htm (accessed on November 6, 2001).

Thomas Warner Letters. [Online] http://www.haemo-sol.com/thomas/thomas.html (accessed on November 6, 2001).

War of 1812. [Online] http://www.galafilm.com/1812/e/index.html (accessed on November 6, 2001).

"War of 1812." *KidInfo.* [Online] http://www.kidinfo.com/American_History/warof1812.html (accessed on November 6, 2001).

"War of 1812." *Studyweb.* [Online] http://www.studyweb.com/links/388.html (accessed on November 6, 2001).

War of 1812–1814. [Online] http://www.members.tripod.com/~war1812/ (accessed on November 6, 2001).

War of 1812—Forgotten War. [Online] http://www.multied.com/1812/ (accessed on November 6, 2001).

The War of 1812 Website. [Online] http://www.militaryheritage.com/home.htm (accessed on November 6, 2001).

Index

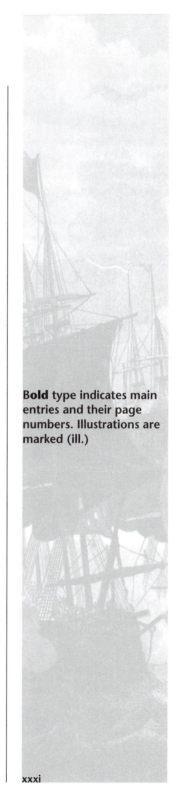

Bold type indicates main entries and their page numbers. Illustrations are marked (ill.)

B

C

Prophet, the. *See* Tenskwatawa

Prophet's Town 23–24, 26, 184, 301, 303–04 (*see also* Tippecanoe, Battle of)

Q

Quasi War 12–13, 92, 254

Queen Charlotte (HMS) 74, 259, 262

Queenston, Battle of 48–52, 64, 168–69, 290–91, 306

Quincy, Josiah 30, **277–86,** 277 (ill.)

R

Raisin River Massacre 61–62, 82, 305

Randolph, John 281

Rattlesnake 126

Red Eagle. *See* Weatherford, William

Red Sticks (*see also* Creeks)
  aided by the Spanish 313, 315–16
  battles involving 82–85, 98–100, 196, 313, 316–17
  British alliance with 195
  First Seminole War and 101
  massacres involving 82–83, 314
  slaves taken by 83
  Tecumseh's influence on 82, 195

Reindeer 126

Republican Party
  founding members of 243
  image of 12, 233
  split within 244

Republicans
  anti-British feelings of 17
  Congress dominated by 31, 280
  military cuts made by 12, 36, 96
  military expansion supported by 94
  political beliefs and values of 10–11, 31, 36, 173, 248, 279–80
  taxes and 11, 31, 95

Treaty of Ghent and reaction of 147

Revenge 255

Revere, Paul 54

Revolutionary War 4, 9, 22, 78, 96

Reynolds, James 42

Riall, Phineas 70, 103–04, 292

Ripley, Eleazer 102

Rockets used by British military 109, 116–17, 206

Ross, Robert 107–08, 110, 115–16, 117 (ill.), 121

Rush-Bagot agreement 247

Russell, Jonathan 135–36, 175, 245

Russian government, peace treaty assistance offered by 72, 93–94, 136, 245

Russian peace commission, members of 72, 136, 245

S

Sacajawea 269

Sacket's Harbor 63–68, 79, 112, 167, 256

Salaberry. *See* de Salaberry, Charles 80

Saratoga (USS) 112–14, 212–15

Savary, Jean Baptiste 120

Sawyer, Lemuel 57

Scorpion 74, 258

Scott, Winfield 49–50, 52, 61, 78, 102–04, **287–96,** 287 (ill.)

Secession 130–31, 200, 282

Secord, Laura 66, 67 (ill.)

Sectionalism 148–50, 179

Seminoles 101, 198

Shannon (HMS) 87

Shelby, Isaac 76, 186

Ships used during War of 1812, types of 60, 95, 123 (ill.), 255

Sioux camp, postwar 155 (ill.)

Slavery
  agreement to promote abolition of 145
  as issue in presidential campaign of 1840 188
  as issue in presidential election of 1852 296

national bank of 31, 93, 129, 155–56
national capital of 128 (*see also* Washington, D.C.)
neutrality of, in Napoleonic Wars 13, 243–44
population of 11–12, 19, 38, 260
sectionalism in 148–50, 179
trade restrictions of, during wartime 95–98
trade restrictions of, prior to war 15–17
war support/opposition in different regions of 150
westward expansion in 18–20, 137, 154, 200, 281
Upper Creeks. *See* Creeks; Red Stick

V

Van Buren, Martin 178, 188, 200, 226
Van Rensselaer, Solomon 49, 291
Van Rensselaer, Stephen 48–50, 52, 290
Vienna, Congress of 137
Vietnam, war in 4
Viger, Jacques 148
Villeré, Jacques 122
Vincent, John 65–66
Virginia dynasty 128, 131, 234, 239, 247
Virginia Plan 231
Virginia Resolution 232
Voter turn-out in 1840 189

W

War Hawks 22, 30, 284
expansionist aims of 174, 234
leader of 171, 237

Madison pressured by 31, 174, 283
members of 17–18, 174
Monroe and 244
Warren, John Borlase 85–86, 107
Washington, D.C.
as national capital 128
as part of special military district 108
British plan to attack 107–08
burning of 110, 111 (ill.), 224, 236–37
Washington, George 10, 156, 231, 242–43, 296
Wasp 57, 126, 211
Wayne, "Mad" Anthony 182, 268, 300
Ways and Means Committee 92, 281
Weatherford, William (Red Eagle) 82, 100, **309–18**
Wellesley, Arthur (First Duke of Wellington) 138
Whig Party 178, 188, 295
White House, burning of the 110, 224
White House parties during Madison's presidency 222
Wilkinson, James 78–80, 154, 194, 268, 270–72, 289–90
Winchester, James 62, 184–86
Winder, Levin 108
Winder, William 108, 110
Wolfe. *See* De Wolfe, James 97
Wool, John 49–50, 52
World War I 4, 208
World War II 4
Wythe, George 172

Y

Yankee 97
Yeo, James 64, 67, 112, 261
York, Battle of 64–65, 107, 224, 236, 273–74